License to Steal

Malcolm K. Sparrow

License to Steal
Why Fraud Plagues America's
Health Care System

With a Foreword by Lawton Chiles

Westview Press
A Division of HarperCollins*Publishers*

Copyright © 1996 by Westview Press, A Division of HarperCollins Publishers, Inc.

Published in 1996 in the United States of America by Westview Press, 5500 Central Avenue, Boulder, Colorado 80301-2877, and in the United Kingdom by Westview Press, 12 Hid's Copse Road, Cumnor Hill, Oxford OX2 9JJ

Library of Congress Cataloging-in-Publication Data
Sparrow, Malcolm K.
   License to steal: why fraud plagues America's health care system / Malcom K. Sparrow
      p.   cm.
   Includes bibliographical references and index.
   ISBN 0-8133-3067-X (hbk.)   ISBN 0-8133-3068-8 (pbk.)
   1. Medical Care—Corrupt Practices—United States. 2. Medicare Fraud. I. Title
RA395.A35764   1996
362.1'0973—dc20   96-16557
                                                                                    CIP

The paper used in this publication meets the requirements of the American National Standard for Permanence of Paper for Printed Library Materials Z39.48-1984.

10   9   8   7   6

Contents

Foreword

During my eighteen years as a member of the United States Senate, I worked hard to pass legislation aimed at improving governmental accountability and ferreting out waste, fraud, and abuse in programs ranging from the defense industry to meat packing and milk production. All along, I have been committed to the notion that anti-fraud strategies must be considered an integral part of the design and operation of public programs.

With respect to our nation's major health care programs, it is easy to understand why, historically, fraud control has not been a central issue in program design. For example, when the Medicaid program first came into existence, some within the medical community labeled it socialized medicine, and many physicians refused to participate. Consequently Medicaid reimbursement policies and procedures were designed to encourage provider participation by eliminating billing problems as a reason not to join. By design, the Medicaid system and virtually all health care programs, both public and private, assume honesty and integrity on the part of both recipients and their health care providers. Reimbursement policies and procedures encourage provider participation by making billing less complicated, facilitating faster payments with less paperwork, and de-emphasizing detection or prosecution of fraud. In such an environment providers were rarely challenged for the accuracy of their billings, nor for the medical necessity of their treatments. Staff in many Medicaid programs became accustomed to an environment in which detection of fraud and abuse was not a top priority.

Nearly thirty years later the situation is quite different, as our experience here in Florida demonstrates. In 1970, when the Medicaid program was initiated in Florida, it served just over 300,000 recipients with a budget of $43 million. Now it serves over 1.6 million recipients and spends more than $6.7 billion. Now, there is no shortage of providers who wish to participate in public programs. Florida has 60,000 within the Medicaid program alone. Many of these providers regard it as their right to supply such services. In fact, we are frequently challenged by providers who are not accepted into the program or by those we try to terminate from the program. For many providers of medical services, the opportunity to serve major public programs seems to be quite attractive.

The time has come for the health care industry to reconsider its traditional assumptions about the degree to which health care providers can be trusted. Of course, we still assume most physicians to be honest, and believe that the majority of fraud can be laid at the feet of a relatively small proportion of providers and recipients intent on cheating a large, complex, and ever-changing delivery system.

But the prevalence of fraud we have witnessed here in Florida has led us to elevate the importance of anti-fraud efforts considerably. We are unable to pinpoint the precise dollar amount of program expenditures attributable to fraud and abuse. Nevertheless, experienced fraud investigators suggest that the more we look, the more we find.

In 1992, as Governor of Florida, I met with the United States Attorney General William Barr to initiate a health care fraud and abuse task force in each of Florida's three federal judicial districts. We convened fraud and abuse work groups including federal, state, and private insurers and practitioners. It was an important first step in developing a more unified, integrated approach. And I recently filed a petition to impanel a statewide grand jury to focus on allegations of fraud and abuse of the state's financial resources. Cases involving health care fraud are being examined. Partly as a result of this focus, I believe Florida has become a leader in implementing reform strategies that show great promise in increasing access to high quality health services and at the same time reducing the costs of those services.

As we pay more attention to fraud, and as we see more evidence of it, so we have to question the adequacy of traditional control systems. We have to understand the historical legacy of the assumptions, policies, and procedures upon which these major systems have been based. In many respects, these historical policies have left the health care system with fragmented and inadequate controls.

Health care fraud and abuse, whether perpetrated against public or private programs, hurt those who are least able to protect themselves—our children, our elders, our poor, and our disabled. The cost of crime also manifests itself in higher insurance premiums, higher taxes for individuals and employers, and, because of the resulting resource constraints, in cutbacks in service for those genuinely in need. Health care reform has become one of the major social and economic issues of our generation and will continue to be so for many years to come. It makes no sense to debate health care reform without giving proper consideration to the adequacy and relevance of the control systems currently used throughout the industry.

That is why *License to Steal: Why Fraud Plagues America's Health Care System* by Malcolm Sparrow is so valuable and so timely. Dr. Sparrow systematically peels back the layers of existing control systems, and shows that in many cases they simply do not provide the protections against fraud that the industry has been counting on. *License to Steal* catalogs the failings of the industry's current approach to fraud control.

From my own experience in working on these issues, I would say that Dr. Sparrow has not overstated nor overdramatized the situation. These issues are urgent, and require the formation of genuine partnerships at the national, state, and local levels to safeguard every dollar spent on improving our health care system. Both in federal and state government I have had the great pleasure to be joined by many dedicated servants with a common mission—working to ensure that the members of the public have access to affordable, quality health care services. An essential part of that mission involves developing a systematic and collaborative effort to understand and solve the problem of health care fraud.

Prior to this work, the issue of fraud control had received very little attention from academia. The analysis contained in *License to Steal* places an important focus on this critical issue and provides us with valuable guidance in the effort to battle fraud and abuse in our health care system.

Lawton Chiles
Governor, State of Florida

Preface

Of all the research projects I have undertaken, this has been the most lonely.

For virtually every other significant area of public policy, academia provides some established body of knowledge, elders and betters who have gone before and defined the field and regular forums for meeting and debating the issues among peers.

Not so with health care fraud control, nor, more generally, with fraud control. The science of fraud control does not exist; it has not been defined. Some academic researchers have observed the phenomenon of fraud within the health care system and provided insightful commentary. But they have not presumed to teach fraud control to practitioners. The health care industry, when it turns to fraud control, still has no manuals.

For four years now I have been attending major national conferences on health care fraud. Despite attendance of seven or eight hundred, I am normally the only "academic" present and have often been asked by other attendees, "What are you doing here?" The reason I have been there seems all too plain: I believe that I have been paying attention to an important public policy problem, which may be costing the country a great deal of money. Nobody knows the precise extent of fraud in the health care system, but prevailing industry estimates set the scale in terms of hundreds of billions of dollars: maybe one, maybe more.

Surely the intriguing question, therefore, is, "Why are there not more serious researchers paying attention to this problem?" One answer, I suppose, is that fraud control does not fit neatly under the rubric of criminal justice, health care policy, medicine, public administration, economics, political science, nor any other well-established academic discipline.

I have felt somewhat isolated too, when asked to "wait outside." Not since high school have I been asked to leave the room and stand in the corridor. What better place to have to stand in the corridor than the Department of Justice, so passersby can wonder what bad thing I did! This exclusion results from being the only nongovernment person in a room when it comes time to discuss some confidential investigation or enforcement action.

I have felt somewhat isolated in this research, even among my colleagues. Countless seminars over the last three years, on various aspects of health care reform, have scarcely mentioned fraud. Fraud, waste, and abuse—if mentioned at all—have been presented more as a question of political rhetoric than a serious intellectual or practical challenge. And, on the few occasions fraud earned a second mention, the context usually included some phrase like "not such an issue under managed care. . . ," the implication being that fraud in the system is no longer a matter for serious concern.

This research project has felt quite risky to me. On several occasions I have asked myself why on earth I would want to take on such a complex and difficult subject; and why would I want to present a message that almost no one will want to hear—a message that scores of professionals have powerful incentives either to reject or ignore. I hope not to remain alone, out on this limb, for long.

Let me say a few words about what this book *is not*. First, it is not what I expected to write about health care fraud. My original interest was the design and implementation of a new class of fraud-detection tools, aimed at early detection of sophisticated criminal conspiracies. I approached the health care industry expecting to find an audience for such ideas and hoping to find appropriate sites for the development of new technological tools. I naively assumed the industry would jump at the chance.

But after I spent two years looking for the right development opportunity, a more important truth began to dawn on me. The industry was not ready for more sophisticated detection tools. Detecting more fraud would create the most enormous headaches for officials. Many of them already detected far more fraud than they could possibly deal with. There was no shortage of fraud and no shortage of detected fraud either. Improving detection capabilities was not the issue—at least, not the central one.

Rather the business of fraud control posed many paradoxical questions that neither the industry nor I seemed able to answer. Was it better to detect more fraud, or less? Was it better to prevent fraud, or prosecute it? Was the issue justice, or cost control? Fraud control, it seemed, presented a series of deep intellectual questions—with profound implications for policy and practice—for which there were no readily available answers. Fraud control was more difficult and complicated than I had realized. Unless the general pathology of fraud control were better understood, I decided, very few would be ready to invest in sophisticated new detection systems.

Any readers who are really curious to know what I would have said about detection systems need not be disappointed. The issue of detection systems is dealt with in Chapter 9 of this text.

The second thing this book is not is a condemnation of fraud-control practitioners. On the contrary. This book is essentially a compilation and rearrangement of practitioners' insights, generously shared. The practitioners are not at fault. They work extraordinarily hard, with inadequate resources, with inadequate support, and surrounded by perverse incentives. It is not the practitioners who warrant scrutiny or need changing but the framework of assumptions, policies, and systems within which they have to operate.

And this is not an attack on the medical profession. The vast majority of physicians with whom I have discussed these issues are horrified when they learn of cynical manipulation of the system by members of their own profession, for gain; and they are disgusted at the thieves who masquerade as health care providers—not least because of the damage they do to public trust in the medical profession.

This book is not just about the federal government either. In some places it may seem that way, because of the number of references to the Medicare program and its contractors. But Medicare does happen to be the nation's largest health care insurer as well as the fourth highest expenditure in the federal budget (after Social Security, National Defense, and Income Security); so it *should* feature prominently. But this book is about the health care industry more broadly: spanning the public (federal and state), private, and not-for-profit sectors. On my travels, one of the most striking discoveries was that the whole industry faced the same dilemmas, and that the fraud-control practices of the major public programs differed remarkably little from those within the private sector.

Regardless of the sector, the strengths, the weaknesses, and the challenges were all pretty much the same; and *they* are the subject for this book.

Malcolm K. Sparrow

Acknowledgments

I have many people to thank for their role in the creation of this book; too many to name them all. Let me at least name most of them by category and just a few by name.

The most important contributors were the formal interviewees—investigators, analysts, claims reviewers, auditors, lawyers, and managers—more than one hundred of them, who helped me understand the realities of fraud control and the constraints under which it is performed in the field. They made time during hectic schedules and, even more generous, they shared their own views and convictions, even when those convictions were at odds with their organization's official position. Their views and convictions largely shaped my own.

Within the Department of Justice, I must thank Attorney General Janet Reno for encouraging me to look into the health care industry as possibly the most critical area where fraud needed to be tackled and for her resolve in keeping the Department of Justice focused on health care fraud, despite the issue's complexity. Also the attorney general's staff, particularly Gerald Stern, Debra Cohn, Joshua Hochberg, Jeff Menkin, and Jim Sheehan for trusting me, including me, and educating me.

At the Federal Bureau of Investigation (FBI), I extend particular thanks to Joe Ford and Bill Esposito. From an outsider's point of view, these two special agents seemed to be the two most responsible for building the FBI's internal commitment and expertise within the area of health care fraud. They also welcomed me in, as an academic, believing that I might help them raise the level of debate on the subject. (I am still trying!)

The National Institute of Justice funded the fieldwork that lead to this book (under grant number 94-IJ-CX-K004). Thanks to Lois Mock, program manager at the institute, for her patience and skill in piloting the project through the bureaucratic maze.

Closer to home, let me thank Jerry Mechling and Tom Fletcher, whose "Program on Strategic Computing and Telecommunications in the Public Sector" at the John F. Kennedy School of Government handled the administration of the project, and who always seem to trust my judgment about what is and what might be important and then push me a little further and faster than I had planned.

Thanks to Corey Copeland and Chari Anhouse for absolutely first-class research assistance. Thanks also to three other Kennedy School colleagues—Hale Champion, David Ellwood, and Tamar Miller—who took the time to review drafts and provide detailed feedback. I took all their comments and suggestions very seriously, as they will see.

Finally, at home, let me thank my wife, Penny, and the children—Henry, Elodie, Nadine, Patrick, Sandra, Natasha, and Sophie—for their forbearance during the time it took to write this book. They left me alone when I needed it and were there when I needed that. They have learned, I think, that this tolerance of theirs keeps the writing time mercifully short.

And special thanks to Patrick, who told all his school friends that *this* book, unlike all the others I have written, might actually be interesting!

Malcolm K. Sparrow

Introduction

The United States now spends more than $1 trillion on health care each year; roughly 15 percent of the gross national product. Losses to fraud and abuse within the health care system have provoked great alarm, particularly during the first half of the 1990s. During 1992 and 1993, with health care reform under debate, no less than nine separate committees within the House of Representatives held hearings dealing with health care fraud and abuse, as did a further five committees within the Senate.[1]

These hearings generated thousands of pages of testimony, drawing from witnesses an apparently inexhaustible supply of horror stories—fraudulent quackery of the most flagrant kind; psychiatric hospitals using bounty hunters to fill their beds; Medicare beneficiaries' homes containing floor-to-ceiling stacks of unwanted and unnecessary medical supplies, delivered by durable medical equipment companies using aggressive telemarketing; laboratories "sink-testing" blood samples (i.e., just pouring the specimen away); and urban communities making a substantial living off various forms of Medicaid fraud.

New York's deputy attorney general and special prosecutor for Medicaid fraud control, Edward J. Kuriansky, testified to what he described as "a feeding frenzy on the Medicaid Program, a period of unprecedented white-collar wilding in which wave after wave of multi-million dollar fraud has swept through nursing homes and hospitals, to clinics and pharmacies, podiatry and durable medical equipment, radiology and labs, and more recently, home health care. Each surge has brought its own special brand of profiteer in search of the next great loophole in the Medicaid system."[2]

These stories are, in part, about the unlimited creativity of men and women determined to steal from the health care complex and their complete lack of concern for the damage they do both to patients' health and to the health care system.

But they are also stories about the failure of controls that are supposed to prevent or detect such abuses. They are stories about just how bad things can get before anyone notices or takes action. They are stories about the inertia and nonresponsiveness of control systems and about the ineffectiveness of the response when it does eventually come.

The proportion of the nation's trillion-dollar health care budget lost to fraud and abuse remains unknown. Conventional wisdom, crystallized in a 1992 Government Accounting Office (GAO) report, puts it at 10 percent (or roughly $100 billion per year). But the 10 percent figure has no basis in fact. The GAO report merely says, "Estimates vary widely on the losses resulting from fraud and abuse, but the most common is 10 percent . . . of our total health care spending."[3] GAO got their estimate from "industry experts," and now "industry experts" get their estimates from GAO.

The 10 percent estimate has been politically useful: high enough to be credible in the face of continuing media revelations about fraud and to justify the "get tough on fraud" rhetoric, yet low enough not to disturb the medical profession too much. The truth is, of course, that nobody knows the true figure, because nobody systematically measures it (rather a critical point, which Chapter 3 of this book considers at length). The true level of fraud losses could be lower than 10 percent, or it could be significantly higher.

Since 1992 the issue of health care fraud and abuse has continued to receive plenty of attention. A broad range of new statutory provisions has been proposed at the federal level,[4] although most of the proposals have since died with the failure to pass health care reform legislation. The rash of congressional hearings continues unabated and seems to be accelerating. There were nine separate hearings relating to health care fraud within just the first seven months of 1995.[5]

The Clinton Administration, determined to "crack down" on fraud and abuse, made health care fraud the number two priority for the Department of Justice (after violent crime). In 1992 the FBI assigned fifty agents to health care fraud. The Department of Justice created a health care fraud initiative and formed a health care fraud unit within its criminal division. By the spring of 1995 the number of FBI agents assigned had risen to 250, with that number due to double eventually. From 1990 to 1994 the General Accounting Office produced twenty separate reports specifically relating to fraud and abuse issues or payment control inadequacies, eight of these in 1992 alone.[6]

In the battle against health care fraud, there have been many apparent successes. The involvement of the FBI increased the level of publicity given to enforcement actions. In 1992 the FBI's "Operation Goldpill" arrested one hundred pharmacists, other health care professionals, and prescription drug distributors charged with carrying out widespread fraud through excessive billings and the illegal diversion, repackaging, and distribution of prescription medicine.[7] Operation Goldpill targeted a particular type of pharmacy fraud involving illegal recycling of prescription medicines.

Pharmaceutical recycling schemes typically work as follows. Physicians set up clinics in a large city. They employ "runners" to recruit poor, or homeless, or drug-addicted, or otherwise indigent people who would willingly spare half an hour to earn some ready cash. Most often these people would be covered by the government's Medicaid program. Each recruit is led to the clinic where the doctor (in a few minutes) diagnoses some fictitious ailment and then issues a prescription for some expensive medication. The doctor subsequently claims an hour's consultation for each patient from Medicaid.

The "patient" is then taken (or sent) to a local pharmacy to have the prescription filled—again at government expense. Upon leaving the pharmacy the patient finds someone just outside with their car trunk open, waiting to buy the drugs back from the patient for $10 or $15. The recruited patients are pleased to accept the cash and may return the next day for a repeat performance.

The buyers are known as "non-men," because they deal in noncontrolled drugs. Through the non-men, the drugs are repackaged and fed back into the pharmacy supply chain, with the recyclers reaping enormous profits, once again at the insurer's expense.

Such schemes have plagued the Medicaid program in particular, especially in the nation's major cities. Operation Goldpill was the first coordinated, nationwide attack on this type of scam; the operation also served as a dramatic announcement of the FBI's new commitment to investigating health care fraud.

Coordinated actions involving federal and state authorities as well as private insurers have succeeded in bringing some major corporations to book. In 1992 National Health Labs, (NHL), one of the nation's largest providers of clinical diagnostic testing, plead guilty to two criminal charges of submitting false claims to government health insurance programs. NHL agreed to pay $111 million to settle the case.[8]

In 1994, another major corporation, National Medical Enterprises (NME), owners of one of the nation's largest psychiatric hospital chains, plead guilty to paying kickbacks and bribes for patient referrals. NME agreed to pay $362.7 million in the largest settlement to date between the government and a health care provider.[9] In addition,

NME paid over $230 million in settlement of suits brought by sixteen private insurers and more than 130 patients.[10]

In 1994 alone, the FBI obtained 353 criminal convictions and collected $480 million in fines, recoveries, and restitutions, plus $32.7 million in proceeds that were seized or forfeited to the government (representing $13.65 for each dollar spent on health care fraud investigations).[11] In the same year the Office of Inspector General at the Department of Health and Human Services, recouped $5.4 *billion* in fines, settlements, restitutions, and other recoveries involving federal health programs.[12] The state Medicaid Fraud Control Units, between them, secured 683 convictions and recovered $42.8 million in fines, restitution, and overpayments.[13]

Despite all the attention and publicity, the increased enforcement resources, and the prosecutorial successes, virtually no one believes the situation is getting better. Many officials in the public and private sectors believe the situation is deteriorating. Not one person interviewed in connection with this research said they thought the situation was under control or even in the process of being fixed. Most shared the conviction that existing efforts to control the problem barely scratched the surface, and how much fraud you found in the system depended only on how hard you looked.

The media certainly have no trouble finding fraud, frequently making medical scams front-page news and maintaining a steady stream of television documentaries exposing fraud in one segment of the industry after another.

It is striking how many vulnerabilities, identified in the past, remain open. One would hope that weaknesses, once identified, would be plugged. But that happens slowly, if at all. A summary article on various health care scams, published in 1992, identified IPLs (independent physiological laboratories), DME (durable medical equipment suppliers), home health care, home infusion services, and psychiatric hospitals (using bounty hunters to fill their beds) as segments of the industry topping the fraud-prone list.[14] Three years later all but one of these (psychiatric hospitals) are still at the top of almost every investigative unit's list.

DME fraud has been endemic since the late 1980s. Recent efforts to control the problem include two major changes. First, Congress approved a prohibition on unsolicited telemarketing by DME companies.[15] Second, the Medicare program consolidated the claims processing for DME claims into four regional sites in order to facilitate monitoring and analysis of claims patterns nationwide. They recognized that DME suppliers were artfully spreading claims activity to avoid detection and were deliberately exploiting inconsistencies in reimbursement rates and levels of scrutiny from state to state.

But, to get around the telemarketing prohibition, some DME suppliers now conduct mass postcard mailings to thousands of Medicare beneficiaries, offering inducements for them to sign and return the postcards. The signed postcard gives permission for subsequent telephone solicitation. HCFA officials complain "they [the fraud perpetrators] can get around those things [new controls] faster than we can implement them."

Consolidating DME claims processing should certainly help broader aggregate monitoring. But that does not mean the system is now well defended. According to the director of monitoring and analysis working at one of the four new DME Regional processing sites: "If I wanted to do fraud I'd call South Carolina [National DME Suppliers' Clearing House] and get a [supplier] number, pay a $75 fee, set up in some office across the street and start billing. I'd bill $5 million in thirty days and walk away. It's mine to keep. Period." Coming from an official directly responsible for monitoring such abuses and as knowledgeable about the defenses as anyone, this statement certainly leads one to question the adequacy of existing control systems.

One of the controls on DME suppliers involves certificates of medical necessity, or CMNs. Insurers require CMNs, signed by a physician, with respect to any DME claim for the more expensive types of medical equipment: wheelchairs, hospital beds, infusion pumps, glucose monitors (for diabetics), oxygen equipment, and home-infusion equipment.

According to investigators specializing in DME fraud, CMNs provide little protection. For one thing, CMNs are not required at all for less expensive items such as surgical strips, gauze, tape, and incontinence supplies. In these areas, unscrupulous DME suppliers make their money by billing for huge quantities, more than any patient could ever possibly use.

With respect to the more expensive items, fraud is still easy. A CMN may certify the need for a wheelchair, but fail to stipulate motorized or non-motorized. The supplier delivers the cheaper version and bills for the more expensive one. A favorite item for this particular method of cheating are lymphodema pumps, used to help circulate blood in order to reduce swelling in cancer patients. One version of the pump costs around $5,000; the other costs only $200. According to the claims processors, the frequency with which the more expensive type is billed greatly exceeds the proportion of cases in which that version would normally be prescribed.

Investigators report that DME suppliers have little trouble obtaining signed CMNs, finding physicians who are either careless about what they sign, corrupt, or corruptible. DME suppliers have also been known to intimidate physicians, refusing to leave their offices until they agree to sign the forms.

One of the regional DME claims-processing sites recently conducted a random review on past claims for 4,000 glucose monitors, all provided by DME suppliers and paid for by Medicare. In more than 30 percent of the cases the patients had never even been diagnosed as diabetic (which is the underlying requirement for Medicare to cover the monitors). Nevertheless, all the claims had supporting CMNs, purportedly signed by physicians.

Home health care companies, likewise, were already under close scrutiny in 1992. Two years later, in March 1994, *Business Week* published a survey of home care services, cataloging abuses within the industry and bemoaning the lack of regulation.

> Home care is largely unsupervised. With ill-defined or nonexistent pricing guidelines, poorly conceived federal regulations, and a patchwork of uneven state and local laws, the home-care industry is primarily accountable to itself. Though the industry has tightened its standards, the guidelines have little or no effect on the thousands of home care companies that don't belong to trade groups. And federal investigators are far too understaffed to meet the growing caseload.[16]

Meanwhile Medicare and Medicaid spending on home health care has risen to $18 billion in 1993 from $8 billion in 1990, and HCFA estimates the tab for home health care will approach $30 billion in 1996.

One recent case shows how a major home health care corporation can perpetrate fraud systematically and nationwide. On August 23, 1995, the National Association of Medicaid Fraud Control Units announced a settlement with Caremark, an Illinois-based home health care company and subsidiary of Caremark International, a multi-billion-dollar a year home health care company.[17] In the largest Medicaid fraud settlement ever involving overbilling and kickbacks, Medicaid received $44.5 million as part of joint federal/state prosecution and civil settlement. Caremark plead guilty in U.S. district courts in Minnesota and Ohio in June 1995, to charges that it defrauded federal health programs by making improper payments to induce doctors and other professionals to refer patients.

One auditor, who worked for one of the top five major Medicare contractors, has specific responsibility for oversight of roughly 320 home health care agencies. Of these, he estimated that roughly 10 out of the 320 were honest. "Everyone out there has some kind of scheme going. They may not all be fraud, but they are definitely abusive." He also expressed the conviction that "when it comes to fraud and abuse," existing audit, detection, and investigative resources "barely scratch the surface."

Pharmaceutical fraud—the focus of Operation Goldpill—does not seem to have abated since 1992 either. Investigators in major U.S. cities describe "whole communities living off Medicaid fraud." For many recipients, they say, Medicaid fraud is a full-time job.

> They can make $150 to $300 per day if they "hustle," getting prescriptions, selling them to pharmacies or getting the drugs and reselling them. The cost to the government is more like $2000 per day for such people, with the providers and middlemen taking the rest.
> They take that Medicaid card like you take a cash card—they just have to make a couple of stops at a physician [to get a prescription] and pharmacy [to sell the prescription, or the drugs] to get the cash.

Health care fraud is committed by individuals, many of whom—acting as health care providers—seem to have little trouble stealing a million dollars or more. It is also committed by *networks* of individuals, often bound together by ethnic ties, sometimes by simply living in the same neighborhood, or—as was the case with Operation Goldpill—all members of the same graduating class at pharmacy school.[18] Health care fraud is also committed by major corporations, although they always prefer agreeing to a financial settlement rather than admitting to their own guilt.

According to Louis J. Freeh, director of the FBI, there is a new kind of player in the game. The FBI has intelligence showing cocaine traffickers in Florida and California switching from drug-dealing to health care fraud.[19] Why? Because health care fraud is safer and more lucrative, and the risk of being caught is smaller. Moreover, if they are unlucky enough to get caught, these criminals know the punishments for health care fraud are likely to be much less severe than those for drug dealing.

No one can listen for long to the accounts of millions of dollars being stolen at a time without asking what on earth is wrong with this system? Why is it apparently so easy for individuals, acting alone, to steal a million dollars or more? How can extensive networks of providers, runners, and middlemen operate fraud schemes for several years at a time, using essentially the same methods, without being closed down or shut out of the payment systems? How could two Russian émigrés, David and Michael Smushkevitch with their associates in southern California, fraudulently bill over one *billion* dollars (for lab tests not performed or not prescribed) and collect over $50 million (very little of which has ever been recovered) before their operation was closed down by the authorities?

While the nation struggles to restrain spending on health care and deliberates over reform, a colossal amount of time and energy is being devoted to debate about fraud and abuse. Yet little progress—in terms of practical improvements—seems to result. The voices in the debate, and their responses to one another, become familiar, predictable, even wearisome; the arguments, all well-rehearsed.

The media exposes scandal after scandal, and Congress responds with hearing after hearing. The Health Care Financing Administration (HCFA) and other major payers get roundly condemned by the press, politicians, and public alike for their apparent incompetence in recognizing or dealing with fraud.

Government officials respond, in turn, by telling how inadequate their powers, how meager their resources, and how difficult the task of picking out bad claims from a universe of hundreds of millions of claims processed each year. Officials plead for more resources and more effective tools, pressing for fraud-control legislation that would grant more effective prosecutorial and exclusionary powers.

The medical associations, with their considerable political influence, claim the problem is not so bad and point out (correctly) that nobody has any hard evidence on the size or nature of the problem. So, they say, it would be rash to take precipitous action that might jeopardize the goodwill of participating physicians, or make yet more onerous the administrative burden for the bulk of perfectly honest doctors. Other provider associations express fears about newly proposed inquisitorial powers, claiming they would be used indiscriminately, thus imperiling legitimate providers who already have enough trouble getting paid for their work. And then not much happens until the next set of embarrassing media revelations, when the whole circle turns once more.

Occasionally, though, it becomes transparently obvious that existing control systems do not work the way we imagine they should. The *Miami Herald,* on August 14, 1994, blasted Medicare for paying thousands of dollars in claims to "Whope of America," a phantom corporation whose corporate address seemed to be a sand trap at the Fontainebleau Golf Club.

> Cheating Medicare is as easy as filling out a four-page form that asks for basic information—name, address, phone number and a statement saying the operators have never been in trouble with Medicare.... Most of the time, the information isn't verified, allowing anybody with a $15-a-month rented mailbox and a beeper to go into the Medicare supply business.[20]

An investigator from the Office of the Inspector General (OIG, HHS) quoted in the article, said:

> What we have seen is a series of health care providers come into existence solely on paper. A company is incorporated using a fictitious name. The company submits a series of claims, usually between $200,000 and $1 million. By the time Health and Human Services becomes aware of the scam, the company and John Doe have vanished.

The article referred to other officials who confirmed that an application to become a Medicare provider would normally be approved automatically, provided it was complete and had a signature at the bottom.

Another phantom company, Bass Orthopedic, comprising nothing more than two rented mailboxes and a phone number, was paid $2.1 million between November 1993 and April 1994. The phony billings listed the names of physicians and hundreds of patients, none of whom had ever heard of the company. When a federal judge ordered Bass's bank account frozen it was too late. Most of the money had disappeared along with the owner. No services were ever rendered.[21]

Another company, Med EO Diagnostic, used the names of dozens of dead patients and a rented West Dade, Florida, mailbox to collect $332,939 from Medicare in May and June 1994. The owner—an unemployed tow truck operator—got caught only because he withdrew $200,000 in cash from the lab's bank account. A bank official became suspicious and called the police.[22]

The same article quoted Senator William Cohen (Republican—Maine) as saying, "The solution doesn't take more legislation, it takes common sense. We have got to persuade the government to do what it is supposed to do." The same point about the use of common sense was made by Bruce Vladeck as far back as 1980. "We might be better served if government policy was made and implemented not by Ph.D.s in economics but by grandmothers employing the skills they practice at the butcher's." [23] Under the Clinton Administration, Bruce Vladeck was appointed to the position of administrator of the Health Care Financing Administration, responsible for federal disbursements under the Medicare and Medicaid programs. *Medicare* spending for fiscal 1994 was $162.7 billion and is projected at $157 billion for fiscal year 1995 and $178 billion for 1996.[24] The total *Medicaid* budget nationwide was $145.9 billion in 1994, of which the federal government pays between 50 percent and 78 percent, state by state, depending on per capita income. The total federal contribution to Medicaid in 1994 was $89 billion, and it is expected to exceed $104 billion by 1997.[25] In fiscal year 1994, the federal expenditure on Medicare and Medicaid combined exceeded $251 billion, which means that HCFA now dispenses roughly *one billion dollars of public funds each working day of the year.*

Administrator Vladeck created a new position at a senior level within HCFA to lead the charge against fraud and probably took fraud control more seriously than any previous administrator. Writing in the *Journal of the American Medical Association* in March 1995, he declared, "For many years HCFA may have appeared ambivalent toward fraud and abuse. When other agencies, particularly the OIG, assumed primary responsibilities for program integrity in Medicare and Medicaid, HCFA often was prepared to defer to them. Those days are over."[26] He also acknowledged "good reason to believe" that the $5.4 billion in recoveries during 1994, was "merely the tip of the iceberg." He described HCFA's new commitment to cooperation with law-enforcement agencies and a new willingness to exercise its rights in suspending payments to providers when there is tangible evidence of fraud. Such a commitment, coming from HCFA, seems refreshing, significant, and long overdue. (The notion that HCFA previously did *not* cooperate with law enforcement may surprise the public, but surprises nobody within the industry.)

However, even the strongest commitment at the upper levels of HCFA may take many years to bring fraud under control. Administrator Vladeck, interviewed by NBC's *Dateline* in November 1995,[27] explained how he and his executive team were trying to "plug the holes in the dike" just as fast as they could, but that they had inherited an extremely leaky dike.

In order to be able to plug the holes—for major government programs and other insurers too—one has to know where and what those holes are. No amount of political rhetoric or upper management commitment can control fraud if the assumptions, policies, and systems upon which the industry relies for fraud control actually do not work: if detection systems cannot detect the right things, if investigative teams do not have the right tools and methods to help them see patterns of fraud clearly, and if "payment safeguards"—for whatever reason—do not actually safeguard payments.

Focus on Criminal Fraud

This book focuses quite deliberately on *criminal fraud* as opposed to *abuse*, all the while accepting the difficulty of drawing a clear line between the two. *Fraud,* according to the Medicare Carriers' Manual and most state laws, is defined as "An intentional deception or misrepresentation which an individual or entity makes, knowing that the deception could result in some unauthorized benefit to the individual, the entity or some other party."[28] The times when fraud and abuse become most difficult to separate are when the "deceptions" or "misrepresentations" relate to the issue of medical necessity rather than some other fact, and when the physician's intentions cannot be inferred accurately enough to distinguish zealous overutilization (based on legitimate, if unusual, medical judgments) from criminal theft.

The reason for focusing on fraud, rather than abuse (or billing errors, or "code optimization," or a host of other gray areas), is that fraud controls play to a distinctively different audience. Control systems may work very well in pointing out billing errors to well-intentioned physicians and may even automatically correct errors, adjust claims, and limit code manipulation. But those same systems might offer no defense at all against determined, sophisticated thieves, who treat the need to bill "correctly" as the most minor of inconveniences. Most competent fraud perpetrators study the rule book carefully—probably more carefully than most honest providers—because they want to avoid scrutiny at any cost. So they "test" claims carefully, making sure they neatly pass all the established system edits and audits. Then, having found combinations of diagnoses, procedures, and pricing that "work" (i.e., trip no alarms and preferably pass through "auto-adjudication" to payment, avoiding human intervention altogether), they ratchet up the volume, carefully spreading the claims activity across different patients and across different insurers so as to avoid detection.

Many control systems are designed with only one audience in mind—honest providers; perhaps error-prone; perhaps not up to date on administrative requirements and regulations; on occasions sloppy and disorganized; often confused by complex or indecipherable rules. For this audience, control systems serve the purpose of correcting errors, testing eligibility, matching diagnoses to procedure codes, checking pricing, and, if necessary, sending claims back for correction.

But effective fraud-control systems must deal with a second, quite different, audience: sophisticated, well-educated criminals; some of them medically qualified; some technologically sophisticated; all determined to steal just as much as they can just as fast as possible. They read manuals, attend seminars, and really appreciate all the help and training they can get in how to bill correctly, how to avoid prepayment medical review, and how not to "stick out" under postpayment utilization review.

That second audience is the one that this text is concerned with. Fraud control assumptions, policies, and systems will be evaluated in terms of their effectiveness in deterring, preventing, and detecting *criminal fraud*.

About This Book

What this book sets out to do is to examine the fraud-control apparatus currently in use within the health care industry and to ask the simple question, "does it work?" If not, "why not?" So the task is to provide an assessment of the assumptions, policies, and systems that constitute the health care industry's approach to fraud control; to understand their strengths and their weaknesses; and to offer some clues as to how controls could be made more effective.

The observations made here represent the observations of an outsider to the field of medicine, previously unfamiliar with the practice of medicine or the workings of health care organizations; but an outsider broadly familiar with criminal fraud and the distinctive challenge of fraud control, in several different contexts. Consequently, this book brings a rather unusual opportunity to explore the peculiarities of the health care industry's approach to fraud control, when compared, for instance, with the financial services sector, credit card companies, or the IRS—all of which have to defend themselves against fraud.

Chapter 1 describes the general nature—or pathology—of the fraud control business, providing an account of what makes fraud-control in *any* environment such a difficult and depressing business. The chapter highlights the following seven characteristics of the fraud-control challenge:

- What you see (i.e., what your detection systems show you) is *never* the problem.
- Available performance indicators are all ambiguous.
- Fraud control flies in the face of productivity and service and competes with them for resources.
- Fraud control is a dynamic game, not a static one.
- Too much reliance is placed upon traditional enforcement approaches.
- Effectiveness of new fraud controls is routinely overestimated.
- Fraud-control arrangements reflect the production environment within which they operate and fail to deal with the multilevel nature of fraud control.

Chapter 2 describes five properties, particular to the health care industry, that exacerbate the problem yet further:

- Insurers are regarded as socially acceptable targets for fraud.
- The majority of health care fraud schemes are non-self-revealing.
- Separation between administrative budgets and funds.
- Respectability of the health care profession.
- Absence of clear distinctions between criminal fraud and other forms of abuse.

Chapter 3 points out the ubiquitous failure of the health care industry to measure the scope or nature of the fraud problem in any systematic or scientific way. The extent of fraud is never measured; merely estimated. In the absence of measurement, debate focuses on the size of the problem, rather than on solutions. Estimates of the magnitude of the fraud problem are too soft to act as a basis for serious resource-allocation decisions. Consequently, massive under-investment in fraud controls result.

Chapter 4 examines the functional units that contribute toward and collectively constitute existing fraud-control arrangements: claims-processing "edits" and "audits," prepayment medical review, post-payment utilization review, audits, and special investigative units. Chapter 4 describes how fraud perpetrators can easily circumvent such controls by billing "correctly" and staying within the confines of medical orthodoxy and policy coverage. Such controls are extremely useful for correcting providers' honest errors, but ineffective as detection apparatus for criminal fraud.

Chapter 5 describes the practices of one small, private health insurer whose claims-review practices represent the antithesis of modern claims processing. This company eschews electronic claims submission and makes extensive use of human claims review with external validation. In short, they look to payment safeguards to keep their costs down, rather than processing efficiencies. This insurer's unique experience provides salutary lessons for the rest of the industry.

Chapter 6 examines the implications of electronic claims processing for fraud and for fraud control. What new vulnerabilities to fraud will emerge, if any, under EDI (electronic data interchange)? Does electronic claims processing pose major new threats, as some enforcement officials believe; or do existing threats merely translate faithfully from one medium (paper) to another (electronic)? And what new opportunities for fraud *control* can be realized given the advent of EDI?

Chapter 6 dismisses popular misconceptions about computer fraud, and rejects the notion that use of the electronic medium will create significant prosecutorial difficulties. The real problem under EDI will be in timely fraud detection, particularly as a consequence of increased vulnerability to high dollar value "hit and run," or "bust-out," schemes.

Chapter 6 also examines the belief—prevalent throughout the industry—that EDI can be made safe through extensive use of automated, up-front controls. This vision for "automated prevention" is shown to be dangerously flawed in that it neglects the dynamic nature of the fraud-control business, seriously underestimates the sophistication and adaptability of the opposition, and overlooks the critical role that humans must play in any effective fraud-control operation.

Chapter 7 considers the advent of managed care and its implications for fraud and fraud control. Several interviewees—particularly senior managers in private insurance companies—expressed the view that the deficiencies of their fraud-control systems under traditional indemnity (fee-for-service) arrangements did not matter much anymore, because the continuing expansion of managed care would soon make them all irrelevant. Many in the industry seem to believe that managed care, by eliminating the incentive for overutilization, would effectively eliminate fraud.

Chapter 7 shows that managed care will not provide a structural solution to the fraud problem, as many had hoped. Fraud will certainly take different forms under the various types of managed care contractual arrangements, but it will not disappear.

Chapter 7 also anticipates difficulties law enforcement will face in dealing with managed care fraud and suggests that the criminal justice system will become less and less relevant to fraud control. At the same time, the new forms of fraud—involving diversion of capitation fees, resulting in inadequate medical care—may be more dangerous to human health than the types of fraud familiar under traditional fee-for-service arrangements.

Chapter 8 pulls together the various recommendations made along the way, presenting a picture of a "model" or "ideal" fraud-control strategy. It describes seven critical features of a successful fraud-control operation: systematic measurement of fraud; resource allocation based upon measurement; clear designation of responsibility for fraud control; adoption of a problem-solving approach to identified patterns of fraud; deliberate focus on early detection of new types of fraud; operation of prepayment, fraud-specific controls; and preservation of some (small) risk of review for every claim.

Finally, Chapter 9 focuses on the detection tools currently used within the industry and identifies the most critical areas for development of new analytic and technological capabilities. This last chapter is somewhat more technical in flavor than the rest of the book, so some may choose not to read it. It will principally interest those readers who work within the insurance profession as well as anyone with responsibilities for defending other payment systems against fraud.

Anonymity

The fieldwork for this research involved a series of interviews at a variety of different insurers—some public programs and some private. (A brief note on how the sites were selected and how the interviews were structured can be found in the Appendix.)

Neither the sites nor the individuals interviewed will be named within this book, for two reasons. First, to preserve the anonymity that interviewees were promised in order to encourage a productive and frank exchange. Second, to avoid advertising specific fraud vulnerabilities in a way that might invite assault. Deliberate vagueness about which vulnerabilities appear within which organizations seems prudent.

All unattributed quotes in this text are from interviewees to whom the promise of anonymity was extended.

Part One

Understanding the Fraud-Control Challenge

1
The Pathology of Fraud Control

Fraud control is a miserable business. Failure to detect fraud is bad news; and finding fraud is bad news too. Senior managers seldom want to hear any news about fraud, because news about fraud is never good.

Institutional denial of the scope and seriousness of fraud losses is the norm. Many interviewees explained how their own views differed from "the official position" of their organizations and how uncomfortable they felt telling what they saw as "the truth," even to their own management. Investigators in Florida described how only recently, after years of media attention to the concentration of fraud problems in southern Florida, had it become acceptable to "speak up" during interagency meetings. Previously, they explained, if you talked honestly about the prevalence of fraud, you immediately got blamed for having failed to prevent it.

Employees closest to the work of fraud control habitually feel frustrated, unappreciated, sometimes ostracized by their own organizations, and deeply resentful of management's deaf ears to the whole subject. As one industry consultant, James Guzzi, told me:

> Senior management does not want to take the time to deal with the issue. It's too troublesome, and with too many other things on their plate to attend to, fraud always gets pushed to the bottom. The only time they pay attention is when there's a scandal involving them, or close to them. If they see a headline case, then they just want to know if their company was involved and whether or not they are going to be embarrassed.

Fraud-control policy tends to be scandal-driven. Management pays little attention to fraud control provided everything is quiet. They finally pay attention when scandal hits, either at home or close to home: But they pay attention for a remarkably short period and with short-term damage control as the primary motivation.

Fraud control—as a science or art—is scarcely developed and little understood. There is little instruction available from academia. And there is not much expert guidance in the field. Guiding principles or practical approaches to fraud control are almost impossible to find in any literature.

The discipline of "Managerial Accounting" gives the subject some attention but treats it as a rare subspecialty. Even specialist texts readily acknowledge the vacuum. Howard Davia (author of *Management Accountant's Guide to Fraud Discovery and Control*) confesses:

> There is no existing, established methodology for fraud auditing. Furthermore, there are no generally accepted fraud audit field standards, or generally available criteria that normally guide traditional auditors in the pursuit of their craft.
>
> Why is this so? There is a lack of such methodology and standards because effective fraud auditing is generally not being practiced.[1]

Under the heading, "Fraud—Pernicious and Largely Ignored," Davia describes the inevitable consequence:

> We cannot overemphasize the fact that entities throughout the world do not adequately recognize the seriousness of their exposure to fraud. The result is that he or she who would commit fraud has, more or less, carte blanche to do so. All entities are at risk, but few perceive the serious gravity of that risk.

Unfortunately, even when accounting or audit textbooks tackle fraud, they deal with it almost exclusively from the point of view of defense against internal corruption (employee embezzlement), rather than from the point of view of institutions defending their payment systems against concerted criminal attacks from *outside*.[2]

So, those who commit to the task of controlling fraud throw themselves into an area that academic literature has virtually ignored,[3] and where practitioners often feel isolated and abandoned. As one investigator testified to Congress: "You have to have guts. . . . There is no body of law or procedure, and you are . . . going out in an area relatively unexplored."[4]

Essential Character of Fraud Control

Before turning to the particular difficulties of the health care industry, what do we know about fraud control in general? What makes fraud control—in any environment such a difficult and depressing business?

Why do so many managers prefer to leave it alone? Why do organizations routinely underestimate or deny the existence of fraud? Why do organizations routinely fail to make proper investment in fraud-control apparatus?

The general pathology of fraud control needs to be understood, as backdrop, before considering the health care industry more specifically. The following seven points represent common experience in fraud control, across many different professions. They represent the core, harsh realities, which any effective approach to fraud control must confront.

What You See Is Never the Problem

Frauds can be categorized as self-revealing or non-self-revealing, depending on whether or not the fact that fraud has been committed shows up by itself some time after the commission of the offense.

Credit card fraud that involves usurping somebody else's account is generally self-revealing: The account holder usually reports the unauthorized activity eventually, when it shows up on their monthly statement. Tax refund fraud, where the perpetrator files a return and claims a refund using another person's identity, will also show up by itself if the real person subsequently files a return. Tax administration systems will notice the duplicate submission. Check fraud, also, usually reveals itself ultimately, provided the legitimate account holder is alive and well and paying sufficient attention to their bank statements to spot illegitimate activity.

Some fraud schemes fall between the two extremes, showing up, but showing up as something other than fraud. For example, many organized credit card frauds are based on fraudulent applications. Perpetrators obtain cards using totally fictitious names, run the cards up to their credit limit, and then discontinue use of those personal identities. From the credit card company's point of view the "cardholder" has simply become untraceable—a common phenomenon with a variety of possible explanations. Most credit card companies classify such losses as "credit losses," being unable to establish fraudulent intent.

But most white-collar fraud schemes *do not* reveal themselves. Examples include most categories of insurance fraud; bankruptcy fraud; and tax refund fraud where the perpetrator uses *his own* identity, or that of a non-filer. All these frauds, provided they go undetected at the time of commission, and provided they escape any post-payment audit, will remain invisible forever.

In relation to non-self-revealing frauds, therefore, *you see only what you detect.* Whatever fraud-control systems do not detect, no one will ever know about (although the aggregate economic impact might become apparent if the volume of fraud is sufficiently high).

The danger, of course, is that organizations vulnerable to fraud lull themselves into a false sense of security by imagining that their "caseload" (i.e., what they detect) reflects the scope and nature of fraud being perpetrated against them. Often it represents only a tiny fraction, and a biased sample, of the frauds being perpetrated. A 1980 study of white-collar crime expressed this basic truth. "Conceptually and empirically, the records of individual events themselves are products of socially organized means of perceiving, defining, evaluating, recording and organizing information."[5] In plainer language: the number and type of fraud schemes that become visible depends as much upon the effectiveness and biases of the detection systems as upon the underlying patterns of fraud.

Detection rates for non-self-revealing fraud types are usually extremely low, typically ranging from a high of 10 percent all the way down to zero. Some organizations simply have no idea they are vulnerable to fraud at all. Seeing no problem, they create no detection apparatus. Having no detection apparatus, they see no problem. Thus some organizations remain completely oblivious to the truth about fraud losses until some outside source surprises them by showing them what they lost.

Other organizations see a problem, but make the serious mistake of allowing the performance of their detection systems (often exceedingly poor) to shape their understanding of the problem and their sense of its magnitude. The inevitable consequence, with extremely serious long-term effect, is that they allow what they see to determine the level of resources allocated to fraud control or prevention. Quite naturally, everyone focuses on the visible part of the fraud problem. The real battle in fraud control is always over the invisible part.

Available Performance Indicators Are All Ambiguous

Nearly every available statistic in a fraud-control environment is ambiguous—at best, ambiguous; at worst, perverse and misleading.

If the amount of detected fraud increases, that can mean one of two things: Either the detection apparatus improved, or the underlying incidence of fraud increased. Few organizations can tell for sure which, or how much of each, is happening. The resulting ambiguity pervades much fraud-control reporting, as noted by Larry Morey (deputy inspector general for investigations, Office of Inspector General, HHS) testifying to Congress in 1993:

> Fraud is invisible until detected. Because of that fact, it is extremely diffi-
> cult to estimate the total monetary loss as a result of fraud in the health
> care industry. While we cannot assign a dollar figure to the monetary loss
> to the Medicare and Medicaid programs as a result of fraud, we can tell you
> that we have noticed a dramatic *increase* in our investigative workload.
> This is caused, in part, by the ever expanding size of these programs. The
> increase in administrative and prosecutable authorities that the Congress
> has enacted is also a contributing factor. Finally, there may also be an
> increase in fraud in absolute terms.[6]

One private insurer, the Travelers, had observed steady increases in their levels of detected fraud from 1987 through 1990. Unable to tell whether this meant more fraud or better detection, they used an interesting technique to try to separate the two factors.[7] They care-fully recreated the old set of detection tools (i.e., as of 1987) and then passed a subset of each subsequent year's claims through that same set of controls.[8] Having eliminated improved detection from the experiment, they still observed a 14 percent increase each successive year. Hence they concluded that the level of fraudulent claims being submitted was actually increasing, even in areas for which defenses had been in place for some time. Without such careful analysis, it generally remains impossible to say whether an increase in detected fraud is good news or bad news.[9]

Many other quantitative measures of fraud control success are ambiguous too. Reactive successes can equally be viewed as preventa-tive failures. Some organizations boast of "record recoveries"; others say they prefer to stop the fraud up front and regard chasing monetary recovery after the fact as a poor second best to prevention. Some orga-nizations emphasize prevention simply to avoid having to admit that their detection systems are ineffective. In fact, if detection systems detect next to nothing, one can always claim preventative success.

The introduction of fingerprinting as a welfare-fraud control in New York State serves as a case in point. New York City and thirty-seven other counties in the state implemented a fingerprint system for wel-fare recipients, designed to detect "double dipping"—claiming the benefit multiple times using multiple identities—by recipients of home relief. In the summer of 1995, during the first two months of the operation, the system only identified 43 cases out of 148,502 claimants. The *New York Times* reported the story under the headline "Welfare Fingerprinting Finds Most People Are Telling the Truth."[10] But there are two quite plausible explanations for the unexpectedly low number of cases—one of which suggests the system accomplished its goal, whereas the other suggests the system was a waste of money. "While the Giulini administration hailed the low number of double dippers as proof that fingerprinting was scaring off cheats, advocates for the poor said the results showed that welfare fraud was an overblown issue." The Giulini administration, which had introduced the measure as part of a more comprehensive crackdown on welfare fraud, pointed to the fact that the number of claimants of home relief had dropped by 30,000 since January 1995 as a result of tougher investigative procedures and the institution of a work requirement.

The article raises the question, unanswerable without much more serious analysis, "Did the creation of a system to fight fraud stop it? Or was there little to begin with?"[11] Either way, the administration will have trouble maintaining a budget for a fingerprint system that prevents fraud but does not detect much, because nobody can say for sure what a preventive system does or does not accomplish.

To complicate things further: Fraud controls usually come in a sequence of phases or stages. The phases of fraud control typically parallel various phases of the claims-processing operation. Detection successes late in the sequence often represent failure at earlier points in the process.

For example, auditors at one Medicaid fraud control unit (MFCU) described what could be called "last-ditch controls," just before checks were sent out. Following the entire claims adjudication process, a magnetic tape was sent over to the state controller's office to generate the weekly payments to providers. Two employees within the controller's office took the trouble to examine the "big checks" and identify providers or services that appeared problematic. The auditors reported that these two employees typically saved the state "between 30 and 60 million dollars each year" and suggested that 30 to 60 million dollars per year, as an error rate, reflected "surprisingly accurate payment for a $15 billion program."

Well, that is one way of looking at it. But when you realize that two employees (maybe costing the state a total of $100,000 per year each) are saving up to $60 million per year, one has to ask how much ten employees would save? With a savings-to-cost ratio exceeding 150:1, it would seem wise to invest additional resources.

The ratio of direct dollar savings to cost, for virtually all fraud-control activities, normally ranges from a low of 2:1, to a high of 50:1 or 80:1. Savings-to-cost ratios are frequently used as a method of justifying the budgets for fraud control expenditures. In calculating the "savings" companies typically combine prepayment savings with post-payment recoveries. (The indirect and unmeasurable deterrent effects are never included in the calculation.) Of course these ratios, as measures of fraud-control effectiveness, are ambiguous too. Higher ratios may reflect unusually effective operations or the existence of huge, untapped reservoirs of fraud.

One hundred fifty to 1 is unusually high, though. To find that kind of return so late in the process suggests serious weaknesses earlier in the process. The existence of such rich pickings so late in the day should surely lead officials to question the adequacy of prior controls. Still, when it comes to saving 30 or 60 million dollars of taxpayers' money, better late than never!

Thirty million dollars is indeed a small fraction (0.2%) of a $15 billion program. If $30 million was really all of the fraud left at this last stage of the process, then the payment system would indeed be "unusually accurate." But a savings ratio of 150:1 suggests nowhere near optimal investment has been made in detection. So the low detection figure (0.2%) more likely represents massive underinvestment in controls.

Another type of measure deserves comment too. The deterrent effect of a particular prosecution or set of prosecutions is often measured by a sudden subsequent drop in the level of claims within that category of services. In the health care industry precipitous declines in claims rates often follow well-publicized cases. One can interpret this phenomenon as the sign of extraordinarily well-targeted investigative effort.

Conversely, one can interpret the drop in claims level as an indication of the prior level of fraud. If the Medicaid claims for medical transportation, for example, drop by 75 percent in an area following a handful of ambulance company prosecutions, what does that tell us about the level of fraud just prior to the enforcement action? That it was probably 75 percent of total billings, or higher.

Congressional testimony from Deputy Attorney General Edward J. Kuriansky (MFCU director for New York State), describes the pattern. "We have often witnessed a pattern of skyrocketing Medicaid expenditures followed by a sudden, sharp dollar decline in the wake of a Unit's investigation of a particular provider group."[12] He cites as an example a reduction in prescription footwear costs, dropping from nearly $30 million to $3 million per year once his unit started focusing on that area.[13] A 90 percent reduction suggests a prior fraud prevalence of *at least* 90 percent (assuming not everyone is deterred).

Some would argue with this interpretation, saying that *legitimate* billings could also be affected by focused law-enforcement attention. Perhaps so—if that attention brings with it any change in policy or clarification of previously unclear regulations. But when a provider or providers are convicted of fraud in a criminal court (which suggests no ambiguity about the illegality of their actions), and that is all that happens, it is hard to understand why legitimate billings should be affected at all. Previous literature on white-collar crime has used such changes in behavior to draw inferences about prior levels of noncompliance.[14]

So, when enforcement actions produce dramatic reductions in claims level, should we be encouraged or disheartened? We should feel encouraged because of the skillful targeting and effectiveness of an enforcement response. At the same time we should feel disheartened because the evidence has shown up yet another area of the health care system riddled with fraud. In the fraud-control business, encouragement and despair routinely go together.

Finally, how should the industry interpret its major investigative successes? Many investigators derive great satisfaction from what they refer to as "tip of the iceberg cases"—where an apparently insignificant tip off or lead is developed, through diligent and painstaking investigative work, into a major case on a massive fraud scheme. Investigators are most satisfied when they know they could easily have dropped the case, or not pressed so hard, because it looked somewhat trivial at the outset. As one investigator put it, "I love it when one [telephone] call blossoms into a massive investigation."

These cases really do represent excellence in investigation. But they also reveal chronic failures of routine detection systems. If major scams are *only* uncovered through tip-of-the-iceberg-style investigations, then routine monitoring is missing the mark. Such cases suggest that discovery of major fraud schemes is more a matter of luck than judgment.

Fraud Control Flies in the Face of Productivity and Service and Competes for Resources

A third feature common to most fraud-control situations is the inevitable tension between those officials responsible for fraud control and those responsible for productivity. Additional fraud controls tend to slow down or complicate routine processes and create too many categories for exceptional treatment.

To the fraud investigators, the "process-oriented" appear narrow-minded, obstructive, blind to the reality of the fraud threat, and self-serving. The process-oriented seem to be preoccupied with processing efficiencies and appear not to care at all about the dollar losses through fraud that might completely eclipse savings achieved through automation or other processing efficiencies.

Officials whose job it is to make processes more efficient or streamlined or predictable, resent the obstacles to performance placed in their way by those who concentrate on exception monitoring. To the managers of the high-volume processes, the fraud investigators seem irritatingly obsessed with an apparently small (and to them, largely insignificant) segment of a colossal transaction load. The processors want to think about the best way to handle the whole load. The investigators or fraud analysts want to think about the best way to handle the exceptions. These are two very different agendas. In some organizations these two groups work very hard to destroy each other's careers, each convinced that they are working in the best interests of the organization.

Where does this tension lead? The savings from processing efficiencies may be small, but they are concrete and tangible. By comparison, the potential savings from enhanced fraud controls may be massive, but they remain uncertain and invisible. Bureaucracies always choose concrete and immediate monetary returns over longer term, uncertain ones. So processing efficiency invariably wins the battle for resources.

The late Congressman Ted Weiss, calling for creation of a national commission to map out a health care fraud strategy, said "I do not understand how we can be cutting funds to oversee federal health insurance programs at a time when costs are rising at the speed of light." [15] The reason "funds to oversee..." get cut is because they represent the easiest, least painful, and most obvious opportunity to cut costs.

The head of the fraud-investigation unit at one major Medicare contractor explained how her most powerful weapon against fraudulent providers was to require documentary evidence in support of every claim. But because electronic submission cannot handle accompanying documentation, that pits her interests directly against those of the claims-processing division, which has to accommodate all the extra claims coming in on paper rather than electronically:

> The real weapon is putting people on pre-pay (which, if they are committing fraud, is the equivalent of putting them out of business), but that hits me hard here within the company. If I require supporting documentation, I get killed inside the organization for increasing processing costs. Over $3 per claim for paper, rather than 5.5¢ for electronic claims submission.
> They all hate me, inside and out. It's a great job.

Pursuit of processing efficiencies can seriously damage payment controls. As one senior HCFA official succinctly put it, "of course, the *cheapest* way to process a claim is to *pay* it."

Dynamic Nature of the Game

The fraud-control game is dynamic, not static. Fraud control is played against opponents: opponents that think creatively and adapt continuously, and who relish devising complex strategies. Which means that a set of fraud controls that is perfectly satisfactory today may be of no use at all tomorrow, once the game has progressed a little. One commentator on the health care reform debate noted: "About 10 minutes after the president signs a bill, Americans will figure out how to 'game' the new system. The cleverest doctors and lawyers in the country will match wits with bureaucrats. Guess who will win?"[16] Maintaining effective fraud controls demands continuous assessment of emerging fraud trends and constant, rapid, revision of controls.

Officials responsible for fraud control often complain that, for every loophole they find and close, the providers seem to find another.[17] Some even respond to this realization by suggesting that closing loopholes merely displaces fraud rather than eliminating it and is therefore a waste of time. (This tends to be their private, pessimistic, somewhat embittered view; never the "official position.")

These complaints suggest a lack of understanding of the fundamental nature of the fraud-control business. Fraud control is like chess. You play against opponents who watch everything you do and adapt accordingly. To win the game you must watch everything they do and counter every play they make.

In many fraud-control situations much fruitless time is spent searching for "the golden bullet": that is, the perfect, final, detection methodology (or econometric model) that will forever hereafter distinguish

legitimate from illegitimate transactions. The health care industry, pre-
ferring medical terminology, searches not for the "golden bullet" of
fraud detection but the "magic pill."

One may as well search for one perfect, final, configuration of
chess pieces, which—without the need ever to make another move—
will guarantee complete defense. All too often organizations vulnerable to fraud make some investment in new edits or auditing systems
and then sit back, relax, and convince themselves that they have
taken care of the problem. Placing faith in a static set of controls and
failing to appreciate the paramount importance of watching how the
opponents respond is as foolish as trying to play chess blindfolded
and with your pieces bolted to the table.

In the fraud-control business, intelligence counts. One investigator, tackling extensive webs of corruption in the hospital construction
business, pointed out that the fraud perpetrators know the value of
watching their opponents. "Counterintelligence is a serious business.
They have their own network and talk about what we're up to."
Enforcement priorities and current targeting strategies are frequent
topics of conversation, formally and informally, at conferences for
provider specialties. At some such conferences, the doors are closed
and careful checks are made to ensure no government or law-enforcement officials are present before the conversation proceeds.
(Investigators hear this, eventually, from honest providers alarmed by
their own profession's behavior.)

Generally it takes committed fraud perpetrators less than a week to
figure out how fraud-control defenses have changed; and only three
months to a year for any new, successful, fraud strategy to become
known all across the nation. Many defending organizations, by contrast, take a year or more to consider and implement even the most
straightforward adjustments in their claims processes.

Overreliance upon Traditional Enforcement Approaches

Another common problem is confusion between fraud *investigation*
and fraud *control*. For many organizations, these activities are one and
the same. These organizations rely on the notion that vigorous pursuit of individual offenders, with well-publicized prosecutions, produces control through the mechanism of deterrence—which it does,
to some extent.

But the strength of the deterrent effect depends on the probability
of getting caught, the probability of being convicted once caught,

and the seriousness of the punishment once convicted. For white-collar crimes all three are notoriously low.

The criminal justice system in the United States has very little capacity for health care fraud cases, even despite recent investments. The case-development cycle takes between two and four years, which is painfully slow given the dynamic nature of fraud. Even once developed, many cases will not be prosecuted.

Within the Medicare program, for example, HCFA officials estimate between 1,000 and 2,000 "good-quality" cases are developed and referred each year. Less than half of these are accepted by the Office of the Inspector General (OIG-HHS), which only has 150 agents in the country dedicated to health care fraud. Of the cases accepted by OIG, roughly twenty or thirty per year are prosecuted criminally.

Even when health care fraud cases have been prepared for prosecution, many do not make it to court. A small number of prosecutors have specialized in health care fraud and will aggressively pursue sophisticated, complex cases. But most prosecutors have limited knowledge of the field and have an overwhelming caseload of violent crimes competing for their attention. Consequently most prosecutors will only take health care cases if they are both of high-dollar value and easy to understand. But "large" does not normally go with "unsophisticated." Most health care fraud cases are either small, or sophisticated. Very few cases are both large and unsophisticated, so very few make it to court, and the ones that do make the system look really stupid, precisely because of the selection criteria: large and unsophisticated, involving perpetrators—not particularly clever—who managed to steal hundreds of thousands or millions of dollars.

This funneling effect creates substantial disincentives for preparation of more cases. It even creates disincentives for fraud detection. "The last thing in the world I need right now is to detect more fraud," said one senior federal official, complaining of the impossibility of getting more than a mere handful of cases to court each year.

The funneling effect frustrates virtually everyone associated with it. Investigators at the field sites routinely referred to the Office of the Inspector General as a "black hole" and complained of their best cases simply "sitting," after referral to OIG, until they went stale. And OIG officers point to stacks and stacks of unopened files and ask how anyone really expects so few of them to be able to deal with this kind of workload.

In the context of an effective fraud-control operation, investigation and prosecution will play an important part. But they constitute just one tool, among many. Feeding the justice system (criminal or civil) is a slow, highly constrained approach to control. Control strategies must incorporate a much more comprehensive set of tools.

Insurers vary a great deal in the degree to which they rely on the process of referring cases to the justice system. In general, the more the members of a fraud unit viewed their job in terms of "making cases," the more frustrating they found their jobs.

Effectiveness of New Fraud Controls Is Always Overestimated

Another common problem is that it always looks as if the next set of fraud-control enhancements to be implemented will solve the problem. Why? Because the new set of controls quite properly reflects the most recent experience of fraud schemes. So the new controls, provided they work as expected, should eliminate most of the instances of fraud that an institution has observed most recently.

As a result, a false optimism is produced, based on the hope that elimination of the types of scams most recently seen will mean elimination of the fraud problem. Unfortunately this assumption fails to take into account the adaptability of the opponents, who take only a few days, or weeks at most, to change their tactics once they find a particular method thwarted.

Often officials deliberately point to some minor recent change as a way of dismissing allegations of vulnerability. However bad the situation *was,* any adaptation in controls—no matter how minor—casts a cloud of uncertainty over how bad the situation *is* or *will be.* Hence the predictable last sentence in so many news stories about health care fraud losses: "Some state officials say that recently enacted controls should help curb abuses in the program."[18]

Officials place unwarranted faith in new controls. Even the designers of new controls, if asked "what would you do as a criminal if you were trying to get around these new controls?" can immediately describe methods of circumventing them. The designers' mistake is to fail to think more than one move ahead, or to imagine that the opponents will easily lose interest and move on to some other target. Having learned the claims-submission business, having developed the necessary cooperative arrangements, and having invested in billing apparatus (people, systems, and software), very few criminals will be easily deterred. They move on only when they are made to adapt so much and so continuously that the target begins to look unprofitable. They have to be *harassed* out of the game.

Often fraud artists move on only when a noticeably easier, more profitable, slower-moving target comes into their sights. For many well-established and sophisticated criminal rings, health care payment systems are exactly that: fat, rich, and slow moving.

Fraud Control Arrangements Fail to Appreciate the Multilevel Nature of the Fraud-Control Game

In many institutions the type of fraud control that is implemented is determined—or, at least, strongly influenced—by the type of transaction-processing environment within which they operate. These can be characterized as high-volume, repetitive, transaction-oriented processes.

Fraud controls implemented within such processes tend to acquire certain characteristics. The underlying transaction-processing system deals with the work *in the same form and usually in the same order* in which it arrives: claim by claim (insurance), return by return (tax), or charge by charge (credit cards). Fraud controls, superimposed upon or embedded within the process, most naturally do the same: that is, they examine the claims, returns, or transactions one at a time and usually in the same order in which they arrive. Thus the fraud-detection systems most naturally use the same unit of work as the underlying processes, which means they operate principally at the level of the *transaction*.

Fraud-control systems operate within environments committed to efficiency and productivity. In order to fit (and to cause no more disruption to the production process than necessary), fraud controls also become high-volume, repetitive, transaction-oriented processes. Many institutions, realizing the inadequacy of relying upon service-oriented clerks for fraud control, turn instead to automated controls. Certain variables or ratios known to be indicators of fraud are calculated and checked automatically so that claims fitting suspicious profiles can be filtered out from the mass for closer inspection, investigation, or rejection.

Whether it be humans or machines that do the monitoring, developing good-quality fraud controls is, for many institutions, synonymous with having a finely adjusted set of filters or branch points embedded within the transaction-processing operation. The most obvious way to improve existing fraud controls is to improve the filters, making them better discriminators through the use of more variables or ratios, or by using sophisticated forms of econometric modeling or discriminant analysis.[19]

There are two major problems with this mind-set—that is, with the fraud-control mind-set that puts its faith in perfecting transaction-based filters. The first problem is that the fraud-control game is dynamic, not static (as already discussed) so any static set of filters has only short-term utility. A set of fraud controls that is perfectly satisfactory today may be of no use at all tomorrow, once the opposition makes their next move. Maintaining effective fraud controls demands continuous assessment of emerging fraud trends and constant revision of controls.

The second problem is that most sophisticated fraud schemes are devised by perpetrators who assume the existence of transaction-level filters, and who therefore design their fraud schemes so that each transaction comfortably fits a legitimate profile and passes through unchallenged. The perpetrators of such schemes accept the constraints imposed by having to fashion each claim to fit a legitimate profile; and then they make their millions by operating on hundreds or thousands of accounts simultaneously, often using computers to generate multiple claims and to incorporate sufficient randomness or variation to minimize the risk of detection.

The opening moves in the fraud-control game consist, therefore, of the defending institution implementing transaction-level filters, followed by the fraudsters adapting all their subsequent strategies to circumvent those controls. These moves could be regarded as a "standard opening" in a game that, like chess, is complex, dynamic, and rich in strategy.

Unfortunately many of the institutions most vulnerable to fraud have not progressed past these standard opening moves. They enjoy a false sense of security based upon the operation of their transaction-level filters, and that sense of security is reinforced through the observation that the process-based filters do reject claims from time to time. A proportion of these rejects indeed turn out to be fraudulent—an observation that demonstrates that transaction-level controls have their usefulness. But such controls generally detect only the casual, careless, and opportunistic fraud attempts; not the serious dedicated criminal groups who quickly progress to a higher level of sophistication.

Medical providers deliberately spread fraudulent activity across multiple patient identities and craft each claim to pass all the transaction-level tests (eligibility checks, pricing controls, diagnosis/procedure code combination, etc.). The smarter criminals are usually careful not to claim too much or too fast for any one patient, knowing that most systems use some *patient-level* monitoring. Patient-level monitoring assesses claims in the context of each patient's recent history, in order to detect sudden accelerations, or obvious overutilization.

Some providers use other providers' identification numbers in order to thwart provider-level checks.[20] Some DME suppliers deliberately use a broad set of "referring physicians." If billing agencies (which are completely unregulated) choose to commit fraud, they have the opportunity to spread fraudulent claims not only across multiple patients but across multiple providers as well.

Investigators report that dishonest providers in the health care industry have become adept at using multiple corporate identities to further frustrate monitoring. One Medicaid fraud control unit recently made a case against an organization fraudulently billing for sonograms (ultrasound images). A small number of patients would have a large number of sonograms taken, and the organization would then bill Medicaid using a long list of Medicaid recipients, none of whom had been seen. The perpetrators, if asked, could usually provide a sonogram to go with each claim, but the pictures were either entirely fake, or were of someone else. One organization used nine different corporate identities in order to conceal the billing pattern. They were detected through undercover operations conducted by the MFCU, acting on ample intelligence that the sonogram business was rotten to the core.

The Smushkevitch brothers' "rolling labs scheme" in southern California used more than 500 corporate identities and tens of thousands of patient identities over a ten-year period of operation.[21]

Payment systems, in order to defend against these kinds of schemes, clearly need to escape the natural tendency to concentrate on transaction-level controls. Transaction-level controls, embedded in the claims processing sequence, accomplish very little for fraud control. They are important and necessary—like the opening moves in chess. But the game for the most part is no longer played at that level.

What Constitutes an Effective Fraud-Control System?

The previously discussed seven points make up a discouraging catalog of why fraud control is difficult. You cannot see what you are fighting against, it is almost impossible to tell how you are doing, and most of the obvious remedies available are easily circumvented. Given the dynamic and constantly shifting nature of the game, how can you ever win? What distinguishes an effective fraud-control operation from an ineffective one?

There is (or used to be) a children's arcade game that presents an almost perfect model. The game consists of a horizontal wooden deck with a set of little mushrooms embedded into it, just flush with the surface. From time to time these mushrooms pop up in a completely unpredictable pattern. The child stands over the game with a rubber mallet in his or her hand, whacking the mushrooms that pop up, just as soon and as hard as possible. It is a game that tests the child's ability to react, fast and accurately, whenever a mushroom pops up. To be good at this game the child needs three simple things: first, to be able to see clearly what is happening, second, to have effective tools in hand, and third, to react quickly.

Effective fraud control demands exactly the same three things. Rather than placing faith in a static set of transaction-based controls, officials should seek to emulate the children that play this game: they are alert, poised, full of keen anticipation, constantly scanning the board for new movement, and proud of their reaction speed.

What counts in fraud control is first, having instruments and systems that enable one to spot early and to see clearly emerging patterns of fraud; second, to have effective tools in hand that can offer some immediate protection to the payment system once a threat is recognized and identified; and third, to react quickly, eliminating vulnerabilities before too much damage has been done. These are the key ingredients of effective fraud control. And three key questions therefore form the basis for evaluating the health care profession's approach to fraud control:

1. What instruments or systems exist that enable payers to see clearly the scope and nature of fraud threats and to spot new threats as they emerge? (And our starting assumption, here, is that reliance on detection systems embedded within claims-processing systems *do not* accomplish this.)
2. Are the available tools effective? Do they effectively eliminate vulnerabilities?
3. How quickly does the system react to new threats? When a new fraud M.O. is identified, how long does it take to curtail the associated losses—days, months, or years?

Within the health care industry it is striking how much officials focus on question 2, rather than on question 1 or 3. Whenever new revelations of scandalous fraud losses appear in the media, officials place the blame fairly and squarely on absence of effective tools. Hence the almost exclusive emphasis, when searching for remedies, upon legislative proposals.

In most fraud-control environments, control inadequacies are much less a function of inadequate statutory powers than they are of inadequate instrumentation and sluggish response.

How Bad Can Things Get Before the System Responds?

For whatever reason, the payment systems within the health care industry are drowning in mushrooms. Control operations seem to have abandoned hope of spotting problems early and cutting them off. Rather they seem content to dip their buckets into the vast reservoir of fraud.

To assess how well the health care industry's controls operate, let us ask question 3 in a slightly different form: just how bad can things get before the system produces an effective response?

In a surprising number of instances, things seem to get quite out of hand before control systems respond. Deputy Attorney General Kuriansky's 1993 testimony before the Committee on Energy and Commerce (House of Representatives) provides some insights. He recounted how Medicaid expenditures for podiatric services in the New York region dropped from nearly $35 million per year to $13.4 million—a 62 percent reduction—following enforcement attention to this provider group and with no change in policy.[22]

New York's statewide clinical lab billings crashed from a high of nearly $170 million in 1988 to just over $20 million in 1992 (an 88% reduction) as a result of a few criminal prosecutions.[23]

And, in November 1985, increased audit attention (by the Bureau of Audit and Quality Control) to the excessive fraud associated with orthopedic shoes achieved an 85 percent reduction in the billing for corrective footwear, estimated to be $47.2 million annually.[24]

A company called Osmomedic of Tampa, Florida, had a highly profitable trade during the early 1990s. Supplying durable medical equipment, Osmomedic specialized in TENS units (transcutaneous electrical nerve stimulators), which use pulsating electrical currents to ease the suffering of chronic pain, such as that caused by arthritis. Osmomedic would buy the units wholesale at $65 apiece and then bill Medicare $685 for each one sold. Medicare "reimbursed" Osmomedic $484 per item. Osmomedic sent doctors to Medicare beneficiaries' homes with the express purpose of having them diagnose arthritis and prescribe a TENS unit. In six months Medicare paid Osmomedic and the doctors (who charged Medicare for their visits) over $500,000.

Prior to the prosecution of Osmomedic, the yearly disbursement by Medicare just for TENS units in Florida had been over $10 million. After just one prosecution, the figure plummeted to approximately $500,000 (i.e., a 95% reduction).[25]

Of course it is good news when enforcement accurately targets fraud-prone areas of the industry. But it does seem extraordinary that the proportion of fraud within any given segment of the industry could ever be permitted to climb well over 50 percent of all billings before control systems intervene.

When the pattern of false billings by National Health Laboratories came to light (resulting in a $111-million settlement) it was not through any systematic detection apparatus. NHL had found an institutional way to defraud the government; they altered the order form physicians use to order blood tests. A standard item on such forms is a SMAC test (sequential multiple analysis computer), an automated battery of tests conducted from one blood sample. NHL amended the form so that two additional tests, one for cholesterol and one for serum ferritin (iron in the blood), were added into the SMAC test and were inseparable from it. Physicians believed that the two extra tests, which they would rarely have ordered separately, had been included in the SMAC test at no extra cost. In fact NHL billed the Medicare and Medicaid programs the standard $18 for the SMAC test, plus an additional $18 each for the cholesterol and ferritin tests.[26]

How long could such practice go undetected, and what was the mechanism of detection? In 1988, before the practice began, the Medicare program paid less than $500,000 to NHL for ferritin tests. In 1990, Medicare paid more than $31 million.[27] Even then it was not a routine audit, or any prepayment review of medical necessity, or any post-payment utilization review that brought the scheme to light. Rather, a salesman who worked for one of NHL's competitors became curious about NHL's unaccountably high profits and growth of revenues. He did a little research, figured out what NHL was doing, and filed a *qui tam* suit under the False Claims Act.[28] The *qui tam* provisions provide a financial incentive for private individuals to initiate action against fraud involving public funds. A private person (know as the qui tam "relator") can bring a civil claim for a violation of the False Claims Act on behalf of the government. The government has the option of taking over the suit or can leave the individual to pursue it alone. The relator is entitled to share in any monetary recovery if the government joins in the suit and takes all of it if the government does not.

The NHL settlement represents a major success for the qui tam provisions and a sorry indictment of routine control systems' ability to spot new patterns and respond in a timely fashion.

In another New York scam, Dr. Surinder Singh Panshi earned the media nickname "Dracula, Inc.: Bloodsucker of the Decade."[29] On August 4, 1988, he was convicted of stealing over $3.6 million from the Medicaid program between January 1986 and July 1988. His scam involved purchasing blood from addicts and Medicaid mills and then falsely charging the state for thousands of blood tests that had never been ordered, referred, or authorized by physicians and were in no way medically necessary.[30] Dr. Panshi had previously been prosecuted in 1986 for false billings and lost his license to practice medicine. So he went into the lab business instead, purchasing two labs in Queens and one on Long Island.

In 1986 the Panshi labs billed Medicaid a combined total of $1 million; in 1987, more than $12 million; and in 1988, over $31 million. By then Dr. Panshi employed a dozen or more "blood collectors" who set up blood-drawing centers in small apartments and prowled the streets in search of donors, paying donors—mostly drug addicts—$10 per vial.

How far could such a scheme go before being closed down? As of February 1988, the three Panshi labs accounted for more than 20 percent of all Medicaid billings by the state's laboratories, even though there are nearly 450 labs in the state. The scam was finally discovered when emergency room physicians in New York hospitals began to see a rash of patients who were anemic as a result of having sold up to a quart of blood two or three times per week. Some emergency room patients would receive extensive transfusions, only to go out and immediately sell their blood again. The problem became so serious that three doctors from Columbia-Presbyterian Hospital published an article in the *New England Journal of Medicine* entitled "Lab-Fraud Anemia." [31]

The media also began receiving anonymous tip-offs, which they passed onto the Medicaid fraud control unit. Despite the extent and rapid acceleration of the scam, it was not detected by any audit, or by any detection system, or by any claims-processing edit or audit, or by any pre- or post-payment review. The payment system had no systematic method—no instrumentation—capable of revealing even such flagrant abuse.

On the face of it, fraud-control systems within the health care industry seem not to notice or respond to emerging patterns of fraud until enormous amounts of damage have been done. The task here is to figure out why.

2
Particular Challenges in the Health Care Field

The general pathology of fraud control, discussed in Chapter 1, makes the job hard enough. Some particular characteristics of the health care profession make effective control harder still.

Insurers as Socially Acceptable Targets

A 1990 study of insurance fraud compared fraud and fraud-control trends in eight different Western countries, including the United States, Canada, and Britain. In all of these countries, the study reports, "a significant minority [of the public] regard insurance companies as large, rich, anonymous, and as fair game for fraud in much the same way as tax authorities."[1]

In the United States, the prevalence of opportunistic insurance fraud—readily acknowledged by the insurance industry at large—is astonishing. Nevertheless the nation was just a little shocked by what it saw when, in 1993, the State of New Jersey staged a series of fake bus accidents in a variety of urban locations. State officials arranged ten minor bus accidents, in each case employing actors to pose as passengers. After each impact, hidden video cameras recorded opportunistic passersby scrambling to get aboard before the police arrived, so they could claim to have been injured in the crash.

In six such accidents around New Jersey, a total of fifty-one people boarded the buses and had their names recorded as having been aboard during the crash. Doctors and lawyers, or "runners" soliciting business for them, were videotaped boarding the buses, coaching passengers on how to feign injury, and handing out business cards.[2] Eleven additional individuals submitted injury claims for injuries supposedly sustained in these six accidents, without even bothering to board the bus at the scene.[3]

One *genuine* accident, not part of the sting operation, occurred when a truck and a car collided just behind another New Jersey bus. Passengers, hearing the bang, assumed the bus had been hit (which it had not). No fewer than twenty-seven of the bus passengers subsequently submitted injury claims.[4]

The rest of the country displays a surprisingly high tolerance for insurance fraud, even though things are not quite as bad elsewhere as they are in the cities of New Jersey. A 1993 public attitude survey conducted by the Insurance Research Council asked members of the general public all across the country whether they thought it was all right to pad insurance claims to make up for past premiums. Nationwide, 19 percent of respondents said they regarded the practice as acceptable. But residents of the mid-Atlantic states (New York, New Jersey, and Pennsylvania) were more than twice as likely (41 percent) to regard the practice as acceptable.[5]

Another question on the survey asked whether it was all right to continue to receive medical treatment after an injury had healed in order to increase the size of an insurance settlement. Nationwide, 9 percent thought it was all right.[6] In the mid-Atlantic states, 20 percent, and among residents of *big cities,* 25 percent of those surveyed said it was all right.[7] The Newark sting operation, conducted in dense urban areas of New Jersey, apparently played to an unusually dishonest audience. More broadly, however, a significant proportion of the U.S. population sees insurance companies as fair game.

With health care fraud, financial losses accrue primarily to insurance companies and to massive government bureaucracies. It is hard to imagine targets that would engender less public sympathy. Tales of insurers peddling high-priced, and in some cases totally worthless, insurance policies certainly do not help.[8] More broadly, many believe the cost-control practices of insurers to be punitive, even immoral, and consequently regard them as having forsaken any claim on honesty in their dealings with policyholders. One physician told the Senate Committee on Aging:

> The insurance companies, particularly Worker's Compensation carriers, appear to create an almost adversarial climate between themselves and honest doctors. Legitimate services rendered by honest providers are often going unpaid. Some honest doctors feel as though they are being encouraged by the insurance companies to break the rules in order to get paid.[9]

Health Care Fraud Schemes Not Self-Revealing

Virtually all health care fraud schemes fall into the category that do not reveal themselves automatically, even after the fact. Many members of the public believe that explanations of medical benefits (EOMBs) provide protection against fraud. Patients, receiving EOMBs, would surely spot the appearance of any services not rendered and would report the activity, just as a credit card holder would report unauthorized activity when they saw it on their monthly statements. Health care fraud advisories continually remind patients to check their EOMBs carefully.

The executive director of The National Health Care Anti-Fraud Association (NHCAA), Bill Mahon, in answer to congressional questions, encouraged the same kind of sensible, prudent, consumer behavior: "I would respond. . . by simply saying we all need to pay as close attention to the insurer's statements of what was paid on our behalf as we would to a monthly credit card bill or a Sears bill to make sure that what was paid for was, in fact, what was provided. No question, we need to be better consumers."[10] But EOMBs do not have the effect one would hope, for a number of reasons. First, they are not sent at all in many circumstances. Use of EOMBs is no longer routine within the Medicaid program. Under Medicare, EOMBs are routinely sent out only when services require a co-payment, or where the Medicare program refuses to cover a service. So, where services are approved and 100 percent reimbursed by the program, EOMBs are not usually sent; in which case Medicare beneficiaries have no way of knowing what was billed under their names. EOMBs have not been used in connection with home health care services—now one of the most fraud prone categories of service—since 1981.

Second, recipients of EOMBs have little or no financial incentive to pay attention to them. Recipients are not, as in the case of a credit card statement, being asked to pay a bill. Third, many recipients cannot decipher the strange, computer-generated forms, and they see no reason to try.

Fourth, fraudulent suppliers find innovative ways to stop patients from reading their EOMBs. In Florida, DME suppliers have paid Medicare recipients $5 for each unopened EOMB envelope. And investigators at major Medicare contractors described how providers were altering beneficiaries' addresses on their claim forms and switching them to post office boxes under their own control, knowing that the claims-processing system would automatically update the beneficiary address before dispatching the EOMB. Typical schemes, these investigators reported, would use around thirty post office boxes, with twenty to thirty beneficiaries being switched to each box. (So the fraudulent activity in such schemes is routinely being spread across upwards of six hundred beneficiaries, none of whom would ever see their EOMBs.)

Fifth, as Louis Freeh, director of the FBI, testified in March 1995, many fraud schemes deliberately target vulnerable populations: "Nursing home and hospice operators exploit the elderly and Alzheimer's patients by fraudulently billing for services, incontinence supplies and medications. Tragically choosing patients who have difficulty understanding or remembering what was and what was not done, much less complaining to their insurer or alerting law enforcement."[11] Despite all of these obstacles, beneficiaries in significant numbers do call their Medicare carriers to complain about bogus or questionable charges. HCFA mandates that such calls go directly into the fraud and abuse unit within the carrier, and "beneficiary complaints" are, for many of those units, the bulk of their work.

But what happens when such a complaint is received is quite surprising. If a beneficiary says a service, reported on an EOMB, was not provided as billed, the investigative unit mails a form or letter to the provider asking them to confirm that the service was, in fact, provided. Depending on the practice of the Medicare contractor, providers may be asked to provide medical records; in other cases they merely have to sign a declaration that the service was provided. Assuming the provider confirms the service, the unit then sends the complainant a letter explaining that the service has been confirmed. That is the end of the matter, unless the beneficiary chooses to appeal the finding. To a complaining beneficiary this makes the government appear extraordinarily stupid. Most beneficiaries drop their complaint at that stage, many of them no doubt feeling the government does not deserve any help. But some, according to investigators, "go ape, call the media, or call their Congressman."

The truth is, EOMBs are not the automatic fraud-discovery mechanism one might imagine. EOMBs are only issued with respect to certain categories of services and generate notoriously low response rates. Moreover the handling of beneficiary complaints, even when they do arise, often lacks the rigor required to uncover fraud.[12]

What about Certificates of Medical Necessity (CMNs)? Within the durable medical equipment segment of the industry, one would imagine CMNs would play a major role in guaranteeing the validity of DME claims. The majority of DME services require a CMN signed by the prescribing physician. The provider must provide his or her unique physician identification number (UPIN). Surely these physicians would be able to confirm whether or not they had actually prescribed an expensive item of equipment—such as a hospital bed or motorized wheelchair?

In theory they could help verify DME claims, but in practice they are seldom, if ever, asked. There is no routine or random verification of CMNs with the signing physicians. And, even once a claim is under review, investigators report that going back and trying to check on CMNs can be extremely frustrating. The director of the investigative unit at one of Medicare's regional contractors for durable medical equipment described CMNs as "totally useless": "Doctors sign them to get rid of suppliers. No sense of responsibility. They are not getting paid for signing or not signing them. And often physicians do not respond to queries when we check up, as it doesn't relate to any claim of *theirs*. So they say 'why should we? Are you going to pay us?'" Moreover DME suppliers intent on fraud tend to submit CMNs under the names of prescribing physicians who are corrupt, lazy, sick, absent, desperate for cash, or dead. They forge signatures where necessary.

The non-self-revealing nature of nearly all health care fraud schemes exacerbates the difficulty of seeing the fraud problem clearly. It makes the question "what instruments or systems exist that enable payers to see clearly?" all that much more crucial.

Separation Between Administrative Budgets and "Funds"

Investment in adequate fraud controls suffers significantly because program administration costs are budgeted separately from program costs (i.e., claims paid). This budgetary separation makes it virtually impossible to consider the notion of "return on investment" in allocating resources for fraud control. Particularly within government programs, even substantial returns cannot justify investments in control if the program funds (which stand to gain from better safeguards) are administratively or legally separate from administrative costs.

In May 1995 the Senate Appropriations Subcommittee on Labor, Health and Human Services held a hearing to consider the findings of the latest GAO study. This particular study had explored the savings to the Medicare program that might accrue if the government purchased commercially available "code manipulation" software packages and installed them within Medicare payment systems. These commercial packages rebundle improperly unbundled procedures and automatically correct a variety of other improper or erroneous billing practices. Senator Tom Harkin opened the hearing with this statement:

> The GAO indicates that it would cost around $20 million to install the private sector technology in Medicare. And they have clearly demonstrated that such an investment would save Medicare taxpayers and beneficiaries over $3.9 billion in five years. So, for every dollar we invest, taxpayers will get $200 return. I call that a bargain. For every day we fail to invest, taxpayers will lose $2.5 million. I call that a scandal. The time to change is now and I will be introducing legislation today to mandate that Medicare discard its outdated system to detect billing abuses and take advantage of this cost-saving technology.[13]

The particular merits and limitations of this GAO study are not the issue here. HCFA contests the conclusions, stating that the software packages tested by GAO incorporate claim-rejection rules that are much more restrictive than existing Medicare rules and whose insertion into Medicare claims-processing systems would therefore be illegal.

What Harkin's statement reveals, however, is the obvious public appeal of notions such as "value for money" and "return on investment" when considering additional fraud controls. A $200 return for every $1 invested looks irresistible. Unfortunately, the practical workings of the budget process cannot even consider such ratios. The Medicare trust fund (for Medicare payments under Part A) is sacred to the American Association of Retired Persons, and woe betide any politician who suggests taking any of it for anything resembling administrative purposes. The Medicare trust fund is maintained by the 2.9 percent Medicare payroll tax, paid half by employers and half by employees.[14] The Medicare program's administrative expenses, by contrast, come out of the discretionary budget from general tax revenues.

Control, or reduction, of Medicare and Medicaid costs has become highly politicized as a key budget deficit-reduction issue. But neither political party dares attack the integrity of the trust funds,[15] so the statutory segregation of funds will persist at least for the time being. Given that segregation, any extra investment in controls has to come from the discretionary budget, whereas any savings directly benefit the trust funds.

Legal or budgetary separation of funds from administrative costs forces fraud and abuse controls into a zero-sum game with other parts of the processing apparatus. Every extra dollar spent on prudent controls means one dollar less spent on processing, automation, customer service, due process, beneficiary services, or a variety of other inescapable obligations. Fraud controls, once in this zero-sum game, invariably lose. Whenever the administrative budget comes under pressure, program integrity controls (given the uncertain nature of the dividends they bring) are always first on the chopping block.

In a 1995 congressional testimony, Sarah F. Jagger of the GAO made a very similar point when she stated that payment safeguards under the Medicare program produce at least $11 for every dollar spent; and yet, on a per-claim basis, federal funding for safeguard activities has declined by over 32 percent since 1989. Adjusted for inflation, the decline increases to 43 percent.[16]

> In large part, the decline in program spending for these activities corresponds to the passage of the Budget Enforcement Act of 1990. That act established limits—or caps—on domestic discretionary spending, including spending for Medicare program safeguard activities. Exceeding these caps in one domestic discretionary account requires budget reductions in other accounts, such as those for education and welfare. This means that even though *appropriating additional funds for safeguard activities would result in a net budgetary gain*, under current law, it would necessitate offsetting cuts in other areas.[17]

Jagger then pointed out that the act included a specific exception to the spending caps with respect to the IRS's compliance activities—which produce much more revenue than they cost—and Jagger urges lawmakers to consider a similar exception for Medicare program safeguard activities.

Pooling fraud controls under the umbrella of administrative costs makes them exceedingly vulnerable to budget pressures. Minor fluctuations in administrative budgets cause major fluctuations in control resources. These fluctuations, say senior HCFA officials, have disastrous effects on the capacity of investigative units. "It takes a long time to train a Medicare investigator. First they have to learn their way around the program. Then they have to learn their craft. Usually they become productive after around three years. But every time we take a budget cut, we lose investigators. Then we have to start over. It's *very* frustrating." Some recent initiatives at the federal level (and a sequence of legislative proposals) have embraced novel ways of producing additional funding for fraud investigation and prosecution, by beginning to chip away at the separation of funds. These proposals, if passed into law, would permit proceeds from court-ordered penalties to be placed in special funds designated for the support of further antifraud-enforcement efforts.[18] Use of these funds would strengthen efforts to fight fraud in much the same way that asset forfeitures are used by law-enforcement agencies against drug dealing.

Creating such funds represents one small step toward a softening of the strict segregation, and focusing on court-awarded penalties allows the step to be made without increasing the administrative budget at all. It is a small step, but definitely in the right direction.

The damaging consequences of segregating funds and the consequent inability to clearly see a bottom line, also afflict the private sector. Even where no legal separation between funds and administrative expenses exists, the practical separation persists and produces the same effects. Private sector insurers, aware of the need to control aggregate claims administration costs, feel they have to choose between investments in payment controls and investments in other functional pieces of the administrative apparatus.

The separation, whether statutory or merely administrative, is powerfully manifested in employee culture and attitudes. Most officials care a great deal, *either* about the costs per claim (where their goals and incentives all relate to efficiency), *or* about payment accuracy. Which one they care about depends on their specific functional responsibilities. Virtually nobody cares about both; and virtually nobody is in a position to act upon the important relationship between them.

One conversation with senior managers at one of Medicare's DME regional contractors vividly illustrates the clarity of the distinction. We were discussing vulnerabilities to very rapid, high-dollar bust-out schemes—particularly involving computer-generated claims—that might arise under electronic claims processing. Considering the possibility of $100 million scams, each of which might only take a day or two to perpetrate, these managers were asked how many times they thought their company would need to fall victim to such schemes before being effectively put out of business. The answer, as obviously true as it is alarming, was "Oh, [company name] probably wouldn't even notice—*it's not our money.*"

These same managers, who confess they might not notice Medicare scams involving hundreds of millions of dollars, can tell to the nearest *cent* how much it costs to process a claim. Virtually nowhere, not even in the private sector, does the common-sense notion of "return on investment" actually drive investments in fraud controls.

Respectability of the Health Care Profession

Society places enormous trust in health care professionals, and rightly so. People need to be able to trust their doctors. Lacking expert medical training, most consumers of medical services are in a poor position to assess the quality or appropriateness of those services. So society honors physicians in many ways, acknowledging the rigor and intensity of their training.

Society pays physicians the compliment, as a profession, of not subjecting medical judgment to scrutiny except by another physician. Physicians expect to be granted exemption from outside scrutiny and strenuously oppose efforts by administrators, investigators, or even managed care companies to question or influence their professional judgment. Defense *of* the profession, *by* the profession, is serious business—as the power, wealth, and political influence of the medical associations attest.

Physicians, therefore, are willing to censure only the most outrageous acts of their colleagues; even then with remarkable reluctance. Revelations about fraud are received by medical practitioners as an attack on the integrity of the profession and on its ability to police itself.

Some commentators have noted the peculiar defensiveness of the medical profession. "If one studies burglars, citizens who avoid breaking into others' homes do not feel that their reputations are being endangered. But if one reports on the frauds committed by doctors, the vast majority of doctors, whose conduct is honest and above board, nonetheless are tempted to complain that their whole profession is being unfairly besmirched."[19] The profession's defensiveness presumably results from the value physicians place on preserving public trust. Society has trusted physicians, most importantly, to subvert their own personal financial interests to their professional obligations. The efficacy of medical practice as well as physicians' own status and financial compensation, depend on preserving that trust. Reports of greedy physicians cheating and stealing, damages it. Burglars, by contrast, do not constitute a profession, do not depend upon public trust; and do not feel the need for concerted effort to resist bureaucratic encroachment onto their professional turf.

The unwillingness of doctors to condemn their own has also been commented upon by judges in criminal court. In 1984 a California ophthalmologist was convicted of performing unnecessary cataract operations on Medicaid patients, stealing more than a million dollars over five years, and leaving several patients blind or with unnecessarily impaired eyesight.

The judge, disgusted by the letters of support the court had received from other physicians appealing for leniency, commented on the fact that not one of the letters paid any attention to the true victims in the case, which he described as "uneducated, Spanish-speaking people, some of whom will never see a sunrise or a sunset again." Rather, the letters of support painted the whole trial as "a contrivance by the attorney general's office."[20]

Some physicians, even when convicted by a jury of a criminal offense, seem to show remarkably little regret or remorse. They often cling to the moral high ground, viewing and presenting themselves as innocent victims of unreasonably complex and meddlesome bureaucratic rules; too busy caring for their patients to watch their own backs.

> Convicted physicians often insist that their crimes were merely the consequence of their being too involved in heady medical matters to attend to the niggling red tape of the programs that were paying them. This not uncommon strain of professional arrogance among medical practitioners may help the guilty deflect the disgrace of criminal prosecutions, the accompanying unpleasant publicity, and assaults on their self-esteem.[21]

The desire and need of members of the medical profession to protect their professional status is perfectly understandable. Their resulting defensiveness, however, has historically inclined the profession and its associations to play down the extent and seriousness of health care fraud and to oppose provision of additional resources for the purpose of investigation and review.

The respectability of the medical profession also presents notable problems to investigators and prosecutors. Investigators, lacking medical training, feel sorely disadvantaged when questioning physicians, whom they frequently encounter as arrogant and condescending.

And most prosecutors still avoid taking cases that require expert medical testimony, knowing such cases will be difficult, expensive, and relatively unlikely to succeed in front of a jury. Some prosecutors still display a broader reluctance to bring physicians—pillars of the community—to trial.

Extension to Other Provider Groups

Investigators concede society's need to trust physicians and acknowledge the integrity of the majority of physicians. However, many of them express outrage when they see the same kind of professional immunity or trust being extended to all kinds of other provider groups not bound by professional ethics of any kind. Investigators view these other provider groups—durable medical equipment suppliers, home health care agencies, medical transportation companies, physiological laboratories, and so on—quite starkly as businesses, run by businesspeople, for profit. Investigators believe health care insurers and payers are naive to assume, as they do with physicians, that for these provider groups the drive for self-enrichment would be subordinated to higher professional obligations. In these other provider groups, investigators see no such professionalism.

Nevertheless, payers accord such groups surprising latitude, paying claims on trust without any routine verification of services provided. In some cases payments are made on the basis of prevailing fees, which began as a compliment to the integrity of professional physicians. Prevailing fees, in many of these industry segments, are "whatever you can get away with."

Despite the absence of any identifiable code of professional ethics, these segments of the health care industry, dominated by big business, acquire aggressive political lobbies and wield enormous power. Home health care suppliers, for instance, are renowned for the effectiveness of their political lobbies. The Medicare program still pays home health agencies for services that are not covered by the program, under what is termed *favorable waiver status*. Favorable waiver status was designed during the 1980s as an interim transitional measure to give providers in the emerging home health business time to learn the rules. The idea was not to penalize home health agencies for "good faith errors," made early on. Under favorable waiver status, provided an agency keeps its overall denial rate below some threshold percentage of claims, any claims that are "denied" as ineligible, will be paid nonetheless. Apparently HCFA tried to withdraw this provision in

1991 but, as one official put it, "they ran into a political buzz saw." Five years later this provision still remains in place, allowing every home health agency to be paid for a certain percentage of services not covered by the program.

Fraud investigators have no trouble naming the most significant trend in health care fraud today: increased involvement in the health care industry of big business, with powerful political allies and no code of professional medical ethics. Investigators report that they are beginning to see corporate fraud being committed within the health care industry at an unprecedented level. Investigators predict that the next few years will reveal cases of corporate health care fraud that will make NME's $362.7 million settlement look tiny.

Unclear Distinctions Between Fraud, Abuse, Overutilization, and Other Activities

Criminal fraud is defined clearly enough. It requires a deliberate misrepresentation or deception, leading to some kind of improper pecuniary advantage. If the deception is as to some objective fact (e.g., if the services were not provided as billed, or were billed as something else) then the boundaries of fraud are fairly clear. But when the deception or misrepresentation relates to the question of medical necessity, the distinctions between fraud and abuse (or between fraud and defensive medicine, or between fraud and well-intentioned overzealousness) become quite muddy. To establish fraud, many argue, you would have to get inside the head of the physician to ascertain the motivation; or, at least, establish such a blatant and persistent pattern of behavior that criminal motivation could be inferred.

No one would categorize phantom providers billing millions of dollars, with never a service rendered, as anything other than fraud. Many other blatant scams, equally, would present neither the public, nor physicians, nor juries any definitional problems. There is plenty of clear fraud. But the fuzziness of the boundaries, away from the extremes, produces a particular problem: it becomes extraordinarily difficult to mobilize unequivocal condemnation of fraud, even when the fraud is quite blatant. Nobody can be quite sure exactly where along the continuum that condemnation, once mobilized, would end. Physicians may find it hard to condemn fraudulent practice among their peers if they cannot construct satisfactory dividing walls between what they might condemn in others and what they do themselves.

Perhaps this helps explain, for the sake of a puzzled public, the medical profession's response to an event such as National Health Laboratories $111 million settlement with the government. Shortly after the settlement was reached, an article appeared in *JAMA*, entitled "Medicare Case Underlines Importance of Physician Compliance with All Rules When Claims Are Filed." [22] Despite the fact that the president and CEO of NHL, Robert E. Draper, pleaded guilty to two counts of fraud and resigned from the company, the article nevertheless interpreted the action of the government in going after NHL as an *extension* of the definition of fraud applied to the health care industry. A former attorney for HHS, Thomas S. Crane, was quoted:

> Up to now, most health care attorneys believed that the only thing that made a *criminal* case was services not rendered or clear fraud. Otherwise it would be a civil case.
>
> This means that for physicians there should be a new sense of caution. What the government is saying is that when a physician signs a Medicare or Medicaid claim form, there is an implied representation that all of the rules are complied with.
>
> Of course, minor mischaracterizations are not going to be prosecuted as criminal cases, but the government is clearly in mind to press the view that physicians are obligated to see that all of the rules are complied with when they file a claim. I think this is a big cautionary sign.

In view of what NHL had done, the idea that the definition of fraud was being stretched seems surprising. NHL systematically, and as a matter of company policy, tripled its billings to the government for SMAC tests by including two additional tests that doctors would not normally prescribe. They redesigned their order forms to mislead physicians as to the cost of these tests.

NHL, in its post-settlement statements, preferred to characterize the whole question as one of expert medical opinion, saying "the tests were done believing they are necessary for a full diagnostic evaluation, are medically sound, and supported by the medical and scientific communities." In other words, NHL claims to have acted perfectly responsibly.

But the general public would have no difficulty condemning NHL's actions. Even if the medical necessity of the two tests were debatable (which it is not), NHL still made an unannounced, unilateral judgment on the question, without any consultation with payers, which happened to triple NHL's revenues with almost no impact on their costs. Of course we should expect NHL to present this unfortunate truth in the best possible light. But why the prevarication from physicians? Can they not recognize this as fraud and join the rest of the public in condemning it? Or do they recognize this as fraud, but think of it as a type of fraud that they thought was safe from criminal prosecution? Assuming the majority of physicians to be honest, why the apparent alarm and the "need for a new sense of caution?" Perhaps it is the absence of clear dividing walls along the continuum that heightens physicians' sense of vulnerability.

The dividing walls are indeed hard to construct. From a practical point of view, the inner workings of providers' minds cannot normally be fathomed. So the existence of criminal intent is usually inferred from other objective, verifiable facts. But neat dividing walls are hard to construct even among objective realities. Even if the services were not provided as billed, what was the reason? Was it a genuine, isolated mistake? Or was it part of a persistent pattern of mistakes resulting from a genuine misunderstanding of the regulations? Was it reckless disregard for the rules? Or was it a deliberate attempt to steal?

These ambiguities do not necessarily appear in other fraud-control situations. If unauthorized activity appears on a credit card bill or a bank statement, there are few plausible explanations other than fraud. In most contexts, determining whether a transaction is fraudulent or not is a binary affair: either it is, or it isn't, with little room for debate. But the definitional ambiguities within health care hamper fraud-control efforts in a number of ways.

First, they contribute to the medical profession's reluctance to unequivocally condemn fraudulent practice.

Second, definitional ambiguities make it much more difficult to measure the problem systematically, because any measurement methodology would have to establish clear outcome classifications. For practical reasons, outcome classifications would have to be based on objective, verifiable realities, none of which precisely fit legal definitions of fraud.

Third, definitional ambiguities provide an excuse for anyone who would prefer, for whatever reason, not to refer suspected fraud cases to an investigative unit. Some state agencies, responsible for administering the Medicaid program, display a marked reluctance to refer cases to the Medicaid fraud control units (which are organizationally separate). Conscious of the need to protect and maintain their provider network, the paying agencies generally prefer to deal with suspicious claims or billing practices through administrative action rather than refer them to the MFCU for investigation.

The difficulty of distinguishing fraud from other, grayer behaviors enables anyone so inclined to avoid the obligation to refer suspected cases of fraud. One state official—who was using this definitional ambiguity to explain a lack of referrals to his state's MFCU—was asked to define the point at which he would be willing to categorize a suspicious claim, or pattern of claims, as potential fraud. He replied: "It's fraud when a judge says it's fraud, and not before." (So much for the effectiveness of *that* referral mechanism!)

Fourth, definitional ambiguities weaken fraud controls. For example, within the Medicare program, carriers and intermediaries generally accept the rule that, in order to prove a provider guilty of fraud, you have to demonstrate that the provider had been previously educated about a particular billing practice. Only that way, the logic goes, can a court be sure the provider knew what they were doing and that it was wrong. This rule is commonly applied for all but the most blatant forms of fraud.

So, in practical terms, when a contractor discovers a provider is cheating, the most common course of action is to write and explain to the provider what they did wrong and ask them to stop. Only if they persist in the same practice, following "education," do they become vulnerable to investigation and prosecution for fraud.

This highly practical rule, based upon prosecutorial experience, substitutes objectively verifiable facts—in this instance, prior education—for the need to probe the mind of the provider in search of criminal intent. It serves to protect honest providers who make honest mistakes. But it protects fraudulent providers too, enabling all but the most stupid and greedy to eliminate their vulnerability to prosecution entirely, simply by heeding warnings if and when they come.

These impediments to effective fraud control—the social acceptability of government and insurers as targets, the invisible nature of the crime, the separation of administrative budgets from funds, the trust placed in providers, and the difficulties of separating fraud from other behaviors—are substantial. Add them to the seven elements of the general fraud-control pathology, and the task of controlling fraud seems complex, amorphous, and overwhelming.

Perhaps this helps explain why health care fraud has not gone away despite all the attention paid to it and why strenuous political and administrative efforts to bolster defenses have failed to provide a cure. Many dedicated, intelligent people—administrators, reviewers, analysts, auditors, investigators, and prosecutors—work long hours seeking to combat the problem. But, at the end of the day, not one of them feels the problem is under control, or that the situation is getting any better. Most feel that their heroic efforts barely dent the surface.

One reason is the enormous complexity of the task, which Chapters 1 and 2 have laid out. Another reason—which Chapters 3 and 4 will explore—is that the policies, systems, and machinery in place to combat fraud do not work the way everyone thinks they do.

3
The Importance of Measurement

VISA International administers and operates the global network that handles VISA credit card transactions. On a busy day, the transaction volume on the network exceeds $1 billion (just like HCFA's). When considering potential investments in new fraud controls, VISA looks carefully at its "confirmed fraud rate," which indicates the proportion of VISA card transaction dollars lost to fraud and never recovered. As of July 1995, that rate hovers around nine basis points (i.e., 0.09 percent of the transaction volume). VISA management likes to keep the rate under 0.1 percent, or ten basis points, which the credit card industry generally regards as a satisfactory level for fraud in the system; the acceptable price of doing business.

The health care industry, which thinks its fraud rate might be 10 percent—a hundred times worse than the credit card industry's—lacks any precise instrumentation on which to base its control investment decisions and makes no serious attempt to measure the problem. Given the obvious seriousness of the fraud problem, the lack of systematic calibration seems both striking and alarming.

Basic decision theory teaches the value of information in choosing between alternative courses of action. Presumably the health care industry might lean toward different courses of action if the true level of fraud losses were 40 percent than if they were only 2 percent. So, to an outsider, for the health care industry to pay some attention to measurement of the problem would seem rational and reasonable; maybe even imperative.

Yet, year after year, the uncertainty remains. GAO, in a 1993 comment on their own 10 percent estimate, declared: "Because of the hidden nature of fraudulent and abusive practices, however, the exact magnitude of the problem cannot be determined."[1] Which means, of course, that the returns on any new or marginal investments in fraud controls are uncertain, and additional investments are therefore much less likely to be made. The same uncertainty existed in 1977, when the Medicaid fraud control units were originally created.[2] At the time the director of the Congressional Budget Office was asked to comment on the financial implications of the formation of MFCUs. She replied, "The unknown magnitude of fraud and abuse presently extant in the programs makes it impracticable for the Congressional Budget Office to project the actual cost impact of this measure at this time."[3] In the late 1970s, as now, the absence of knowledge left different parties free to make their own, partially self-serving, estimates. In 1979, the Inspector General's Office of HHS estimated Medicaid fraud and abuse to be $468 million, with the caveat that the number was "incomplete and probably low." Responding, HCFA *recommended* an estimate of only $100 million. The IG diplomatically commented, "All agree numbers are soft. IG considers HCFA estimate low."[4]

In the absence of hard facts, estimates from investigative units are normally at least double or triple the size of corresponding estimates from paying agencies, and much energy is wasted squabbling over the truth. Investigative units, closer to the realities of the streets and short of resources, aim high. Paying agencies, defensive about their own control systems, eager not to offend their network of providers, and protective of their program's public image, aim low.

The situation has not changed. Consider, for example, the different estimates of the level of fraud in the New York State Medicaid program. What proportion of the $20 billion Medicaid bill for that state is lost to fraud? Senator Donald Halperin, testifying to the New York State Senate in 1993, bemoaned the lack of agreement and clearly felt that consensus around a reliable estimate would greatly facilitate efforts at control.

> During the last few years, there has been disagreement between the Office of the Special Prosecutor for Medicaid Fraud Control and the Department of Social Services regarding the approximate level of Medicaid fraud. The lack of consensus. . . is troubling because it doesn't provide an accurate assessment of the degree of the problem. A consensus forecast would aid in determining strategy for reducing Medicaid fraud. Agreement on the nature and scope of the problem would also be beneficial in developing and formulating staffing levels and overall appropriations.[5]

Halperin described how the New York Department of Social Services tended to minimize the problem, acknowledging that around $125 million might be at risk, but expressing considerable confidence in their latest processing system enhancements; meanwhile the Office of the Special Prosecutor (the MFCU) claimed that Medicaid fraud and abuse activities were rapidly escalating and were costing the state up to $2 *billion* every year; sixteen times as much.[6]

The failure to systematically and routinely measure the scope of fraud is characteristic of the whole insurance industry—not just health care—and is not limited to the United States. Michael Clarke's comparative international study of the insurance industry, published in 1990, commented that

> despite the vigorous and extensive efforts of some insurers to detect and control fraud, there is no evidence that any insurer has undertaken research to establish the real extent of fraud in any given area of risk. It would certainly be possible to employ standard sampling techniques to pick out a representative set of insureds and to investigate each claim's history with exhaustive care, using the best available means of fraud detection (which, it should be said, are fairly effective).[7]

Given the absence of such systematic measurement, Clarke pointed out that "It is always likely, therefore, that the sophisticated fraudster is at least one move ahead in this process, and possible that entire categories of fraud are being ignored: beyond standard deterrent and defensive tactics, insurers are relying on the mistakes of fraudsters and on what they already know about them."[8] Picking transactions at random and auditing them as thoroughly as possible is much more than an academic idea. For many regulatory and compliance agencies it is a familiar operational tool for discovering what they do not know; for scanning the horizon in search of noncompliance problems that might have entirely escaped their attention. A program of rigorous random audits acts like the smoke or paint aimed at the "invisible man" in various Hollywood movies: it makes the invisible visible.

The IRS, for example, established its Taxpayer Compliance Monitoring Program (TCMP) precisely for the purpose of detecting patterns of noncompliance. Every three years or so the IRS selects 50,000 tax returns completely at random and subjects them to a rigorous line-by-line audit.[9] The object is not to make cases but to get reliable information about patterns of noncompliant behavior, of which the IRS might otherwise remain completely oblivious.[10]

The danger of self-delusion threatens all agencies that have to deal with noncompliance problems that are not self-revealing. The mechanism of delusion goes like this. The agencies focus on what they think are the central problems. As they do so, they learn more and more about those problems, and they become yet more central in their thinking. As time passes, the agencies work on the problems they know about; and they learn about the problems they work on. Trapped by the circularity, agencies focus more and more carefully on things they always focused on before, just because those are the problems that happen to be in their sights. They fish in the same place, year after year, because that is where they caught fish before.

Meanwhile new patterns and types of noncompliance emerge, all potentially out of sight. If there is no system or machinery to help uncover new problems, the problems may go unnoticed for years. TCMP is a piece of machinery designed specifically to help the IRS identify new areas of noncompliance. TCMP's strength lies in its random selection. The whole point is that the selection is not focused on known problems, or influenced by any existing IRS biases.[11]

Conducting random audits is usually as unpopular internally as it is externally. Auditors often regard random audits (which they characterize as "studies") as a waste of time, claiming they could raise more revenue if only they were allowed to focus on known problem areas. In fact, they *would* raise more revenue focusing on known problem areas, but that argument misses the whole point. The principal value of random audits by the IRS (or—for that matter—random searches by Customs, or random audits of health care claims) is that random audits provide information about types of noncompliance that existing targeting might be missing. Random audits provide the opportunity, over the long term, to reassess the level of resources devoted to control; to redirect those resources; to adjust audit selection formulas; to target investigations and audits more effectively; and to select enforcement actions that will have the greatest impact on significant areas of noncompliance.

In the 1970s, the Bureau of Health Insurance (a precursor of HCFA) ran a random audit program. Program validation teams conducted rigorous random validation audits, guided by exactly the same philosophy as the IRS's TCMP program. However the practice had disappeared by 1980 and has never been reinstated. No doubt, sometime when resources were tight, someone decided that the program of random audits did not pay for itself and was therefore a prime target for elimination. Measurement programs will always be vulnerable to short-term, short-sighted cost benefit analysis.

Industry officials point to a wide variety of activities that seem, to those officials, to accomplish systematic measurement of the fraud problem. None of them, however, provides effective measurement of the size of the fraud problem.

Quality Controls in Claims Processing

Most insurers perform some random sampling of processed claims. But the purpose of the sampling is to measure the accuracy and consistency of the human claims examiners. These quality-control procedures test procedural compliance, accepting the claim as presented, and do not attempt to check the veracity of the information in the claim itself. As one manager explained, within the context of quality controls, "we regard the claim as a legal document and assume that what it says is true; we are measuring the performance of our staff."

A 1984 study of fraud control within the AFDC (Aid to Families with Dependent Children) and Medicaid programs expands the point:

> Thus, while the Quality Control data may be a measure of managerial accuracy and may reflect the types of mistakes which are being made, they are not a measure of fraud problems. The review process does little to distinguish between intentional and unintentional client errors, and the reviewers are given few opportunities to probe beyond the data contained in the files.
>
> The Medicaid Quality Control system checks a sample of Medicaid claims, but error findings indicate only that a payment violated a program rule (e.g., by paying for a service not covered, by paying an incorrect amount, etc.); QC reviewers do not check to see if the service was in fact provided as claimed.[12]

Quality-control processes at the eight field sites varied in the frequency with which they were conducted and the proportion of claims checked. But in every case the purpose was to check the consistency and accuracy of either the entire system or individual claims examiners. Most QC processes specifically measured individual performance as part of the reward or promotion system and to provide feedback and training as necessary. In every case the method used was essentially to have a supervisor or senior claims examiner repeat the processing steps with respect to a randomly selected set of claims and then, by comparing results, measure the examiner's discrepancy rate.

Use of quality control-procedures demonstrates that the role and value of random selection within measurement processes is understood and accepted. But quality controls measure and detect internal errors, not fraud. A fraudulent claim will pop out of such a process only if, by some fluke, it was processed incorrectly. Even then, it would probably not be identified as fraudulent.

In fact, perfectly accurate claims processing serves fraud perpetrators rather well. Perpetrators like to confront systems that are 100 percent predictable and that behave the same way, claim after claim, week after week, month after month. As Clarke points out, "the essence" of any fraudulent insurance claim "is to appear normal and to be processed and paid in a routine manner".[13] One of the surprising truths of the fraud control business is that *fraud works best when claims processing works perfectly*.

Surveys of Fraud Cases

Several interviewees pointed to industry surveys, such as those conducted by Health Insurers of America Association (HIAA), as "measurement" of the fraud problem. HIAA periodically surveys member organizations and publishes aggregate profiles of the fraud experience within the industry. But the profiles represent industry's aggregate investigative caseload, not the underlying universe of fraud. The profiles, therefore, reflect the biases and capacities of the detection systems and the policies and preferences of insurers, as much as the nature or scope of the underlying problem.[14]

Random Mailing of EOMBs

Insurers, for a variety of reasons, sometimes mail EOMBs out to consumers on a random basis. One state Medicaid agency randomly mailed a small number of EOMBs, even though the response rate was extremely low and scarcely ever resulted in the detection of fraud. They did it because they thought HCFA required them to do it; not as a measurement device. They made no attempt to interpret the aggregate response. Given the ineffectiveness of EOMBs in soliciting useful information, aggregate results would not have meant much anyway.

At one major private insurer, staff made a random selection of 200 claims per week (100 from the western half of the United States, and 100 from the east) and dispatched payment verification letters. These letters, sent to the insurance certificate holder, included details of the provider, the date of service, and the dollar amount paid. Certificate holders were asked to reply only if there was a problem. Response rates averaged fifty per quarter (i.e., 2 percent), with twenty-five per quarter (1 percent) returned undelivered. Most responses resulted from misunderstandings or queries about genuine treatments and did not lead to financial recoveries or savings. Once again, little was made of the results, and no one was able to state a clear purpose for the practice.

The closest to any real explanation offered for the practice was that the payment verification letters provided management with a general sense of quality assurance. In other words, the fact that this practice failed to reveal extensive fraud or abuse was taken as reassuring evidence of the effectiveness of their control systems. But the fact that this instrument did not reveal any substantial problem can be interpreted two ways: either there was no big problem, or the instrument was poor. Without rigorous follow-up on all the nonresponders (98 percent), one cannot possibly tell the difference.

The payment verification letters used by this company were more readable than most EOMBs, but still rather dense and bureaucratic. Few recipients would have had much inclination or incentive to respond. So little reason exists to believe that such letters produce any better feedback than EOMBs. With low response rates and without rigorous follow-up of nonresponders, such systems provide little useful information and certainly no scientific measurement.

One of the major Medicare contractors was preparing to embark on an experiment with what they called "notices of utilization" (NOUs). Twenty thousand NOUs were to be sent out to Medicare beneficiaries, and 4,000 more were to be sent to physicians. The notices would relate to a random selection of claims for home health services, at a rate of 2 percent of total volume. The experiment had been requested by HCFA, with the purpose of establishing whether NOUs should routinely be used in the home health care segment of the industry. (Home health services, being 100 percent covered by Medicare, do not routinely generate EOMBs).

But once again, the plan did not provide for follow-up rigorous enough to establish fraud. Patients were asked to reply only if there was a problem. As usual, presumably, response rates would be low and meaningful interpretation impossible. Once again, the object of the exercise was not scientific measurement of the level of fraud. Rather the purpose was to perform cost/benefit analysis of the NOU procedure itself, to ascertain whether NOUs (designed to be more user-friendly than traditional EOMBs) would pay for themselves if used routinely within home health care.

This particular experimental program began early in 1995. According to the program's administrators, the experiment generated vociferous complaint from the home health care lobby, who characterized it as "unfairly bothering our clients." In any case, the experiment was never intended to provide a valid measurement instrument and could not be used as such in its planned form.

Implications of the Absence of Measurement

Previous commentators have observed the lack of systematic measurement within the health insurance industry, but have not dwelled much on its implications for fraud control. Without knowing the level of fraud in the system, it is extremely difficult to establish the appropriateness of particular fraud controls or to decide what level of resources should be invested in controls. Perhaps most important, without any clear sense of the magnitude of the problem, neither the medical profession nor society at large can determine what level of inconvenience (from additional verification procedures) should be tolerated for the sake of preserving or restoring program integrity. If the size of the problem cannot be accurately gauged, then it is unlikely to be adequately addressed.

Without measurement, the debate focuses on the *size* of the problem, rather than on *solutions*. Different parties make their own estimates and expend considerable energy defending "their position" against others'. A 1993 article in *The Lancet,* for example, attacked the White House's acceptance and use of the standard 10 percent (or $100 billion) figure.

> Where does that figure come from—even allowing the enigmatic "up-to"? The General Accounting Office, so called watchdog for Congress, estimated last year that fraud consumes 10 percent of the country's health care spending—which would more or less dovetail with the $100 billion figure from the White House. Solid data in support of that estimate, however, are extremely soft.
>
> . . . Given the hefty rewards, the difficulty of concealing large-scale medical fraud, and the rapacity of the legal profession—which gets a big cut of the winnings—the $100 billion estimate of fraudulent billing warrants deep skepticism.[15]

In other words President Clinton should either put up some solid facts, or drop the subject. Without proof of the problem, the medical profession refuses to contemplate more stringent controls.

How Measurement Changes the Nature of the Discussion—Fraud in the IRS Refund Program

The IRS recently discovered how measuring a fraud problem can completely transform the game. By 1993, the IRS knew it had a tax refund fraud problem in the electronic filing program. The earned income tax credit (EITC) enabled low-income working families with dependent children to claim up to $2,211 even if no tax had ever been withheld from their wages.[16] The EITC was more a welfare payment than a tax refund, but was administered through the tax system. The advent of electronic claims processing, accompanied by the offer by commercial banks of refund anticipation loans, meant that tax return filers could get over $2,200 cash in their hands within forty-eight hours, without ever having paid any taxes.

From a fraud perpetrator's point of view, this was easy money and fast. In April 1993, at the end of the 1993 filing season, NBC's *Dateline* exposed massive EITC scams, where residents of housing projects, who would not normally file tax returns, were being paid $400 cash for the use of their name and social security number by scam artists who would then submit hundreds or thousands of fraudulent refund claims based upon the credit. Dependent children would be "borrowed" or "invented" as necessary. Through the criminal circulation and use of lists, some children appeared as dependents on up to five hundred separate tax returns. The IRS electronic filing system, coupled with refund anticipation loans, paid up fast and reliably. There was little systematic check of the veracity of EITC claims.

In the worst scams, criminals set themselves up as electronic return originators (EROs), submitting electronic claims themselves. One ERO submitted 18,000 individual tax returns during one filing season (roughly a $36 million scheme), every one of them based on fictitious taxpayers, fictitious earnings, fictitious children, or some combination of the three.

IRS detection systems did catch a certain number of fraudulent claims. But as the "detected schemes" figures accelerated rapidly from $7.5 million in 1989 to $67 million in 1992, nobody knew whether the detection systems were getting better or the problem was getting worse. During the 1993 filing season, the detected fraud schemes jumped to over $136 million. Once again, nobody knew if that was good news or bad news.[17]

Inevitably Congress held a series of hearings following the media revelations, during which IRS managers were condemned for their organization's apparent incompetence and, at the same time, asked to guarantee that the problem would be brought under control. The IRS was unable to state the magnitude of the problem with any certainty, so was caught in the classic fraud-control dilemma: they could either play down the problem, claiming to have the situation under control (in which case they would get no additional resources to deal with the problem); or they could play up the seriousness of the problem (at the risk of making the service look incompetent) and ask for the necessary investments in controls.

As usual, in the absence of the facts, the first option (play down the problem) seemed more attractive, but offered little hope for effective future control. The IRS needed significant systems improvements as well as reassignment of substantial examination and audit resources to bring the EITC problem under control. Without the facts on the table, the most likely prospect was for the IRS to be embarrassed year after year by revelations about fraud vulnerabilities in the filing system, without ever being able to obtain or devote the resources necessary to deal with the problem.

So, in the fall of 1993, the IRS resolved to measure the problem systematically, each year from 1994 onward. In the first two weeks of the 1994 filing season (January), the IRS randomly selected over 1,000 of the returns claiming the earned income tax credit. They held up the refunds just long enough to send an IRS criminal investigator to the doors of the taxpayers' homes. The investigator arrived with a simple survey form in hand, saying, "We plan to issue your tax refund, but I'd appreciate it if you'd answer just a few simple questions." Did the dependent children really exist? Particularly if the filer fell in the category "Male: Head of Household," what evidence could be found that any children lived in the house? Could the person's employment or earnings be confirmed?

The investigators were not asked to make cases; just to use their common sense and get the basic facts so the results could be compiled into a meaningful measure of the fraud problem. They were required to validate any information the taxpayers provided by checking with third parties. They would verify the employment with the employer. If there was any doubt about the children's residency they would talk to neighbors. If there was a spouse or other relative who might also claim the children as dependents, they would make contact with them. After making their inquiries, the investigators were asked to make their own best judgment as to the nature of any error or omission and to classify any misrepresentation as intentional or unintentional. If the EITC was erroneous in any way, the form was passed to the examination division for a formal review, after which a "best and final" judgment would be made in each case.

The results, once compiled, showed that 38.8 percent of the claims for the EITC were either inflated or entirely unmerited, with 26.1 percent of the total EITC budget going into the wrong hands.[18] Even with the most conservative definition of fraud, 19 percent of the EITC claims had been classified as outright fraud.[19]

The EITC budget for the 1993 tax year (i.e., for the 1994 filing season) was roughly $15 billion.[20] So the survey results suggested that roughly $4 billion of this was getting into the wrong hands, and the piece of this loss due to outright criminal fraud exceeded $3 billion.[21]

During the 1994 filing season the IRS's detection systems found only $160 *million* worth of refund fraud.[22] So, had the IRS continued to rely on information coming from their detection systems, they would have underestimated the magnitude of the fraud problem by a factor of twenty. In other words, their detection systems showed them no more than 5 percent of the problem.

What changed once systematic measurement of the problem had been instituted? Well, fortunately, IRS managers resisted the powerful temptation to discount or discredit their own study (the thought did cross their minds when they saw how bad the results were) and faced up to the true magnitude of the problem. They encouraged the Treasury Department and congressional overseers to do the same.

Now the nature of the discussion changed altogether. The debate was no longer over the size of the problem, but how to fix it. During the remainder of 1994 the IRS scurried to make some critical multi-million-dollar investments in control systems and a number of painful and difficult policy changes that would enable them to slow down payment of certain refunds to give time for extra checking. They strengthened the eligibility requirements for electronic return originators and devoted an extra 1,700 staff *years* to detecting and preventing refund fraud.[23] Having discovered how hard it was to recover EITC payments after the fact, the IRS instituted a whole new operation using tax examiners in a pre-refund mode rather than in their traditional, more leisurely, retrospective mode. To avoid any impression of being "anti-EITC," the IRS also sent out notices to 420,000 taxpayers who appeared to qualify for the EITC but had failed to claim it.[24]

The policy changes were by no means easy. The lending banks and other tax filing intermediaries lobbied hard politically and mounted a well-orchestrated press campaign in an attempt to keep things just as they had been during 1994. For the refund anticipation loan (RAL) business to be profitable, IRS refund payments had to be fast and predictable. The new controls made them slower, much less certain, and many more of them were stopped altogether, leaving the lending banks exposed on their loans.

Two months into the 1995 filing season *USA Today* ran a front-page headline, "IRS Puts on the Brakes: Anti-Fraud Slowdown Angers Filers." The *story* was that the implementation of new IRS fraud-control measures claimed innocent filers and businesses as victims.[25] But deep within the text of that story, the simple facts were told: "The [Earned Income Tax] credits have been a popular source of fraud. An IRS study last year found that 20 percent of 1.3 million returns claiming the EITC were fraudulent. Another 20 percent had mistakes that inflated the payments."[26] The headline could have been "Thirty-Nine Percent of $20 Billion Tax Credit Program Goes to Wrong People."[27] But perhaps the media were not accustomed to such revelations coming from the defending agency itself and may not have known what to make of it. The norm, after all, was to have outsiders blast the agency, and then for everyone to join in the spectator sport of watching agency management squirm uncomfortably in their seats as they tried desperately to provide reassurance.

Valid, scientific measurement of the problem enabled the IRS to hold up the problem for congressional overseers and other stakeholders to see. It allowed them to say, in effect, "this is the problem: what price—in terms of inconvenience as well as resources—are you prepared to pay to help us deal with it?"

During the 1995 filing season, the IRS held true to their commitment and repeated the measurement survey. The problem had not gone away, but in just one year it had been cut almost exactly in half. The 1995 survey not only provided feedback as to the effectiveness of the new controls; it also showed the IRS exactly which categories of tax returns remained problematic, enabling them to focus additional resources in those areas ready for the 1996 season.

In 1995, for the first time ever, the number of EITC filers claiming dependent children dropped when compared with the previous year. The total number of children claimed also dropped.[28] The Senate "Budget Bulletin" reported in July 1995 that "the refunded portion of the EITC is $2 billion lower than originally projected (perhaps due to increased IRS scrutiny of returns claiming the EITC this year)."[29] 1995 was the first year the EITC had ever come in under budget. All but the harshest congressional critics applauded the IRS's efforts in bringing EITC fraud under control.

Why Measurement Is Not Done

Given the transforming effect of rigorous measurement, why does the health care industry fail to take it seriously, or even to consider it at all?

Few officials say rigorous measurement shouldn't be done. Some say it can't be done (i.e., it is technically too difficult). But most say *they* can't do it and give a variety of explanations why not.

One of the most common explanations is shortage of resources. "We don't have the time, or the money." Another explanation stems from short-term, short-sighted, cost benefit analysis: "We'd get better return by focusing on known problem areas" (the same objection that IRS auditors raise to the TCMP).

HCFA does have a formal procedure in existence for conducting random audits of Medicare claims, presumably for measurement purposes. "But," as a senior official explained, "we have 125,000 complaints a year from beneficiaries. All existing resources are spent following leads. We've never had the resources to do both."

Within the private sector, resource constraints had similar effects. One senior investigator said his company never did systematic measurement through random audits and *could never* do it, because "we are all too busy ... we'd have to hire outsiders to do it ... we only have fourteen people here and plenty of work to keep us busy."

Paradoxically—assuming a fixed level of fraud-control resources— the worse the fraud problem, the less likely it is to be measured. The more fraud there is, the busier everyone will be, as well as being less inclined to "waste time doing studies."

The technical objection—that scientific measurement couldn't be done—is often raised by senior managers. The same objection was raised by some when the IRS considered measuring the EITC problem. In the health care industry definitional ambiguities (between fraud, abuse, waste, errors, differences of medical opinion, and overutilization) present substantial technical difficulties, which should not be treated lightly.

Oddly enough, nobody at the field level raises the technical feasibility objection. Investigators and auditors accept readily that rigorous investigation of a random sample of claims would teach them a lot that they do not already know about the extent and nature of fraud. Many people at the field level say they would like to do it, but never have the time.

Some senior managers are not so sure that they, or their companies, would really like to do it. The vice president for audit for one major Medicare contractor explained carefully how all their various types of audit did something other than measure the fraud problem. External audit examined the procedures of external business affiliates. Internal audit focused on separation of functions, system security, and opportunities for employee corruption. Quality review processes were all aimed at procedural adherence. None of these procedures was designed to detect fraud attacks by claimants, or to measure the level of fraud in the system.

Faced with this glaring omission (which left the contractor with absolutely no idea whether their fraud problems were any worse or better than anyone else's) and asked whether his company might consider instituting a program of random audits for systematic measurement, the vice president for audit commented: "There is no reward for finding fraud. There are no out of pocket losses for us [as a Medicare contractor]. Why would we put ourselves in this painful position? We have to think about our shareholders." The head of the special investigative unit at the same company, explaining that no one within the company wanted to devote resources to a "study," added:

> Let's not make a wave. No one's upset. No one here is complaining about [fraud]. Business is good. We're making money. [Fraud losses] are not operating expenses. It's just someone else's money that's passing through.
>
> Besides, what would happen if we did do such a study? What if this became known? The newspapers are watching us. They'd love a story like that.

Making the commitment to measurement demands enormous courage on the part of managers. In November 1993, when the leadership of the IRS gathered to consider whether or not to approve the random sampling of EITC-based refunds, the decision was far from painless.[30] Commissioner Richardson had been appointed by President Clinton and knew that the Earned Income Tax Credit Program, which the president hoped to expand considerably, constituted a central plank in his welfare reform plans. If the discovery were made that the EITC program was riddled with fraud, that would be grim news indeed for the administration. But the commissioner was resolved to do whatever it took to restore the integrity of the program, even if that meant exposing its weaknesses first.

What clinched the IRS executive committee's decision to approve the plan, was when the chief financial officer remarked, "Let's see if I have got this right. It seems to me that the worst possible situation to be in—for *us* to be in—is to believe that we have a huge problem, but not be able to prove it to anyone." Which is precisely the situation in the health care industry.

The IRS commissioner and executive committee went on to make the commitment to measurement, and the president learned how serious the fraud problem within his favorite program had become. But the IRS then obtained and committed the resources necessary to address the problem, which would never have happened in the absence of unambiguous measures.

Resource Allocation, in the Absence of Measurement

If the true scope of the health care fraud problem were actually known, one would expect resource allocation for controls to be based upon that knowledge. But in the absence of such knowledge, how does the industry decide what level of resources to invest in fraud controls?

Most industry officials agree resources allocated for fraud control are pitifully small. But they fail to establish any rational basis for meaningful increases. In 1984, John Gardiner and Theodore Lyman stated:

> Our case studies, GAO reports, and Congressional hearings have found repeatedly that the agencies administering welfare programs [including Medicaid] place little emphasis on fraud control; when cases of fraud or abuse are discovered, the most common responses are to cut losses (terminating a recipient's enrollment or a provider's participation in Medicaid) and to try to recover overpayments. Rarely are defrauders prosecuted. More broadly, these studies indicate that fraud control efforts rarely approach a level of optimality, one at which further investments in control would exceed resulting benefits, or one at which additional control efforts would materially infringe on recipients' and providers' rights.[31]

A private insurer that operates nationwide set the budget for their specialist fraud unit (special investigative unit [SIU]) at $800,000. The unit produces recoveries and direct savings of between $2 million and $3 million per year; a savings-to-cost ratio of roughly three to one. And company policy, according to the unit's director, is "zero tolerance for fraud"; they "aggressively pursue every case that comes up." The investigative unit is busy enough that they hardly ever have time to go out and search proactively for cases. They work almost entirely in reactive mode.

But this insurer's claims volume exceeds $2 billion per year, and management quotes the standard GAO 10 percent estimate when asked how much fraud they think there might be within their system. In other words, they think (but do not know for sure) that they might be losing around $200 million per year to fraud. Of that $200 million in potential losses, $2.5 million is recovered or saved by the SIU.

The obvious question, it seems, is why is this special investigative unit not forty or fifty times its current size? Saving $2.5 million looks terrific when compared with the $800,000 budget, but looks terrible when compared with the estimated $200 million losses. So, what would persuade management to increase the size of the unit? Apparently management would be prepared to increase the size of unit, they said, if the existing unit was clearly unable to cope with its workload: a situation which, they claimed, did not exist.

But why was the SIU, if it was truly far too small, not over-whelmed? Two reasons surfaced. First, the SIU's reactive workload was driven by referral mechanisms that were not very effective. Most referrals received from claims processors or from medical review were quirky and unusual, often product of fluke or coincidence rather than *system*. Examiners or reviewers would notice something suspicious and make a referral, even though they were examining the claim for some entirely different reason. Keeping up with the relatively slow flow of referrals, therefore, was more a function of the size of the pipe than the depth of the reservoir.

Second, clear evidence emerged of a dynamic equilibrium connecting proactive and reactive work. As soon as the investigators had a spare moment, they would go and "beat the bushes": talk to claims examiners, educate medical reviewers, and hold discussions with law enforcement agencies or other insurers. Whenever they engaged in any of these proactive activities, they were rewarded with a rash of cases and referrals that made them so busy that they had to suspend any further proactive work for the time being.

Investigators described how just a little beating of the bushes produced a significant volume of high-quality fraud cases—which meant it would be a long time before they would get a chance to beat the bushes again. Had the SIU been able to dedicate some of its resources exclusively to proactive work, then this SIU would soon have been completely overwhelmed with the resulting caseload.

Investigators had plenty of evidence for their conviction that a "huge, untapped reservoir of fraud is sitting out there." In support of that contention, they offered the following observations:

1. Small investments in proactive outreach produce a large volume of quality cases. "The more we go out and ask and prod people, the more referrals we get. And when we do a presentation or something, and then we get a flood of calls over the next week or so, they are all good referrals. I mean they are *good* calls."

2. Over the years, the number of referrals the unit has received from outside sources, such as the FBI, seems to rise in direct proportion to the resources invested in health care fraud by those outside agencies. They see absolutely no sign of diminishing returns on investment.

3. Their own investigations reveal the weakness of the company's detection and referral systems. "When we get a report and look into it and start digging, it usually turns out that our exposure is huge compared with the little thing that was reported. And we didn't find it because we detected the big pattern; we found it because we got lucky with some little piece."

4. The majority of cases they investigate involve blatant behavior, with little attempt at concealment or subtlety, and most are detected because the perpetrators were careless, excessively greedy, or stupid. Investigators are painfully aware of the fact that they lack both the time and the methods to tackle the professional white-collar versions of the crime. All their time and energy is consumed dealing with amateurs: "What scares me the most: how blatant it is. It's too easy. They are not careful about hiding their tracks. The stuff we detect is obvious. Not well hidden at all. It's just dumb junk."

5. Finally, these investigators had obtained, from a law-enforcement agency, a list that had circulated among various telemarketing operations. The list showed which insurance companies were easy to defraud and which were tougher. This particular group of investigators' company was on the "easy" side, perhaps in part because investigative resources were so limited.

The annual budget for their fraud unit ($800,000) represents 0.04 percent of the claims volume. They spend at the 0.04 percent level to deal with a problem they think might be costing them 10 percent.

Massive underinvestment in fraud-control resources seems to be the industry norm. The budget for fraud control within the Medicare program is set incrementally each year. From $24 million in 1993 it rose to $32 million in 1995. With the total Medicare budget in the neighborhood of $160 billion,[32] $32 million represents an investment in fraud control at a level below 0.02 percent of overall program costs.

These investments, small as they are, pay off handsomely. The special investigative units at Medicare contractors all save more than they cost. Some turn in savings-to-cost ratios as high as fourteen to one. The aggregate ratio for the program (calculated across all Medicare contractors) is roughly three to one. Nowhere is it less than two to one.

Among private insurers, the savings-to-cost ratios for fraud units are climbing each year. Annual surveys of antifraud programs conducted by HIAA showed the ratio of savings-to-budget for dedicated fraud units, aggregated across responding companies, to be 6 to 1 in 1990; 7 to 1 in 1991; and 9.5 to 1 in 1992.[33]

The commentary with these figures concludes, "This increasing cost/benefit ratio indicates that companies are becoming more efficient in their anti-fraud programs." [34] The increasing ratio could mean companies are becoming more efficient. Or it could mean that there is more and more readily identifiable fraud year after year. Or it could represent an increasing focus on monetary, rather than judicial, outcomes. Whatever the reason for the rise, these figures provide compelling demonstration that existing investments in fraud control represent money well spent.

A similar study on fraud controls among disability income insurers showed return ratios of fourteen to one in 1991; thirty-two to one in 1992; and forty-four to one in 1993.[35]

Medicaid spending in 1994 totaled $145.9 billion for 34.6 million recipients—13 percent of the U.S. civilian population.[36] The federal government contributes 50 percent of administrative costs and between 50 percent and 78 percent of benefit costs, depending on each states' per capita income. The federal government pays a larger share of the costs of the Medicaid fraud control units, providing 90 percent of the MFCUs operating costs for the first three years ("start-up period") and 75 percent thereafter.[37]

The federal budget for the MFCUs in 1994 was $62 million.[38] Adding in the states' share, total spending on the MFCUs runs at roughly 0.05 percent of total program budget. The federal government offers to pay $3 for every $1 the states invest in the MFCUs, with a cap for allowable federal reimbursement at 0.25 percent of the states' annual Medicaid budget. Despite the $3 for $1 offer, most states have, for many years, chosen to operate at a funding level far below the reimbursement cap.

A clear pattern begins to emerge, spanning both commercial and public health insurance programs. The extent of fraud is never measured; merely estimated. The estimates are too soft to act as a basis for serious resource-allocation decisions, so resources devoted to fraud control have to be based on something other than the perceived size of the problem. In practice, control resources are budgeted incrementally, with significant increases likely only when a fraud unit is visibly drowning under its caseload.

But most such units are not drowning; which seems a little puzzling at first. Despite their tiny size, most fraud units manage to keep up with the volume of referred cases. How is that possible? If they are really far too small, why are they not overwhelmed with their work? The most likely explanation—which Chapter 4 explores in detail—is that the referral mechanisms just do not work very well and produce only the merest trickle of cases (when compared to the underlying size of the problem).

The Medicaid fraud control units provide an interesting case study with respect to referral mechanisms and their effects on workload. Because the MFCUs are separate and distinct from the paying agencies, their referrals tend to be relatively formal, quantifiable, and subject to record.

Senior managers were interviewed at each of three different MFCUs, (which I will refer to here as MFCU-1, MFCU-2, and MFCU-3.) All three managers believed their units were understaffed and that the fraud problem was much greater than evidenced by their own activities. But managers at two of these units (MFCU-2 and MFCU-3) reluctantly confessed that their units were not particularly busy. In fact, they said, they would dearly love to receive more referrals—especially good-quality ones—from their respective state Medicaid agencies. But the referrals just did not come in any great numbers.

The director of MFCU-3 said he even wondered at times if the unit was too large, given the lack of fraud referrals from the health plans and Medicaid agency. "There are times when I think we're bigger than we should be, because of our lack of quality fraud cases. We're still very busy investigating patient abuse,[39] but have to scrounge around for the fraud cases." He spoke often of the unit's "desperation for getting better referrals." In January 1994, he wrote to the corresponding state

Medicaid agency to express alarm at the fact that they had generated only seventeen referrals in the previous two years (1992 and 1993 combined)—a rate of just one fraud referral for each $100 million expended by the agency.

Staff at the MFCU-1, however, had quite a different attitude. They too considered the number of referrals coming from the state agency pitifully low. On average, they received around twenty referrals per year from the agency. But they nevertheless managed to prosecute between 100 and 150 cases per year. They simply did not rely on agency referrals. They adopted a proactive stance and went out into the streets to dig up cases for themselves. And everywhere they looked, they found plenty.

The net result: MFCU-1 felt "terribly strapped," according to its director. The unit was funded at a level of 0.11 percent of program costs—higher than most, but still significantly below the federal reimbursement cap. But the factor that determined how busy they were was not the size of the unit, but their proactive stance. "When we open up one of these cans of worms we find so many cases that could be worked that we do feel short staffed. We have hundreds of pending cases, which leaves us little time to go out and generate more."

The dynamic equilibrium between proactive and reactive work becomes more familiar: A small amount of proactive work generates a huge caseload, which then constrains further proactive work. One of the unit's more experienced investigators claimed that, in over fifteen years of service, not once had she been assigned a case! Every case she investigated had generated so many other leads that she constantly had to pick and choose which ones to pursue and which to drop.

MFCU-1's management displayed uncommon energy for proactive work. They routinely sent undercover agents out into the streets, just to "find out what's happening"—a practice that both the other two units considered beyond the scope of their duties. In fact the director of MFCU-2 stated the conviction that his unit was *supposed* to be reactive and that anything resembling "fishing" for fraud, or "going out looking for new M.O.s" (Modus Operandi) would be censured.

MFCU-1's investigators, armed with Medicaid cards, go out and shop for medical services just to get a sense for which providers' practices are legitimate and which are not. They hang around seedy storefront clinics until they figure out what happens there. They go in and ask for drugs or prescriptions. In their city, many providers engaged in fraud have begun to take X-rays and to draw blood from patients routinely, in a deliberate attempt to weed out the undercover agents.

They know MFCU agents will not risk exposure to repeated X-rays or want to have their blood drawn under less than ideal conditions.

The investigators who work the streets, day in and day out, offer the most depressing account of what they find. Several of them estimated that, putting hospitals aside, as much as 50 percent of the state's remaining Medicaid budget was lost to an epidemic of street-level fraud.

Meanwhile, the corresponding state Medicaid agency claimed that tighter controls on eligibility and some up-front edits within the claims-processing system effectively controlled fraud, bringing losses down to no more than 2 percent or 3 percent. (If you ask MFCU-1's investigators about the effectiveness of the new eligibility controls, they laugh and point out that anyone can rent a valid Medicaid card for $2 a day from any of the city's homeless shelters.)

The director of MFCU-1 noted that the number of referrals from the state agency had dropped even further since they implemented the new controls. This fact did not bother him particularly; it was just an observation. He had long since written off the state agency (and the whole claims-processing system) as a meaningful source of fraud referrals.

So, given the absence of measurement, what *does* determine the level of resources dedicated to fraud controls? The general answer, it seems, is that sufficient resources are allocated to handle the reactive workload, with little or no spare capacity for proactive work. And why then is the level of investment so low, scarcely ever reaching even 0.1 percent of program costs? Presumably because the reactive caseload is tiny compared with the size of the problem. And why is the reactive caseload so small if the fraud problem is so serious? The most likely explanation would seem to be that the fraud-detection and referral systems do not work very well.

Chapter 4 examines existing detection and referral systems in detail, to establish more precisely what they can and cannot accomplish.

4
Assessment of Fraud-Control Systems

When news of scandalous fraud losses comes to the fore, industry executives often deflect criticism from their own agencies through what might be termed *defense by display of functional apparatus*. They counter suggestions of wide-open vulnerability to fraud by listing all kinds of apparatus, in operational use, aimed at fraud prevention and detection. When their critics accuse them of failing to adequately invest in fraud controls, they respond that those critics only count the resources devoted to specialist investigative units and fail to acknowledge all the other controls embedded within the claims-processing system.

Defending the New York State Department of Social Services (which handles the state's Medicaid program) the executive deputy commissioner, in 1991, produced a fine example of defense by display of functional apparatus. His claim was that fraud losses might reach $125 million, but they certainly did not reach the New York MFCU's estimate of $2 billion. He argued that the Department of Social Services used an impressive array of apparatus to control fraud, including identification processes (computer profiling and targeting, undercover investigations, and audits); front-end controls limiting program access (provider enrollment controls, prepayment edits, utilization thresholds); and extensive application of technology (including Medicaid card swiping and ordering systems, and various computer matching programs.)[1]

To see if the traditional mix of systems really works to detect or control fraud, we must inspect each one in turn. The traditional types of controls, commonly used throughout the industry, are claims processing, involving human claims examiners as well as automated edits and audits; prepayment medical review; post-payment utilization review;

and audits of one kind or another. These systems are supposed either to reject fraudulent claims up front, or to detect them and refer them to specialist fraud units for investigation.

Claims Processing

The bulk of today's health care claims are processed within high-volume, highly automated environments. Claims are fed into the processing stream through one of three mechanisms. Claims are received either

1. On paper forms, and data entry is performed by human data entry clerks
2. On paper forms, but the forms are typed so they can be read by an optical character reader (OCR), eliminating much or all of the human data entry task
3. In electronic form directly from the provider or billing agency, eliminating the paper forms altogether

Most payment systems can receive claims through more than one of these mechanisms; many payment systems combine all three.

Once the claims have been fed into the processing stream, what happens to them thereafter is the same, regardless of the form in which they arrived. The amount of data entered into the automated payment system is cut to the minimum required for processing and paying the claim. So, if it was a paper claim, textual explanations or comments will not get beyond the data entry stage. (The original claim forms, or captured images of them, may be kept for inspection by claims reviewers when necessary). The data entered from paper claims matches precisely the minimal data fields used for electronic claims submission; nearly all of them consist of numeric codes.

All claims then pass through a series of automated edits and audits. *Edits* generally test for data entry errors by checking that entries have been properly formatted and fall within acceptable ranges on a field-by-field basis. System *audits* test a variety of conditions to determine whether or not the claim should be paid.

The automated audits are arranged as a sequence of separate software modules, each with a different function, although the precise sequence varies from system to system. The standard modules (in no particular order) are:

1. Data entered correctly? Have all the necessary fields been properly filled in? Do they pass basic syntactical and relational checks? Do the data fall in valid ranges?

2. Prior authorization? Was prior authorization required for this procedure? If so, does the system have a record that the necessary authorization was obtained for this procedure by this provider?

3. Procedure code matches diagnosis? Does the procedure make sense, given the diagnosis code entered? (Commercial software packages perform this function, providing a matrix of permissible combinations.)

4. Qualifying provider? Is the provider approved? Enrolled? Within the network? Qualified for this procedure? Is the provider on suspension, or review? Is the provider required to submit supporting documentation for this procedure? Are the provider's rates approved and on file? (Involves "look-up" to provider record files.)

5. Qualifying recipient? Is the recipient enrolled? Eligible? Covered for this procedure? Subject to deductible? (Involves "look-up" to recipient record files.)

6. Pricing? Is the price within the approved range for this procedure? Is the price approved for this provider? Is the pricing for this procedure set on the basis of "prevailing rates within the industry?" Is this price within the approved range for this specialty and geographic area? (Again, commercial software packages provide tables of ranges, by zip code, by specialty, by procedure.)

7. Service limitations? Does the recipient's insurance provide coverage for this number of incidents of this type of service within a given time period? (Involves interrogation of patient claim history files.)

8. Duplicate claims? Has this claim been submitted and paid already? Is there another claim for this patient for a sufficiently similar procedure at or around the same time that would cause this claim to be considered a duplicate submission?

9. Code manipulation? Does this claim present an unallowable combination of procedure codes; either because the procedure items should be rebundled, or because the combination of procedures does not seem medically appropriate? (Again, commercial packages provide two-dimensional tables of disallowable combinations).

If a claim passes through all of these modules without a problem, it will be paid automatically, without any further human intervention.

Most systems hold payments for a few days so they can be paid in a weekly batch cycle, when computers automatically dispatch direct deposits, or print and mail paper checks.

If the information content of a claim raises a flag within any one of the nine audit modules, then the processing system will do one of the following three things:

1. Auto-reject: The system generates a notice of rejection which is sent back to the submitter normally through the same medium—paper or electronic—as the claim submission. Rejection notices always include a summary explanation of the reasons for rejection.
2. Auto-adjust: The system corrects an error, adjusts pricing, or rebundles procedures, then passes the claims through for payment.
3. Claim suspension: The system transfers the claim to a queue for human review. The claim is then examined by a claims examiner or by the medical review team, depending on the level of medical knowledge required for the review.

How do such systems contribute to fraud control? And what do they *not* do? These audits and edits enable the system to pay the right amount to the right person for the service claimed. They serve to correct billing errors and inappropriate billing procedures. And they reject claims if one or more of the provider, the recipient, or the procedure is somehow ineligible.

Clearly such systems do not do anything to verify that the service was in fact provided as claimed, or that the diagnosis is genuine, or that the patient knows anything at all about the alleged treatment. Rather, they assume the information presented is true and consider whether or not that information justifies payment of the claim.

None of the nine standard modules is targeted on fraud. Generally no attempt is made to create rules or logic that would pick out suspicious claims for closer scrutiny or to detect claims containing some deception or misrepresentation. The industry does not use fraud-specific prepayment edits or audits of any kind; fraud-specific edits and audits do not exist.

Nevertheless, some fraudulent claims are rejected as a result of the system's prepayment edits and audits. But fraudulent claims are rejected if, and only if, they are billed incorrectly; that is, if the procedure does not match the diagnosis; if the provider, beneficiary, or procedure is ineligible; or if, by some mischance, the service billed overlapped with some other incompatible service (for example, inpatient services overlapping with outpatient services).

In each of these cases the most likely outcome is auto-rejection, with the reason carefully laid out in an explanatory note to the fraud perpetrator. The perpetrator appreciates the education and does not make the same mistake again. Although the perpetrator gets wiser, the paying organization generally does not. There is no system for monitoring rejected claims, so no human within the paying organization notices the classic pattern of test a little, learn a little used by fraud perpetrators. Some insurers monitor aggregate rejection rates for providers, so that they can pick out the ones that seem to be having a really bad time and offer them some extra special education (billing instruction). But, provided the fraud perpetrators learn the billing rules as fast as anyone else, there is no reason why they should show up.

Which is not to say that claims-processing operations produce no fraud referrals at all. In fact they do produce some. But claims-processing operations produce fraud referrals only insofar as they involve human beings scrutinizing claims. Fraud referrals result from the extraordinary capability of the human brain to spot patterns that it was not looking for. Referrals come from data entry clerks, who notice such oddities as white-out on the claim form, misspellings of medical terms, signs of illiteracy, unnaturally round numbers, names spelled inconsistently, apparent relationships between provider and patient, and so on.

At none of the field sites examined did processing systems make fraud referrals. Systems suspend claims for human review—which leads to the possibility of a fraud referral. But the logic and criteria for suspension focus on billing procedures, not fraud. So fraud referrals, when they come from the claims-processing operation, generally come by accident. They come because, for one reason or another, a *person* looked at the claim form and became suspicious.

Some referrals come from data entry clerks, despite the fact that these clerks have no incentive to spot fraud and usually very little relevant training. They also come from claims examiners following the system's suspension of a claim. But that too happens more by accident than design. Claims examiners invariably commented that their fraud referrals had nothing whatsoever to do with the reason the claim was originally suspended. They resolved the suspension according to established procedures, but—given the opportunity to look at the claim documents—they noticed something else about the claim that made them suspicious.

Claims-processing systems seldom incorporate effective fraud-referral mechanisms. The edits and audits do nothing to verify the information in the claims. And the opportunities for human beings to become suspicious are dwindling with every week that goes by. The proportion of claims coming in electronically rises constantly, and the majority of these go through auto-adjudication—which means there is no human intervention or inspection *at any time* between claims submission and payment.

Even when claims do come in on paper, they increasingly come in neatly typed, on standard forms that minimize the amount of textual information. Use of high-speed optical character readers (OCR) removes the human data entry function, except for the occasional correction of numbers that the OCR machine was not able to read reliably.

Modern, high-speed claims-processing systems are not set up to detect or refer fraud. They are set up to process claims, fast and efficiently, and to ensure correct billing. Virtually the only times when such systems raise suspicions of fraud are when human beings have the opportunity to contemplate the claim in its entirety and to ask the kinds of questions that only human beings can ask.

Even claims that are patently absurd will be paid, unless, of course, they happen to contain one of the specific procedural billing violations that trigger rejection. What follows is a case in point, described by a member of a fraud unit at a major private insurance company.

> The other day we had [a claim] come up here [to the fraud investigation unit] for some other mechanical reason, not because of the content of the claim. And [when we read the text of the claim] we rolled around. It was a guy who went to Africa and "fell out of a wet tree" and sustained an injury to his scrotum. So he spent thirty days in the hospital. But he never went to the hospital until two days after the accident. And we paid. Then he sent in a report some time later saying he'd really been in the hospital thirty-two days, so could we pay some more. So we paid. Now, what is a wet tree, and what was he doing up it?

No one could expect highly automated claims-processing systems to display common sense, to become suspicious, or to ask the kinds of questions that humans ask. And they don't, which is why they generally fail to detect fraud. The best one would hope for claims-processing systems is that they would ask all the questions that machines can ask.

Sadly, there is good reason to believe they sometimes fail to ask even the questions they are supposed to ask; sometimes for good reasons, sometimes for bad.

The state agency associated with MFCU-3, for example, showed the "diagnosis to procedure code" module in flowcharts of their system's edits and audits. But they admitted, when asked which commercial software package they were using for this function, that they had not yet purchased one and had not yet filled in the two-dimensional table connecting diagnoses with permissible procedure codes. They had been paying claims for years with this whole module effectively turned off.

System edits and audits are frequently turned off. Limited budgets for claim examination force managers to limit the number of automatic edits and audits in order to limit the claim-suspension rate. Under the Medicare program, HCFA pays for a maximum suspension rate of roughly 9 percent of claims.[2] Most contractors, if they turned all their edits and audits on, would easily exceed that percentage. Most Medicare contractors, in fact, suspend claims at higher rates than HCFA budgets allow, making up the costs with savings elsewhere.

A part of Empire Blue Cross/Blue Shield's recent troubles arose from turning off automated edits, resulting in claims being paid without being properly checked. An inadequately maintained computerized provider file was causing too many rejects and suspensions. So Empire used dummy codes to effectively override the provider-verification system, which resulted in roughly 5 million claims being paid without this control operating.[3]

A 1995 GAO study[4] found that Medicare could save millions of dollars (under Part B) simply by operating commercially available software packages designed to detect and correct various well-known forms of "code manipulation."[5] The study implied that Medicare was not even protected in these *obvious* ways.

In fact, HCFA already provides carriers the specific code combinations they need to do this job and requires them to implement controls sufficient to prevent such abuses. But the carriers have no financial incentive to maintain such controls.

GAO, in their experiment, reprocessed 200,000 paid Medicare claims using four different commercially available code-manipulation packages. The results suggested that the Medicare program might have saved a further $604 million in 1994 alone, had modern code-manipulation defenses been installed and operated.[6]

Code manipulation, although generally classified as abuse rather than fraud, is a high-stakes game. When Aetna first installed a commercial software package to detect code manipulation in 1991, they announced shortly afterward that they were saving $2 million each month in exchange for the $325,000 annual license fee for the software.[7]

Commercial software vendors now find sales opportunities on both sides of the code-manipulation game. Providers and billing agencies can install software that deliberately unbundles codes, and some packages will even suggest alternative diagnoses that would result in increased reimbursement rates. In defense of these so-called "billing optimizers," vendors claim their goal is to prompt coders to consider conditions or treatments they might have overlooked, so that providers get all the reimbursement they are rightfully owed.[8] Nevertheless, such systems are clearly designed to provide an opportunity to alter a medical diagnosis for financial reasons.

With computer software manufacturers servicing both sides of the code-manipulation game, the winner generally turns out to be the side that has the latest version or the more sophisticated software. Code manipulation, and control of such abuses, is a game of "dueling systems."[9]

The various modules built into claims-processing systems may help to control code manipulation. They certainly help to ensure billing correctness. However, these modules do little for fraud control. Overall, the model for claims suspension and review is *systems select: humans inspect.* The criteria upon which *systems select* seldom have anything to do with fraud.

Claims Examination and Development

Once humans have a chance to inspect claims, the prospects for fraud detection and referral improve tremendously. Humans, given the opportunity, often notice the unusual or incongruous.

But the central task of claims examination and development turns out to be quite routine. Claims examiners mostly follow prescribed sequences of actions and decisions, usually specified in manuals on their desks. "If this, then look up that. If that, then do this." These prescribed procedures enable the examiner to resolve questions of eligibility, coverage, medical appropriateness, or whatever it was that caused the claim to be suspended. Examiners' actions largely consist of searching reference materials or interrogating other databases in order to follow a decisionmaking path that was too complex or unusual to be incorporated into the automated claims-processing system.

So claims examiners and developers are "programmed" to resolve the more complex cases, but they focus on precisely the same issues as the edits and audits in the processing system. They just deal with the more complex cases.

Prepayment Medical Review

The term medical review is used in various ways. Usually it means "claims examination requiring medical knowledge." So medical-review teams include nurses, senior examiners (who have picked up some medical knowledge), and a small number of doctors available for consultation (either in-house or externally as consultants). Medical review focuses on issues of medical appropriateness and medical necessity and does so within the confines of an insured's policy coverage. Medical-review teams assume the information content of the claim to be true, even though they may request medical records to establish or substantiate medical necessity.

The courses of action open to examiners and medical reviewers are:

1. Request additional medical documentation to support the diagnosis, or to establish medical necessity
2. Deny the claim, stating reasons, and have the system generate a rejection notice to the claimant
3. Approve the claim, accepting it as valid
4. Compromise, or cutback, based on the level or limitations of coverage and on the examiners' professional judgment as to what is reasonable in the circumstances

"Refer to fraud unit" does not normally appear on the reviewers' list of formal options. Their formal task is to resolve specific issues; and their list of issues does not include verifying the truthfulness of the claim. Nevertheless medical reviewers do make fraud referrals from time to time—just like claims examiners—as an accidental by-product of human claims inspection.

Many managers interviewed regarded their medical-review teams as a major weapon in their efforts to combat fraud. But medical review and fraud detection are two quite distinct sciences. Medical review cannot act as a useful filter for fraud detection. When medical reviewers spot fraud, once again it is *because they are human and because they are looking at the claim*; not because it is their job.

To illustrate how separate the sciences of medical reivew and fraud detection are, consider the following simple fraud scheme. Pick a genuine patient, who suddenly got sick and developed an expensive but perfectly genuine medical history. Now take a thousand other patient identities and replicate the same billing history, maybe a month later, claim by claim. For these other thousand patients, provide no services. If the system paid all the original patient's claims without objection, the chances are it will pay the same medical history a thousand times over—for a thousand fake illnesses—without so much as a hiccup.

To escape attention from medical review, a fraud perpetrator has only to base their false claims on medically plausible diagnoses and procedures and to stay comfortably within the confines of policy coverage.

An Experiment in Automated "Claims Examination"

The routineness and predictability of the claims-examination function was made vividly clear through an experimental application of personal computers at one of Medicare's regional DME contractors. They had a whole roomful of personal computers (486s) neatly arranged around the walls, which the contractors had programmed to do the work of claims examiners and medical reviewers. They called the approach the "Automatic Transaction Processing System" (ATPS).

During my visit to the ATPS room, some of the computers were "sleeping," having resolved all of the suspended claims in their queue and having no work left to do. Others were working away, and, by watching the screen, one could just about keep up with what they were doing. The computers logged into various other mainframe systems, including Medicare's central database of beneficiary histories (HIMR);[10] triggered an inquiry of some kind and waited for the response; logged out; dialed up another system; and so on. These PCs were following claims-resolution procedures, as per the manual, just as claims examiners and medical reviewers do. They just did it faster, more reliably, and much more cheaply.

The designers of the ATPS had taken the list of suspension codes and picked off the ones whose resolution procedures were easiest to automate. Having demonstrated success with the simpler ones, they were working their way down the list to more complex ones. The idea behind this innovation is really quite clever. It is much easier to equip a PC with a wide range of communications packages and have it interrogate mainframe systems one by one, than it would be to integrate the different mainframe systems with each other. So the designers of ATPS programmed the PCs to perform all the mainframe inquiries and built in the decision logic that human examiners would have followed. The cost of resolving a suspended claim dropped to 5.5 cents per claim using the PCs, from $3.85 per claim employing human examiners and reviewers. Meanwhile "accuracy," as established by quality-control procedures, rose to 100 percent.

The ATPS demonstrated ingenious use of modern technology and a highly innovative way of processing inquiries that demanded access to a range of incompatible mainframe systems. But the system also clarifies the true nature of claims-examination medical review. Three key observations should be made: First, none of the PCs in that room ever called a beneficiary or provider on the phone. Second, all the information the PCs used in claim resolution was internal to the payment system (including central Medicare databases). Third, none of those PCs ever made a fraud referral, even after resolving hundreds of thousands of suspended claims. In fact "fraud referral" or "forming of suspicions" appeared nowhere on the list of possible outcomes.

Surprising Lack of Fraud Awareness

Some examination and review procedures seem to ignore the possibility of fraud altogether. For example, when claims are suspended for medical review, claimants are frequently asked to provide medical records in support of the claims. What happens if providers do not supply the requested documentation within the time period allowed (typically sixty days)? What if they never respond at all?

Of course that particular claim will be denied. And, from the point of view of claims examiners or reviewers, that would be the end of the matter. Their job would be finished, because the unit of work for the whole claims-processing system is *the claim*. Examiners and reviewers have no reason to be curious about providers who allow their claims to drop rather than simply providing a copy of supporting documentation.

But the units of work for fraud control are fraud *schemes*, fraud *problems*, fraudulent *providers*, or fraud *patterns* or *methods*. In the control business, intelligence about any of these is a most valuable asset. Fraud investigators would have every reason to be curious, to follow up, and to find out why a provider so casually allowed an account receivable to slip.

Fraud investigators would be especially intrigued, given the surprising volume of responses that never come back. One state Medicaid agency reported that between 40 percent and 50 percent of the requests for supporting documentation went unanswered. In each case, the claim was dropped from the system and no follow-up inquiries were made. That was the end of the matter.

In stark contrast, examiners at one small private insurer—who displayed a much greater level of fraud awareness—asserted "we never let one of those drop. . . if they don't respond we want to know *why*." These examiners would first mail a reminder. After that they would call. If the provider still didn't respond, they would visit the provider's office to discuss the claim.

At a major Medicare contractor, medical review procedures showed a particularly surprising lack of fraud awareness. The medical reviewers themselves were fraud aware and made occasional referrals. But the medical review procedures seemed to institutionalize a lack of curiosity. This contractor's medical review was focused on particularly troublesome segments of the industry and upon known or suspected patterns of abuse and overutilization. (For example, one project focused on the specific problem of home health care agencies billing for two-person visits, when the service provided only called for one-person visits.)

Having picked a specific segment or practice for attention, the medical review section would introduce screens (selection criteria) into the claims-processing system to pick out a random sample of around sixty pertinent claims. With respect to those claims, the medical-review team would mail out, or have the system generate, a standard letter requesting a variety of supporting documentation. When the responses came back in they were examined by medical-review nurses and the aggregate results were examined. If this process confirmed a billing or utilization problem, the team would try to correct the problem, using education as their tool of choice—which, they said, "mostly fixes the problem."

At first sight, this detailed examination of a random sample of claims, within a high-risk segment, looks quite promising as a fraud-detection system. But this unit scarcely ever made fraud referrals. Under what conditions would they refer a provider for investigation? According to the head of the unit "we would refer a case for investigation if, from the documents sent in, there was clear evidence of fraud." But who would be stupid enough to send "clear evidence of fraud," in the mail?

What happens if no documentation is received, or if a provider fails to respond at all? Next to nothing. If the provider does not respond within sixty days, the claim is deleted from the system, which means the system rejects the claim and *erases all record of its existence.*

Such procedures accomplish nothing with respect to fraud control. Fraud perpetrators remain perfectly safe in the face of these kinds of reviews. If they are unlucky enough to receive a request for supporting documentation, they can simply ignore it. Or, if they prefer, they can take the trouble, and up to sixty days, to send in suitably fabricated documents.

The director of this medical review unit—which virtually never makes a fraud referral—was very aware of fraud and said that "sixty to seventy percent of all our providers are crooked." But the procedures the unit uses were nevertheless designed as if the fraud problem did not exist.

Does that mean these procedures are useless? No, absolutely not. They accomplish their design purpose. They help to control overzealous billing that pushes the limits within the rules. They also help to identify erroneous billing or utilization practices by honest providers who did not know they had strayed outside the limits of policy coverage, and who are happy to have the error of their ways pointed out. But fraud perpetrators represent a different audience; they know exactly what they are doing wrong and deliberately stay within the confines of policy coverage and medical orthodoxy.

Post-Utilization Review

Long after the claims have been paid, the post-payment-utilization review function takes the opportunity, outside the pressure of payment cycles, to examine aggregate statistical profiles of providers and recipients. Those that stand out in a statistical sense will then have their medical utilization and claims patterns scrutinized more closely.

The Medicaid program calls their post-utilization review system "SURS," which stands for Surveillance and Utilization Review Subsystem. The origins of SURS date back to 1970 within the Department of Health, Education, and Welfare, where the objective was to perform comprehensive statistical profiling of providers and recipients.[11] By 1995, the emphasis in most SURS units, and in most other post-utilization review units, had shifted almost exclusively to *provider profiling.*

Various commercial companies now sell profiling systems to assist in utilization review, and many health insurers build their own versions in-house. These profiling systems all operate essentially upon the same philosophy and differ only in the number and types of variables they use to characterize provider behavior and the degree of sophistication with which they use statistical methods.

The general philosophy is straightforward. First the system divides providers into groups by specialty and by geographic area. Then it chooses a series of variables through which one might characterize providers' "behavior." These can be general variables (e.g., the number of procedures per patient visit, the average number of times each patient is seen per month) or specialty-specific variables (e.g., for obstetricians, the percentage of births by caesarean section; or, for home health care agencies, the proportion of home visits requiring two staff members rather than one).

For each variable, the system calculates the distribution for the particular specialty and geographic area. Using that distribution, the system assigns a score for each provider that indicates how far their behavior deviates from the mean. The system then picks off the few providers that lie at the extreme tails of the distribution (paying attention to whichever of the two tails seems to be more suspicious; usually the one that represents more expensive behavior). Some of the more sophisticated systems assign scores for each variable and then combine them into composite scores for each provider. The composite scores are used to rank-order providers within any specialty, bringing to the top of the list those whose behavioral profiles appear most unusual.

One of the Medicare contractors I visited had an unusually effective utilization review (UR) unit on the private (commercial) side of their business, which seemed to offer tangible results in terms of cost control. It is worth examining how they operated, as an example of best practice.

The director of this UR unit was one of a rare and valuable breed in the health care control business—a suspicious nurse—combining broad medical knowledge with a deep skepticism about provider integrity. She expressed the view, "the best thing that has happened in this business is that in the last four years the public's trust in the medical profession has been eroded."

Her unit thought in terms of projects, deliberately identifying areas where problems emerged and evaluating their own interventions by subsequent declines in billing levels. The units projects under way included examination of the following issues:

1. Mammograms being reported as "medically necessary" rather than "routine" in order to get higher reimbursement rates.
2. Nuclear cardiology scans of questionable medical necessity and accompanied by code manipulation; specifically unbundling.
3. Overuse of EEGs and nerve conduction studies.
4. Quality of X-ray film: Some providers were using such poor-quality supplies that the results were of no medical value. The insurer was only prepared to pay for good-quality film.
5. Overuse of ear tests (tympanometry and acoustic reflex tests), without medical justification.

Potential problem areas were often identified through statistical trend analysis on the aggregate utilization rates, showing which procedures' or specialties' average billing rates had accelerated sharply.

Once a problem area had been identified, analysts would pick out the extreme providers, usually those that lay more than two standard deviations above the mean, and do a random record review. For each project undertaken, between fifteen and two hundred doctors would be selected, and they would each be asked to provide supporting documentation for between ten and fifty claims. In total, the unit performed roughly 400 such provider audits per year.

If physicians failed to respond to requests for records, the unit would enter a provider flag into the claims-payment system, suspending payment on all of that physician's future claims until they complied. That "usually gets their attention." The unit director described how, when they began to put pressure on a particular problem area, articles would appear in the local medical press discussing the issue and seeking to clarify the rules.

Physician audits took a lot of time however, so the unit used a variety of other methods too. With some problem areas they would just pick off the top few providers and send them a letter saying, in effect, "we are watching you: desist, or else." The unit sends out between six and seven thousand such letters each year, using an automatic letter-generating facility built into their profiling system, which was designed in-house. Roughly one-third of providers receiving such letters call back to discuss the issue, and billing rates usually drop off or flatten out immediately.

This unit has the power to formally exclude participating physicians for repeated violations, but the unit's director says the procedure is bureaucratic, difficult, and expensive. She has other methods that are much more effective. She refers some cases for fraud investigation to the SIU, and the two units worked unusually closely together. She could also ask providers for money back, extrapolating from the audit sample to their whole claims volume. Once they have been found out, she says, it is amazing just how easily they pay up.

Most potent of all, she could insert a flag into the claims-processing system, suspending all of a provider's incoming claims, which amounts to informal exclusion from the payment system until the provider supplies information or explanations. This is an unusually tough approach, and one that clearly helps to control costs. But which is the target: fraud or abuse? And what are the issues: unusual utilization patterns or criminal deception?

Some fraud schemes may produce unusual utilization patterns. Moreover any specialty or provider group that becomes riddled with fraud might show up, in aggregate, through trend analysis. But what of fraud in general, which hides among the mass of legitimate activity? What does a fraud perpetrator need to do to avoid detection by post-utilization review?

To avoid detection, fraud perpetrators need only avoid excessive greed and make sure that their provider profiles are reasonably typical for their industry segment. In particular, they should avoid extremes of utilization behavior. The cutoffs used most often are 2 standard deviations from the mean, which—assuming something like a normal distribution—means only the top 2.3 percent of providers in any one category are likely to face scrutiny.

Fraud perpetrators may also choose specialties that are high volume (so that significant fraud losses do not shift the mean noticeably), or where fraud, abuse, or overutilization are already rampant (so that newcomers are less likely to be among the outliers).

Whatever services are or are not provided, a fraud perpetrator can avoid vulnerability to post-utilization review altogether by mimicking, claim for claim, the billing patterns of any legitimate, honest provider. The honest provider delivers the service; the dishonest one does not. Post-payment utilization review cannot tell the difference.

The degree to which post-utilization review turns out to be a useful device for fraud control depends upon the degree to which fraud perpetrators use anomalous billing patterns. Of course, the smart ones do not. So only the excessively greedy or stupid fraud perpetrators get caught this way.

Once again, this is not a criticism of post-utilization review procedures per se. The principal purpose of utilization review is to review medical utilization patterns, both on an aggregate basis (to help formulate policy changes or provide necessary provider and recipient education) and on an individual provider basis (to eliminate medically inappropriate or unreasonably expensive treatment patterns).

As a fraud-detection methodology, however, post-utilization review procedures, with their strong emphasis on provider profiling, have certain limitations that must be understood.

First, they detect fraud only where it produces anomalous billing patterns, as discussed already. They are much better suited to detecting waste and abuse, which do not amount to criminal fraud.

Second, utilization review generally leads to scrutiny of only a few extreme outliers within each provider category, leaving the bulk quite safe from detection, even if the bulk is rotten.

Third, most utilization-review units prefer to inform and educate providers when they detect anomalous billing patterns, rather than investigate. So, as with prepayment medical review, fraudulent providers remain safe from investigation, provided they change tactics when warned.

Fourth, utilization-review procedures come long after the fact and are useful only in the context of a continuing relationship between payer and provider. Utilization-review systems operate in batch mode, periodically processing three to six months of claims data at a time. Due to processing constraints the resulting profiles may not be available for some time after the period in question and may then not be updated in a frequent or timely manner. The claims data forming the basis for provider profiles is usually at least three months old, and in some cases it is more than a year old.

Post-payment utilization review therefore comes too late to be useful in combating the increasing number of fraud schemes run by fly-by-night operators. Storefront businesses, which fraud investigators say are increasingly prevalent, bill fast and furious, creating extremely anomalous billing patterns, but then disappear with the money long before post-utilization review catches up with them.

To counter the threat of quick, high-volume, "hit and run"–type schemes, the only sure defense is prepayment provider profiling— which would monitor each provider's aggregate billing patterns and acceleration rates *before* claims are paid. None of the sites visited had any form of prepayment provider profiling or any (prepayment) method of watching for sudden surges in billing from individual providers.

Analogous defenses in the credit card and banking industries are commonplace: they consist of spending pattern analysis and acceleration rate monitoring, with preapproval intervention and verification procedures. Consumers experience such control systems when, at the point of sale or at an ATM machine, they are required to speak by phone to an authorization representative from their credit card company, before their credit card purchase is approved. Such systems monitor the transaction patterns of credit card or account holders as well as the *selling* patterns of merchants and are set up to intervene, prepayment, when the transaction pattern becomes sufficiently suspicious.

Audits

When post-utilization review establishes a provider's behavior as extreme or peculiar in some regard, a formal audit may result. The normal audit procedure, for Medicare contractors, is to select a few claims (fifty or so) and audit each one. Some carriers, when they find overbilling, project the results from the sample onto the provider's whole claims volume and then seek to recover the amount of the projected overbilling. Other carriers, however, do not project sample results and reclaim only the overpayments from within the sample.

A 1994 GAO report, which examined the effectiveness of post-utilization review under the Medicare program, commented on the effects of these audits:

> Even when audited, however, a provider has virtually no chance of having to fully reimburse Medicare for overpayments received from carriers that do not project when calculating overpayment estimates. We do not understand how such carriers' routine forgiveness of providers' debts to Medicare can be considered educational in a way that would benefit Medicare. The lesson taught in these situations would appear to be that, even in the unlikely event of a Medicare audit, providers will not be required to repay much of what they owe.[12]

Whatever the effectiveness or ineffectiveness of these audits, their number has been dropping steadily each year. In 1992, roughly eight out of every thousand Medicare providers would be audited in this way each year. But recent reductions in funding for medical review have resulted in the proportion dropping to three per thousand (i.e., 0.3 percent) in 1995.[13]

Part A of the Medicare program—which covers hospitals, nursing homes, home health agencies, rehabilitation clinics, hospices, and a few other miscellaneous types of *institution*—uses a rather different form of audit, called a "Medicare audit." Medicare audits focus on the cost reports of the institutions, upon which the Medicare reimbursement rates for that institution are based. The audits look for a wide range of costs that ought not be included on the Medicare cost report: excessive charges for lunches, cellular phones, cruises, vehicle expenses, or salaries for people who spend most of their time working on something other than Medicare business. All expenses included in the cost reports are supposed to be related directly to health care for Medicare beneficiaries.

How effective are such audits in uncovering fraud? The most important point to realize is that these audits do not examine claims at all; they examine cost reports. The focus is solely on the mechanism through which reimbursement levels are set, and not on the subsequent use of those rates when submitting claims.

The head of one audit unit—with forty auditors working for him doing nothing but Medicare audits all year—explained that Medicare audits rarely establish fraud as such and are not designed to do so. They are obliged to give four weeks' notice in advance of the audit. Even so, he said, many providers refuse to provide documentation or pretend they can't find it.

If auditors find any misreporting, they make adjustments in the cost reports. If the *same thing happens three years in succession*, then they can refer the case to the Office of the Inspector General for investigation! So all the providers have to do is change the nature of their misreporting from year to year.

Half of the auditors in his unit focused exclusively on home health care agencies. These auditors each recovered an average of $1.8 million per year in overpayments. Nevertheless, these audits hardly ever established fraud or referred suspected fraud for investigation, in part—as the head of the unit explained—because they did not really expect juries to be able to deal with financial statements and accounting conventions. Cases under Medicare Part B, involving false claims, were comparatively easy to investigate and prosecute.

Another type of audit under Medicare involves managed care companies. These audits seek to establish the financial security of the company in order to minimize the danger of that company going out of business or being unable to deliver adequate care once the managed care contracts have been signed. Once again, the purpose of such audits is not to find fraud.

One senior auditor at HCFA, commenting on the various purposes of the different audits, explained:

> We would comment that this is the job the CPA firms who do audits for managed care companies are hired to do. They do a *financial* audit. For medicare purposes, CPAs or other auditors do a *medicare* audit. The prime purpose of neither type of audit is to detect fraud. A medicare audit is performed primarily to verify that costs claimed on the cost report are related to patient care, necessary, prudent, reasonable and properly allocated to the medicare program.[14]

Of course, if fraud is discovered during an audit of any kind, it will be referred to the proper authorities. But the *purpose* of the audits is not to find fraud; the audits focus principally on other issues.

Private sector insurers also use audits for a variety of purposes. They do random claims audits in order to check the accuracy of the claims examination process (as discussed in Chapter 3). But these audits are focused on procedural correctness (quality control) and do not include external validation, so they are unlikely to detect fraud.

Private sector insurers also perform internal audits, which are designed to protect the company against employee corruption, by guaranteeing separation of duties and adherence to security policies. They also perform external audits, designed to establish the financial viability of business partners.

In general, in both the public and private sectors, audits are not designed to find fraud, and they seldom do. Just like claims examination and medical review, audits may reveal fraud occasionally. But that is not their purpose.

Special Investigative Units

The investigative units sit at the end of the referral pipeline; their cases coming from EOMB-stimulated beneficiary complaints, from data entry clerks or claims examiners, from prepayment medical review, from post-payment utilization review, or from auditors. A small number of tip-offs from other insurers, from law-enforcement agencies, or from anonymous telephone calls augments the total referral volume.

Any reasonably astute fraud perpetrator avoids all the standard detection methods by billing correctly, by using orthodox treatment/diagnosis combinations, and by avoiding excessive greed, which might put their billing profiles at the statistical extremes for their specialty. As Joe Ford, one of the FBI's pioneers into the field of health care fraud investigation, pointed out in 1992; "For the most part, the audit systems established by the various Federal and State regulatory agencies do not detect this type of criminal activity."[15] Ford was absolutely right. And his point helps explain the assessment, made by an experienced SIU investigator, that the referrals SIUs receive are, on the whole, just "dumb junk." Existing referral mechanisms detect only the stupid, careless, or excessively greedy fraud perpetrators. The SIUs' incoming workloads represent only the tiniest fraction of the total fraud volume. And that explains why these units, so ridiculously under-resourced, are *not* generally overwhelmed by their caseloads.

Most investigative units work predominantly in reactive mode, just about keeping up with the work that comes to them. Whichever mechanism produced the referrals, the investigators' job is the same: to investigate and to make cases. Following a traditional enforcement model, most of these units count their workload in terms of the number of incoming complaints or referrals and count their successes in terms of the number of cases made, settlements reached, aggregate dollars recovered, and convictions obtained.

Investigators in these units may work extremely hard, and be quite expert at what they do. But what of effective fraud *control*—and the child with the rubber mallet in hand? How much can SIUs help their organizations see clearly and respond rapidly to emerging fraud threats? Clearly, if the SIUs remain in reactive mode, fed by largely ineffective referral pipelines, they will see the truth only dimly, partially, and probably very late. The extent to which they gain any better understanding of the scope and nature of fraud depends on the extent to which they deliberately engage in proactive outreach and in intelligence gathering. To find any time and resources for such activities, SIUs have to find ways to escape the demands of their reactive workload.

Two out of three Medicaid fraud control units examined during this research relied principally on referrals and did little or no proactive outreach, or intelligence gathering. SIUs at private insurers typically try to devote some resources to proactive outreach, but find that, as soon as they do, they generate so many cases that the resulting caseload drives out further proactive work for at least a couple of months.

MFCU-1 was the only unit that systematically engaged in intelligence gathering. For them, development of informants, undercover operations, and deliberate inquiry into different industry segments was a way of life. Of course, being desperately short of resources, management struggled constantly to protect the capacity for proactive work from the resource demands of their caseload. They ultimately did much less proactive work than they would have liked.

In order to preserve even some minimal proactive capacity, MFCU-1's managers made strategic selections of enforcement targets, focusing or targeting investigative resources on problematic segments of the industry, rather than selecting cases solely on the basis of their individual seriousness (which is the enforcement norm). By contrast, the other two Medicaid fraud control units were extremely cautious about the idea of targeting: "If it starts to look and smell like targeting, they won't like it at all." They thought targeting might make them vulnerable to accusations of discrimination against certain providers or provider groups.

Even the small amount of resources MFCU-1 managed to carve out for proactive work and intelligence gathering profoundly effected their view of the fraud problem. Unlike many other units, they always worked with a huge queue of high-quality cases. They had become respected nationwide for their effectiveness in generating and prosecuting health care fraud cases. (Of course, what their intelligence activities revealed about the scope of fraud on the streets, the corresponding Medicaid state agency steadfastly refused to believe.)

The investigative units at major Medicare contractors were almost entirely consumed by incoming beneficiary complaints (which made up roughly 90 percent of their workload) and tended to report their workload in terms of the "number of open complaints." A small percentage of these complaints did develop into substantial cases, but most turned out to be misunderstandings of one kind or another.

Using beneficiary complaints as the units of work can make fraud units dysfunctional. Processing complaints is an unambitious and minimalist view of what the unit should be doing. More worthwhile objectives would be tackling serious fraud or, better still, patterns of fraudulent behavior. These more ambitious conceptions of the job would substantially enhance the contributions SIUs can make to fraud control.

Also, given the volume of beneficiary complaints and the trivial nature of many, speed and efficiency in disposition of the complaints can supersede effective fraud investigation as the unit's principal goal. In which case, *disposing of cases*, in isolation from each other, might come to be seen as more important than *investigating fraudulent practices* with a view to control.

The GAO's 1992 general report on health care fraud complains that investigation of Medicare beneficiary complaints too often receives short-sighted, blinkered treatment—serving case disposition better than it does fraud control.[16]

The report cites the example of one Medicare beneficiary who was visited in her home by a nurse and doctor, neither of whom she knew. They claimed Medicare had sent them. Later that day a supplier delivered several medical items. The woman had neither ordered nor needed the equipment and told the supplier to take them away. Later she received notification (an EOMB) that Medicare had paid the physician for a home visit and the supplier for the equipment. So she complained immediately to the Medicare contractor who, upon receipt of the complaint, requested refund of the payments from the physician and the supplier (totaling roughly $700) and took no further action.[17] The complaint had been adequately "disposed of."

The GAO happened to review the case later and pushed the contractor to investigate further. With a little deeper inquiry, the contractor then discovered over $450,000 in potential overpayments to these same providers. The contractor also found another medical supply company operating at the same address as the first, but under a different name and Medicare provider number.

Whenever investigative units fall into a case-disposition mode, they lose most of their value for fraud control. If they also develop an appetite for monetary recoveries (which is the safest way to preserve the unit's budget) then they can often end up doing little more than recovering monies paid to fraud perpetrators.

But surely recovering money paid to criminals is a valuable objective. Yes, indeed it is. But if that becomes the primary accomplishment of a fraud investigative unit, then their contribution to effective fraud control has dropped virtually to zero. Fraudulent providers are notoriously eager to pay money back, once they have been caught cheating. With such a small proportion of their fraudulent activities ever being detected, quick repayment accompanied by a profuse apology for the "mistake" is a small price to pay for ensuing peace and quiet, which enables them to continue their fraudulent activities.

One fraud investigator described how she happened to be at a dialysis clinic one day when an ambulance pulled up outside. Three patients climbed out and walked into the clinic under their own steam. She asked for, and obtained, their names. Checking the claims histories later, she found that the transportation company had billed more than $70,000 over several months for services to these three patients, on the basis that they were wheelchair-bound (which they visibly were not). The investigator called the Office of the Inspector General, who declined to pursue the case. Subsequently an overpayment of $75,000 was requested from the transportation company. The transportation company delivered a check the very next day, without argument: "just like that!" And they stayed in business.

The ease and rapidity with which some providers pay back seems disconcerting. It suggests, perhaps, that fraud-control apparatus normally finds only a thin sliver of the providers' cake, and these providers would much rather give up the sliver than have anyone go looking for the whole cake. Fraud perpetrators, both individuals and major corporations, will always prefer to settle the case, quickly and amicably, than to have investigators delve into their general practices.

Lack of Coordinated Control Strategy

When the control apparatus is examined piece by piece, it becomes clear why effective control remains elusive. The fraud units, however dedicated and competent, are incredibly small when compared with the size of the problem. They work largely or exclusively in reactive mode, generally managing to keep up with the trickle of cases produced by a collection of highly ineffective and vastly overrated referral mechanisms. Add to this situation the lack of functional coordination and the absence of any coordinating strategy tying together the efforts of the various functional units, and it becomes clearer still why the health care fraud problem seems to be getting worse, not better.

A revealing question to ask of any insurer is "who here is responsible for fraud *control*?" The question is usually met with bemusement and bafflement. The standard answers are either "no one," or "everyone" (which in practice means "no one"). As Senator Donald Halperin pointed out in testimony about New York State's Medicaid program: "Overall, there is no single individual or agency in New York State with overall control to ensure that programs work, money is not wasted, and dollars are not stolen."[18] Even if detection and referral systems worked well and were backed up by effective investigation, would the sum of the detection, referral, and investigative functions constitute effective fraud-control apparatus? No, it would not. There has to be a brain, or a team of brains, playing the fraud-control game. Whoever is responsible for fraud control has to be able to see the whole picture, collecting and collating intelligence from many different sources, systematically measuring and monitoring the shifting patterns of fraudulent behavior. And, like a chess player, that person or team needs to be able to coordinate the various functional pieces of apparatus like chess pieces on a board, to defend against each attack and to wear the opponents down.

Existing arrangements within high-volume claims-processing operations provide little opportunity for the exercise of any integrated, concerted fraud-control strategy. Each unit does its own traditional thing, with management assuming that the sum of the pieces constitutes an effective control plan.

The bigger the claims-processing operation, the worse communication and coordination across functional lines tends to be. Larger organizations have more clearly drawn functional boundaries and less frequent communications across those boundaries. Prospects for coordinated intervention using the whole range of available tools—investigation, administrative action, prepayment and post-payment review, adjustment of edits and audits, education—are perhaps worst of all where the investigative units are organizationally separate from the claims-processing operation. That is, in the Medicaid program.

Medicaid fraud control units are required by law to be separate and distinct from their respective state Medicaid agencies.[19] Organizational separation serves two purposes. First, it protects the MFCU budget from the onslaughts that would inevitably result from zero-sum competition with all the other administrative functions. Second, it protects the integrity of any corruption investigations involving employees of the Medicaid agency.

With these ends in mind, federal regulations governing the activities of MFCUs stipulate that no official of the Medicaid agency will have authority to review the activities of the unit, or to review or overrule the referral of a suspected criminal violation to an appropriate prosecuting authority; and that the MFCU will not receive any part of its budget either from or through the Medicaid agency.[20]

Separation of duties comes high on the list of standard protections against internal theft, fraud, embezzlement, and corruption.[21] If functional duties are properly separated, individual employees can only commit fraud by colluding with others.

Unfortunately, functional segregation also cripples the prospects for any coherent, coordinated multifunctional response to external fraud threats. Most of the major frauds perpetrated against health insurance programs come from outside, not from inside. So functional segregation—especially to the degree of creating distinct organizational entities—sorely hampers the prospects for effective control. (This does not constitute an argument for bringing MFCUs back under the management of Medicaid agencies. Under present circumstances, that would just kill the MFCUs capacity for effective fraud investigation, which is what they currently do well. In fact it would probably kill some MFCUs altogether.)

In order to foster effective cooperation, the Medicaid regulations require the Medicaid agency to assist the MFCU by "referring all cases of suspected provider fraud; by providing records, information, or computerized data without charge and in the form requested; and, upon referral from the unit, initiating any available administrative and judicial action to recover improper payments to a provider."[22]

But three major impediments prevent the MFCUs from getting along with the Medicaid agencies. First, the expected tensions between the fraud-control and claims-processing functions (explored in Chapter 1, The Pathology of Fraud Control) manifest themselves even more powerfully given the organizational separation. Second, the constant possibility of having the MFCU investigate employees or management of the Medicaid agency for corruption can poison the relationship. Third, the preoccupation of the Medicaid agency with protecting their provider network (in order to be able to deliver services) appears to the MFCUs a poor excuse for failure to refer cases of suspected fraud and for a general lack of cooperation.

The net result is undisguised hostility between MFCUs and Medicaid agencies, noted as long ago as 1980 by the GAO. The GAO attributed the hostility, in part, to "mutual distrust, concern over loss of control of fraud investigations, and personality conflicts."[23] When the two functions lie beneath some common senior management (i.e., within the same organization) they at least have to feign some degree of cooperation, despite irreconcilable goals and cultures.

Some of the more experienced MFCU investigators felt the tension between their two roles: in one case acting as investigators of the payment agency itself, and in the other case collaborating with the payment agency in protecting against external attack. But nearly all

MFCU investigators were angry, to one degree or another, with the Medicaid agency. A senior manager at MFCU-1 complained how the Medicaid agency seemed to close its ears to the extensive insights collected through his unit's intelligence-gathering activities and investigations."We freely offer them the benefit of our experience—just take it—experience accumulated by taking lashes across our backs. But they are not interested." He added that he thought "they'd be happier to be rid of us than they would of the Medicaid thieves . . . so they could continue shoveling money out of the back of a truck."

Managers at MFCU-2 believed their unit could provide valuable information to the Medicaid agency about fraudulent practices, which they thought the agency could have used to improve their controls. But, when asked what formal or informal mechanisms existed for the passage of such information, one manager said, "None. It's a massive bureaucracy. It would be hard to know who to tell."

Within the Medicaid program, prospects for integrated, coordinated, fraud-control efforts appear bleak indeed. Little information flows between MFCUs and Medicaid agencies. The MFCUs have a tough time finding out what internal controls (edits and audits) are operating at any one time and have virtually no opportunity to affect the allocation of review resources within the claims-processing system. What MFCUs offer to fraud control, they do pretty much in isolation.

In other organizations, where the SIUs come under the same roof and same management, the sources of tension are the same; but the obligation to find some commonality of purpose makes the tensions less sharp and less visible.

The trend within the industry, and especially within major government programs, is toward greater functional specialization. For example, the plans for the "Medicare Transaction System," now scheduled for implementation in 1999,[24] call for consolidation of processing operations into a smaller number of bigger sites. Ancillary functions such as customer services, appeals, and fraud investigation will be contracted separately. The precise extent to which these different functions will be segregated is still under discussion; but the degree of functional separation will undoubtedly increase, not decrease.

The development of modern claims-processing systems—highly automated, high-volume, highly efficient—seems likely to exacerbate whatever functional separations already exist and to diminish yet further the prospects for coherent, effective, multidisciplinary fraud-control strategies.

5
The Antithesis of Modern Claims Processing

Fraud investigators throughout the industry readily acknowledge that they only see a small fraction of the fraudulent claims running through their claims-processing systems. They realize the fragility of detection and referral mechanisms. They bemoan the primacy of efficiency as the goal for the claims-processing system. And they see staff in other functions as oblivious of the fraud problem. The investigators, closest to the realities of the streets, know full well that their fraud-control apparatus—fragmented and understaffed—barely scratches the surface.

Against that depressing backdrop, the confident claims of managers at one particular company—which I will refer to here as Company X—came as a stunning surprise. Managers at Company X claimed that their fraud-control systems detected around 80 percent of the fraudulent claims submitted to them. They felt they had fraud under control. No other company I visited came anywhere near making such a claim.

Could such a confident claim be true? Perhaps they were deluding themselves. Or perhaps they had such terrible detection apparatus that they really had no sense of the magnitude of the fraud problem. Or perhaps, conscious of the company's reputation, they were merely putting forward a highly favorable official position. Of course, they could not prove that they stopped 80 percent of the fraudulent claims, because they, like everyone else, had no systematic method of measuring the overall level of fraud and saw only what their detection systems showed them. But Company X differed from all of the other insurers in several ways, not just in its confidence about fraud control. Its entire claims-processing apparatus was quite unique and, in many respects, represents the antithesis of modern claims processing.

Background

Company X's business is confined to one state, and they have just one policyholder—a labor organization—with around 17,000 certificate holders under that policy. The health benefits are the same for each certificate holder, but each family can choose between four or five different options with respect to deductibles.

Certificate holders obtain coverage for their family, with an average of 2.25 people covered per certificate. The average age of those covered is 56 years. Any resident of the state can join the health insurance program, but they must first become a member of the labor organization holding the policy. (The organization's rules permit anyone to join as a nonvoting member, although voting membership is reserved for particular categories of workers.)

The company also runs roughly 4,600 Medicare Supplemental Policies (privately issued policies that cover deductibles and copayments not normally covered by the Medicare program). The company receives a total of $46 million in health insurance premiums and pays out $36 million annually through the issue of roughly 90,000 checks. The company's corporate parent and affiliates offer a range of other insurance products, but the health insurance operation is self-contained and employs roughly thirty people. The employees all work in one open-plan office, and they all know each other personally. This, as health insurance goes, is a tiny operation.

Evidence of Success

In the absence of formal measurement, no one can tell exactly what proportion of fraudulent claims are detected. So how can anyone be sure that this company does any better at controlling fraud than anyone else? What signs or indicators can be taken as evidence of more effective control? Between them, the managers at Company X came up with the following list of indicators:

Company X Often Catches People the First Time Around

When the company discovers someone trying to defraud them, they write the suspect a letter outlining the facts as the company sees them and warning them to desist. But the company also reviews the relevant claims history to check for any previous occurrences of fraudulent behavior. In the majority of cases, the review of previous history finds no past pattern of fraud, which would suggest that the fraud was detected at the first attempt. In other words, Company X seems to be able to catch fraudulent practices early.

By contrast, other insurers digging into false claims usually find established patterns of fraud. In fact, most fraud investigators relish what they call the "tip of the iceberg" cases: where investigation of an apparently isolated false claim leads eventually to the discovery of multimillion-dollar patterns of cheating. Such cases reveal the diligence and persistence of investigators, but they also show late detection of a pattern of fraud.

Tips Received from Outside Rarely Reveal Anything New

Of the tips the company receives from other insurers, from law enforcement, or from informants, only one in ten tells them of a vulnerability or fraudulent practice of which they were unaware. In six out of ten cases, the tip involves a provider who does not do any business with them. In three out of the remaining four cases, Company X already has the provider flagged as problematic and under scrutiny. So, where someone outside the company tells them of a provider who cheats, they are already aware roughly 75 percent of the time.

Company X Often Tips Off Other, Bigger, Companies

The converse is not true. Staff recalled seven instances where their own methods had uncovered fraudulent providers, and where they had been able to tip off larger companies facing much greater exposures. In each case the other (larger) company had not already identified the problem.

Company X Is Highly Active in Flagging Problematic Providers

Company X, despite their comparatively small size, is one of the most active participants in flagging troublesome providers for the sake of warning other insurers. They flag the problematic providers on national databases set up by industry groups to facilitate information-sharing between insurers about fraud cases and investigations.[1]

Feedback from Chiropractic Community

Company X uses some chiropractors as consultants to help with "medical review" of chiropractic claims. These consultants report back that the word within the chiropractic community is "don't bother trying to cheat company X. It's too hard."

Feedback from Law Enforcement

Feedback from the law-enforcement community confirms that Company X has earned the reputation of being a hard target. Lists obtained from fraudulent telemarketing operations always show the company on the "difficult" side.

Limited Losses to Major Fraud Schemes

Company X, like many other insurers, was defrauded by the Smushkevitch brothers' rolling labs scheme and also by National Health Laboratories. In both cases the company spotted the problems and cut off payment before accruing any heavy losses.

In the "rolling labs" case, Company X paid out around $5,000, which represented only 1 percent of the claims they received. A claims examiner caught the problem early and flagged the providers. Company X had therefore been independently denying claims for several years before they learned from the rest of the industry just how much damage had been done elsewhere.

With National Health Laboratories, Company X had paid only $1,000 for the unnecessary ferritin tests when they noticed the pattern. They immediately wrote to NHL explaining that the extra tests were neither requested nor necessary and asking for their money back. "NHL paid it back, just like that." So, whereas other insurers lost millions to NHL, this company lost nothing at all.

Stable Premium Rates

Perhaps the most encouraging indicator of the Company X's fraud-control success is the fact that the company has not had to raise its health insurance premiums in eighteen months—a fact that makes the employees extremely proud. Many other factors could obviously contribute to their cost-control success. Nevertheless, such success in recent years is rare indeed.

What Company X Does Differently

So, what accounts for Company X's apparent success? How do the assumptions, policies, and systems used at Company X differ from industry norms?

Integrated, Professional Claims Examination

First of all, Company X has developed a professional role for its claims examiners that incorporates and integrates the normally separate functions of medical review and fraud detection. At Company X there are no functional divisions, no formal organizational chart, and no formal budget for claims processing. They spend whatever they need to spend to ensure accuracy of claims payments. And they regard accurate claims payment—not processing efficiencies—as the key to effective cost control. The company rigorously measures payment accuracy (through quality-control procedures), but does not measure or seek to minimize processing costs per claim.

The examiners have, on average, ten years of experience in medical claims examination and over five years with this company. Very little staff turnover means little cost in retraining. So the company invests, instead, in continuous training and "upskilling" for existing staff, encouraging them to obtain additional qualifications. A specified sequence of training experiences, spread over two years, acts as minimum qualification for the title *senior examiner*, and the company promotes only from within. Company X regards claims examination not as a clerical job but as a profession and rejects the typical union-shop environment.

All the claims examiners meet for half an hour every Wednesday morning to discuss fraud trends, changes in payment policy, or to talk about each other's suggestions. Often a visiting speaker will be called in for these meetings to teach the claims examiners about developments in medical practice or medical research, or about new methods used by fraud perpetrators, or to discuss new methods for fraud detection. Examiners are encouraged to nominate items for the agenda. Often they will bring in advertisements for medical services they have clipped from newspapers or magazines (e.g., for cataract surgery) and figure out together what the provider in question seems to be doing. They are particularly curious about the advertisements that seem to offer free medical services, because providers often try to bill insurers for such services. Different teams of claims examiners actually compete to see who can find the greatest number of suspicious newspaper and magazine advertisements—the prize being something like a box of doughnuts for coffee time.

The examiners' mission statement—which they formulated themselves through another internal competition—reads, "our mission is to provide quality claims service through the process of prompt, fair, and accurate evaluation of our insureds' claims."

That sense of purpose, managers explain, makes for a much more interesting job than the typical production-line environment, obsessed with throughput. "The goal here is to pay accurately and to establish that as a norm." And "paying accurately," managers say, is quite different from "cost control." The company wants to pay the right amount: not too much, and not too little. So, when they measure payment accuracy, they make no distinction between overpaying and underpaying. If circumstances warrant, Company X does not feel bound by "usual and customary" rates, often finding a way to pay more. Also, to avoid unnecessarily inconveniencing providers, a senior examiner first reviews any claim that would be reduced by more than 20 percent or $500. Other insurers, they say, are much quicker to shift the burden of proof to the provider and wait for them to appeal before reviewing such decisions.

The claims examiners review every single claim that comes in. Not just those selected by an automated system. Not just 7 percent of the total volume. But every one. What about the ones that come in electronically? There are none; Company X only takes paper claims. The work is divided among sixteen claims examiners and four senior examiners. When an examiner receives a claim they become responsible for its handling and payment from start to finish. So the examiner's role includes data entry, medical review, fraud detection, and claim disposition.

The claims examiners take responsibility for a zip code or combination of zip codes (usually specifying an area by the first three digits of the zip code) and handle all claims from customers (patients) living within that area. Focusing on a small geographic area allows the examiners to get to know their clients well and to spot any unusual localized patterns of activity.

For instance, one examiner recently noticed claims relating to three auto accidents within her area, all of which bore the same provider name and the same insurance agent's name (the policies had all been sold by the same agent). A little investigation revealed the beginnings of a fraud scheme coordinated and executed *by the agent,* and involving colluding physicians.

The claims examiners rotate for three-month periods through a small "technical claims" section, where they do major case review, third-party recoveries, and generally exercise their hypercritical skills on more serious cases of fraud and abuse. These attachments enhance examiners' investigative skills. Then they are sent back to their regular claims-examination tasks, better able to recognize the early signs of cases that would turn out big and expensive if left unattended.

Investigative training is encouraged and formally recognized. Managers recognize that some examiners have better investigative skills and instincts than others and deliberately allocate the better ones to the fraud-rich zip codes.

Examiners are encouraged to take responsibility for medical review as well as fraud detection. On medical questions, as on anything else, they can always ask the senior examiners for help. If the senior examiner cannot make the determination, then they refer the issue to an outside consultant—one of a panel of physicians retained to offer advice as needed. One physician comes in routinely once a week, to go through any unresolved issues that require review of medical records. Consultants are available to the senior examiners by telephone at any time.

According to their manager, the claims examiners relish the business of fraud control. "They get excited if they find some dollar figure that has been altered." And, reflecting on their success in shutting off NHL's unwarranted ferritin tests, she said, "That was a big thing for the staff [when they discovered how hard others had been hit]. It really encouraged them to go after other labs that might be doing the same, or similar, things." The idea that claims examiners would identify with an opportunity, as a group, to go after a particular fraud problem; and that they would be capable, as a group, of delivering concerted action on such an issue across the whole population of claims seems most unusual.

As an instrument for fraud control, this claims-examination function is clearly exceptional. They review every single claim. They have a formal meeting every week, to discuss any new trends or problems they have observed between them and to formulate appropriate intervention strategies. Just by turning their chairs around to face each other, they can pool their knowledge and experience informally, anytime they choose. The examiners pride themselves on their ability to detect fraud and on their ability as a team to shut fraud out completely once they detect it.

Single Point-of-Contact Service for Customers

Company X's second major departure from customary practice concerns customer service: how they conceived it, how seriously they took it, and its practical outworkings.

Company X's customers were the certificate holders, or insureds, not the providers. Claims examiners were careful to treat providers respectfully and properly, but that was not their primary concern. The primary concern was to look after the insureds and to make sure they felt looked after. By contrast, many other insurers—especially in public programs—focus more on maintaining their provider network and spare more time trying to keep the providers happy than the patients.

High-quality service to the customer was the basis of Company X's marketing strategy. Their rates were reasonably competitive, but their distinctive mark was the focus on customer satisfaction. Most of their customers were self-employed and paid their own premiums, so they had a great deal of choice when it came to choosing a health care plan. Quality service was what attracted customers to Company X, and what kept them.

With the allocation of claims to examiners by zip code, the examiners acted as service representatives for each of their customers, providing a single point of contact. They would give their own names and telephone extension numbers to their customers, and they would always interrupt routine claims-processing tasks to take telephone calls. (Each examiner had a backup partnership with another, so if one became overloaded, the second—who would also develop some knowledge of the area—could help out.) If a patient became really sick, or was hospitalized, the examiners had the authority and discretion to send flowers or a teddy bear with a friendly note saying "get well soon."

It seemed ironic to hear insurance claims examiners complaining of a lack of professionalism on the part of physicians. The examiners at Company X deplored the use, by physicians, of software packages that systematically test the upper price tolerances for each procedure. These packages bill high so the claim is rejected. Then they resubmit the bills, gradually lowering the price until the claim is paid. The software packages then record the optimum billing level for future use. As the examiners put it, "we try to pay the right amount. Why shouldn't they just *bill* the right amount?" The use of such software packages is perfectly legal, but the examiners felt it showed that many physicians did not share the examiners' sense of service.

Examiners being in close contact with their customers certainly helped the cause of fraud control. Examiners said they talked to the customers "all the time." If there was anything at all suspicious or unusual about a claim, the examiner would call the patient immediately to check the facts. If a new diagnosis appeared for any particular patient, the examiner might call to discuss which types of future treatment would be covered by the policy and which would not.

One examiner caught a fraudulent claim for services not rendered because the patient's weight was incorrectly recorded on the claim form. The examiner knew the patient was pregnant and had been watching her weight rise (on various claims) over the previous few weeks. A fraudulent claim, submitted by a physician who had never seen the patient, listed her weight wrong.

Examiners have no qualms about checking up on hospitals either. They know that hospitals solicit business on the basis of waived copayments. Company X's view of this practice is that Company X should pay exactly 80 percent of the aggregate liability, so if a hospital waives a copayment, then Company X wants to pay exactly 80 percent (not 100 percent) of what is left. Once company X suspects any hospital of waiving copayments, they routinely call all of their members who use that hospital to establish the precise nature of the agreements made up front.

Examiners had no compunction at all about contacting their members, and nobody ever complained about it. Quite the opposite: friendly, high-quality service was Company X's major selling point.

Fraud-Control Philosophy

Company X had no separate budget for fraud control. A recently enacted state law required every health insurer to have a special investigative unit, so Company X now employs one woman as director of the SIU; but she has no staff. Rather she works with, and among, the claims examiners, who do the bulk of the fraud-detection work. Once a fraud case is opened, however, the SIU director takes it over and sees it through to disposition.

Company X does not employ any specialist investigators. The company values investigative skills a great deal, but prefers to employ medical-claims specialists and teach the necessary investigative skills. The director of the SIU rarely goes out on inquiries. When she needs some footwork done she uses private investigators retained under contract. The company places no budgetary constraints on the use of outside investigators. The SIU director uses them when she sees fit, and the vice president for operations occasionally reviews the expenditures.

But not all that much effort goes into the traditional case-making form of fraud investigation. In fact, Company X has not yet brought a case to court, either civil or criminal. They generally do not consider civil action worth their while, because the legal expenses normally outweigh the potential dollar recovery.

They do believe in criminal prosecution for fraudulent providers, but have never managed to get a case to court themselves.[2] They find prosecutors disinterested in their small-dollar losses, which usually fall well below prosecutorial thresholds. Their dollar losses are small partly because Company X is such a small company, and partly because they tend to detect fraud schemes long before significant losses have accrued. Often Company X detects fraudulent providers and warns other, bigger companies who then develop very significant cases from the information based on their own (much greater) losses.

In the absence of any significant case making, investigative work serves a different purpose. When they do use private investigators it is usually to find out what is happening and to confirm the examiners' suspicions, rather than to make cases. So the investigative function serves predominantly as an intelligence-gathering exercise.

With so little emphasis on case making, the claims examiners and the SIU director focus on early detection and prevention instead. The tools they use to procure compliance include:

1. Sending letters to providers demanding money back once a claim or claims have been established as illegitimate
2. Putting providers *on review,* so that all their claims get flagged and scrutinized even more carefully
3. Requiring second opinions (which they are prepared to pay for) in the case of medical procedures prone to abuse
4. Referral of a corrupt provider to the state medical board (although they say they scarcely ever get any feedback, or see any follow up)

5. Making providers substantiate claims by requesting provision of medical records

They use the fifth tool liberally, requesting supporting documentation of one kind or another for 20 percent of the claims submitted. This obviously holds up claims payment, but Company X still manages to keep their average claims payment turnaround time down to four days. If the claim results from an accident, the request for additional information normally goes to the certificate holder. Otherwise the requests go to the doctors.

All the managers agree on one central point of their fraud-control philosophy: They "don't ever let a doctor go." They say they become very suspicious about doctors who cannot produce convincing medical records. Once a claims examiner has requested records or other supporting documentation they will keep reminding the doctor until the requisite records appear. Some doctors eventually ask them to drop the claim and forget it. But they persist until the claim has been established either as legitimate or illegitimate.

And, if a claim turns out to be illegitimate, then the physician or provider responsible will be put on review; a status under which every claim filed must have supporting documentation. Any provider caught cheating even once will remain on review until the examiners decide that the provider has mended their ways sufficiently to be trusted once again.

Doesn't giving examiners almost complete control over a particular geographical area open the door to employee corruption? What of prudent *separation of duties,* for the sake of corruption control? The management at Company X is well aware of that possibility, but feels the risk is adequately controlled. The director of the SIU considers it her job to monitor for any signs of corruption. Throughout the day she moves around the claims examiners' area, helping out, answering queries, updating the examiners' "fraud watch files" (a compendium of current fraud concerns). Even so, she deliberately maintains a little professional distance in case she ever has to investigate one of her own examiners. She also performs various other precautionary audits from time to time, such as running the file of payment destination addresses against the personnel records to make sure payments are not being diverted. Examiners do not have complete control over their areas anyway. Several days a month one examiner's claims will be handled by their backup. The backup arrangement kicks in if any examiner is too busy, or goes away for vacation or training.

To avoid corruption, for the most part managers count on the professionalism and integrity of the claims examiners. They pay them like professionals, not clerical workers. And they have never had (at least never discovered) an internal corruption problem. The open-plan everyone-knows-everyone environment, coupled with the professional culture, would make it a tough place to operate internal schemes unnoticed.

Attitudes Toward Technology

Company X regards claims examination as an essentially human business. Although they use a variety of software packages to assist in claims examination, they emphatically reject the idea that claims examination can be done by computers. They refuse to contemplate electronic claims submission, concerned that the loss of experienced human scrutiny would tear the heart out of their approach to payment accuracy.

Reluctantly they admit that electronic claims processing will probably come to them, as to the rest of the industry. But for now they are holding off and will do so just as long as they possibly can. If industry pressures force them to move to EDI, they say, they will experiment very cautiously and only in well-protected areas of their business.

Even with their Medicare supplemental policies they resist further automation. Most Medicare supplemental policy issuers set up electronic systems to pay claims automatically once the base Medicare payment is approved. Not Company X. They prefer to review the claims, because they often find Medicare has paid in error. They do not want to pay the $1 fee per claim for automatic processing; they would prefer to retain the opportunity to review the claims themselves.

Going electronic with Medicare supplemental policies would also mean "going on line with eligibility" (creating the facility for billers to query the customer database remotely, without the company's knowledge). *On-line eligibility,* managers say, might make life just a little simpler for honest billers, but it also opens up huge new opportunities for the dishonest.

To illustrate their argument management points to a new phenomenon in fraudulent billing: the computer-generated fraud scheme. These schemes use what one examiner called "perfect claims," generated by personal computers. Another examiner called them "canned records," where the computer reproduces the same claim time after time, but substitutes different patients each time. Each claim is correct in most particulars, except they often miss patient identifying characteristics such as height, weight, or condition. The diagnosis, the treatment, and the price all look perfectly normal.

Examiners at Company X said these schemes were increasing in frequency and were quite easy to detect in their environment because the claims would all come in at once, would all go to the same examiner, and would all be far too similar. When it happened, a quick telephone call to one of the patients would confirm the claim as bogus—at which point all the others would be pulled from the claims process and turned over to the SIU for investigation.

Managers at Company X suspected (quite correctly) that there was nothing in most electronic claims-processing systems to detect such schemes. Provided the claims were billed correctly and medically orthodox, they would all slide straight through auto-adjudication to payment, without human intervention.

The examination process at Company X naturally achieved such monitoring by valuing, nurturing, and unleashing the extraordinary pattern-recognition capabilities of the human brain and by allocating claims to examiners zip code by zip code, giving one examiner the chance to see the whole scheme (assuming all the claims came from one locality). Even if fraud perpetrators deliberately spread their "patients" across several zip codes, they would get caught at break time when the examiners met around the coffee machine.

Managers at Company X showed no interest in electronic claims processing as a cost saver, or as a way of keeping premiums low. They regarded their fraud-detection and prevention capabilities as the best method for accomplishing those objectives. In fact, they regarded effective fraud control as one major source of their competitive advantage.

The company recently considered a proposal to install a document-imaging system with OCR capability. The vendor's pitch was based on the fact that the company could reduce the number of claims examiners from twenty to three, to which one manager responded, "Now why would we want to do that? May as well shoot yourself in the foot." The proposal was soundly rejected.

The company is not antitechnology. Examiners do use technology in the course of processing claims. While they visually review the claim, they enter the fields required to process a payment into their own computerized payment system. The system incorporates a commercial rebundling package, which checks for various standard forms of code manipulation. Another commercial package checks the procedure code against the diagnosis and the diagnosis against the age and sex of the patient. Finally a commercial pricing package, which checks the price of the procedure against a table of prevailing rates in the appropriate area, is used. Whatever these software modules offer, they offer *to the examiner*. There is no automatic claims rejection, or automatic correction. The examiner takes the information and uses it as he or she sees fit.

The director of the SIU also uses modern data-analysis tools to help her spot fraud problems. One of the natural forms of analysis, given the way Company X is set up, is by zipcode. A pattern of abuse by a particular specialty often starts off on a highly localized basis and then spreads. Monitoring specialties by zip code gave Company X one useful way of spotting such trends early.

For example, data analysis revealed two zip codes in which the frequency of septoplasties suddenly shot up. Septoplasties involve repair to the cartilage structure of the nose, usually following an accident. The procedure code for septoplasties was being selected by providers as a way of disguising cosmetic nose surgery as medically necessary operations. The tell tale signs that fraud was being committed was the fact that these were newly established certificate holders, who, within the first month or two of coverage, would report an accident (like walking into a door) that damaged the nose but no other part of the body.

The director of the SIU also values technological assistance when investigating providers suspected of fraud. Once interested in a particular provider, she will normally take an extract of the last three years' claims from the processing system and download them onto a workstation for manipulation that uses a variety of modern database query tools. She also uses, and encourages the examiners to use, on-line access to various national databases such as NHCAA's provider database, the INDEX (ACE) system for information about road accidents, and INFOTECH for background inquiries about individuals or businesses.

Lessons for the Industry

Without systematic measurement, nobody can be absolutely sure that Company X really did a better job of fraud control than anyone else. But the evidence seems compelling. Company X routinely detected schemes that other systems would never notice. They suffered minimal losses in major cases and frequently acted as the early warning system for other larger corporations.

But—in looking to draw some useful lessons from company X's unusual approach—it would be foolish to conclude merely that *small is beautiful*, and to recommend fragmentation of the massive systems that now dominate the industry. Much of the health insurance industry continues to move toward consolidated, high-speed processing and could not possibly contemplate breaking up highly efficient claims-processing operations into multitudes of small, friendly, personable claims-examination units. Any such recommendation would (and should) be rejected as an absurd irrelevancy for the bulk of high-volume claims processors.

And no antitechnology lessons should be drawn from Company X's experience. For one thing, they used technology extensively, even though they eschewed electronic claims submission. Moreover, electronic claims submission is undoubtedly here to stay. Returning to paper-based and manual claims-processing operations is not a viable option for most companies.

If the lessons drawn from Company X are to be genuinely useful to the industry, then they have to be as relevant to large, automated processing systems as they are to small, paper-based ones. Smallness, or rejection of EDI, are not the important issues here. Being small is only one of many ways in which Company X runs against the grain. Some of the other ways in which they deviate from industry norms present serious challenges to all insurers—large or small, automated or manual.

Primary Focus Should Be Payment Accuracy

Perhaps the most fundamental challenge to industry norms is Company X's focus on payment accuracy as the principal source of effective cost control. Most other claims-processing environments seem to breed an obsession with administrative cost control, which often has the effect of stripping resources away from prudent payment controls.

The management at Company X is convinced that the rest of the industry has focused primarily on the wrong thing, and they believe that rapidly rising costs throughout the industry result, in part, from that error. If a $500 claim comes in for treatment, which matters more? That it costs $0.87 to process rather than $7.00, or that the item actually delivered might have been the version that costs $150 rather than the one that costs $500, or that the service might never have been delivered at all, or that the diagnosis might be fictitious and the service might have been completely unnecessary?

Management at Company X took the view that it was worth spending whatever it took to validate claims. For them, it was always money well spent. Company X deliberately avoided calculating how much they spent on processing per claim, because they did not want anyone's attention focused on that issue. As purchasers of services, they felt they should use their common sense on behalf of their customers. And common sense, for them, meant checking to see they got what they paid for and that the patient needed the service. If that took a couple of well-placed telephone calls and the inconvenience of record review, so be it. That's what they thought any sensible purchaser would do.

Ideally, of course, one should not have to choose between processing efficiency and effective fraud controls. Ideally, the costs of fraud control would be measured against the resulting savings, providing a clear sense of the return on investment. Including fraud controls under the umbrella of administrative costs opens the way for processing efficiency to drive out prudent controls.

Every insurer in the industry, whatever their budgetary arrangements, can usefully reconsider the degree of emphasis they place on processing efficiency versus the degree of emphasis they place on claims verification and fraud control. Company X has positioned itself at one end of this spectrum, placing their emphasis fairly and squarely on payment accuracy. They took care to organize their operations efficiently too; but would never allow processing efficiencies to limit or restrict the level of payment reviews.

Most of the industry lies at the opposite extreme and appears to have forsaken many prudent payment controls for the sake of processing efficiencies. It is time to seriously reconsider the balance.

Humans Analyze: Systems Support

Most high-volume claims-processing operations use automated systems as their central backbone. Electronic claims feed directly into the system, and data entry clerks feed paper claims into the system as well. The system rejects some claims automatically, amends others, accepts most, and kicks some out for human inspection. The system's edits and audits decide which claims need to be examined by humans and for what reasons. So the general model for claims review is "systems select: humans inspect." Humans inspect only if the system selects.

Chapter 4's review of standard referral systems confirms what Company X also believed: that systems currently in use cannot generally detect fraud. They do not spot interesting or unusual patterns. They never get suspicious. And they never make telephone calls just to check out the facts.

At Company X the model for fraud control might be stated "humans analyze: systems support." Company X still used technology, but the automated systems served the examiners, not vice versa. The examiners were responsible for keeping abreast of emerging fraud patterns and trends, and they then used the systems to pick out claims for more detailed review. (Examiners also used a variety of other technological tools to support their investigation of those claims.)

By contrast, under the "systems select: humans inspect" model, the system is effectively in charge, and routine edits and audits remain unchanged for months or years, unresponsive to emerging trends. And the humans who do the claims inspection have little or no control over claims-selection criteria. Effective fraud-control demands the alternative model, with human beings playing the fraud control game intelligently and creatively and using technological tools in support. (Chapter 8 develops this concept in considerable detail.)

Fraud Detection Demands Routine External Validation

The customer service orientation at Company X made it natural and easy for examiners to call patients, agents, and providers. By so doing they introduced information beyond that contained in the claim itself, for use in claim determination.

By contrast, an automated processing system's edits and audits have only the claim information itself to work with (plus cross reference to other internal databases). Such systems never make their initial selection of claims for review or referral on the basis of any external information. And most subsequent claims-examination procedures involve prescribed sequences of internal checks, rather than reaching for external validation of any kind.

Some provider groups make an enormous fuss when insurers start contacting their patients to verify treatments and services. They may have the right to make a fuss if they really feel such inquiries breach their notion of patient/physician confidentiality. However, unless the claims were properly verified, Company X would simply refuse to pay them.

Ultimately none of Company X's providers objected to the company's claims-examination practices, because providers were well treated, and they were promptly and properly reimbursed. Generally, that is exactly what honest providers want.

The fact that Company X is small offers some additional benefits; for example, the thorough integration of fraud control, customer service, and medical review into the claims-examination process. These additional benefits may not be so readily realizable within larger systems.

But three basic principles seem critical and apply equally to all health care claims-processing systems: payment integrity should never be sacrificed to processing efficiencies; the role of human inspection in fraud detection should never be underestimated; and fraud detection requires routine external validation of claims information. These three points might sound sensible; even obvious. But they separate Company X from most of the rest of the industry.

Part Two

Current Developments

6
Electronic Claims Processing

Health care insurers in the United States process roughly 4 billion claims per year. Hence the appeal of electronic claims processing, which promises significant savings in administrative and processing costs. Electronic claims processing, once fully implemented, will save an estimated $8 to $10 billion dollars per year in administrative costs, by eliminating many of the people and all of the paper previously involved in the claims-payment process. "The vision is that EDI systems could process routine claims without human involvement, after input, and electronically transfer payment to a health care practitioner's account."[1] By 1998 virtually all Medicare claims and related transactions will be transmitted by standardized electronic means. In 1994 roughly 72 percent of Medicare claims were received electronically[2] (80 % of Part A claims and 55 % of Part B claims),[3] up from 36 percent in 1990. So far, government programs have lead the way into electronic claims submission, with the private sector insurers tagging along behind. The industry at large expects the vast majority of health care claims throughout the United States to be handled electronically by the year 2000.

Electronic data interchange (EDI) acts as an enabler of the shift from paper to electronic medium and has been defined as "the computerized exchange of business data in an accredited standard format between two enterprises and their underlying business systems."[4] The EDI standards are developed and maintained by the American National Standards Institute (ANSI) "Accredited Standards Committee X12," with participating membership of over seven hundred organizations, including state and federal government agencies.[5] HCFA required Medicare intermediaries to start using the X12 standard in October 1993.

With so much pressure to cut costs in health care administration, the shift to electronic media receives almost universal approval.

The potential for significant reductions in the administrative costs of paying medical claims has everyone from the Health Insurance Association of America, both Democratic and Republican members of Congress, the Secretary of the U.S. Department of Health and Human Services and even the President of the United States calling for the rapid development of a "paperless" claims processing system in health care.[6]

Two Views of EDI's Effects on Fraud

Some officials express the conviction that EDI makes no difference to fraud. "However they might hit you electronically they can hit you *now* on paper." Only the medium changes, some officials say; not the types of fraud committed. Some go so far as to suggest EDI will make fraud control easier by facilitating the implementation of more automated controls. (Which is true, in part, as Chapter 9's discussion of detection systems explores.)

Most managers in companies operating high-volume, highly automated claims-processing systems see nothing in particular to be concerned about. EDI finally bridges the gap between their own systems and those of their external business partners. As such, EDI appears a natural and welcome extension of their own internal technology investments: the final piece in the electronic puzzle, making paper claim forms completely redundant. (To be rid of the need to mail paper checks, companies can add a direct deposit capability so that payments too can be made electronically.)

Others in the industry seem genuinely alarmed by EDI, or—more precisely—by what they think EDI will do to fraud. One would expect Company X, with their heavy emphasis on human scrutiny, to resist EDI. But they do more than resist it; they dread it. EDI, they say, will destroy their ability to detect fraud, and the administrative cost savings will in no way compensate for the tide of fraudulent claims they expect to wash over their system should EDI be implemented.

Company X is not alone in their reservations. A senior Medicaid fraud investigator, who said he had been trying to tell everyone about the dangers of electronic claims submission for more than ten years, warned, "With EDI, thieves get to steal megabucks at the speed of light and we get to chase after them in a horse and buggy. No rational businessman would ever invent a system like this." The industry work group helping to guide and promote EDI (called "WEDI") included in its 1993 report a warning of the dangers of running ahead with inadequate caution: "Without proper front-end safeguards, EDI can also increase the private and public systems' exposure to health care fraud, creating the potential for losses far greater than any administrative savings."[7] The NHCAA task force on electronic data interchange issues also reported widespread but by no means unanimous concern: "Talking with health care fraud experts in the health care industry, they are of the opinion that the implementation of EDI is giving the health care practitioners a license to steal. There is much concern that the people responsible for implementing EDI are not addressing the health care fraud issues."[8]

Whether or not EDI offers a license to steal, it does provide a different mechanism for stealing. The important question is whether the change of mechanism affects how much thieves can steal, and how fast. The task for this chapter is to clarify the impact of electronic claims submission on opportunities for fraud and also on opportunities for fraud control.

Popular Misconceptions

When the general public think about computer crimes, they often imagine hackers gaining access to mainframe computer systems from their own personal computers, taking control, and then manipulating payments to their own advantage. Protecting against external attacks by hackers becomes, therefore, a matter of system security. Such security issues belong within the domain of technical experts, who have to protect each piece of the system, access point by access point, to prevent or monitor the incursions of unauthorized outsiders.

In fact such crimes are extremely rare,[9] and are never the major threat in implementing electronic payment systems. The major worry—the one that makes people within the health care insurance world so nervous—is that the system will work perfectly, fast and efficiently, time after time, claim after claim after claim, while the incoming claims themselves may be false.

Fraud works best when claims-processing systems work perfectly. Fraud perpetrators submit claims containing false information, and they rely on the system to dispatch payment, predictably, as if the information were true. In other words, the major problem is not that criminals will be messing with the operations of the system, but that they will be relying upon it to process false claims without the slightest hiccup.

Prosecutorial Difficulties

Several interviewees suggested that electronic claims processing would make the lives of investigators and prosecutors more difficult. Under electronic claims submission, they suggested:

1. There would be little or no trail of physical evidence acceptable to a court with respect to the submission of false claims
2. The Mail Fraud Statute—commonly used when fraudulent claims have been sent through the mail—would be rendered irrelevant
3. There would be no signature on the claim, which would make it impossible to prove personal responsibility
4. It would not be possible to establish the *origin* of an electronic claim, because electronic signals could be introduced at multiple points along the way

Surprisingly, no one interviewed was able to provide a single example either of an investigation thwarted or of a prosecution dropped because of any one of these impediments. So perhaps, in practice, these difficulties may not be insurmountable.

In fact, investigators described various innovative ways of circum-navigating these obstacles. Some had found that courts were very happy to accept paper printouts of electronic claims data as the "best available" physical evidence, especially if the printouts were designed to imitate—for the sake of jurors—the familiar paper forms. Other investigators said the lack of reliable signatures was no great loss, because signatures on paper claims had been of little value anyway. Physicians habitually delegated the job of signing claim forms to billing clerks, allowed the use of rubber stamps, or just left the signa-ture space blank. Neither investigators nor prosecutors seem to have relied much on the signature in the past.

Other fraud-control domains experience similar uncertainty over the importance of signatures. The IRS, with their electronic filing pro-gram, requires a separate signature document for each electronically filed tax return, although they do not wait for it to arrive in the mail before processing the electronic return. By contrast, the Massachusetts

Department of Revenue, in their electronic filing program, dispensed with signatures altogether and invest nothing in searching, like so many others, for acceptable signature alternatives.

Detection Difficulties

The serious risks with EDI relate not to investigative or prosecutorial difficulties but to detection. In essence, electronic claims processing creates the situation where an electronic signal received by an insurer triggers an electronic payment, often with no human intervention. The promise of administrative cost savings rests on the assumption that the majority of claims will be handled without any human involvement at all. Only those that are somehow exceptional will be flagged for review, with resources for review strictly limited.

The IRS created a very similar situation with their electronic refund program: An electronic signal received by the government triggers an electronic (tax refund) payment, in most cases without human intervention. Both in health care and in tax administration, electronic claims processing offers substantial opportunities for speedier service. But increased speed of payment, coupled with the removal of human judgment, presents some very special risks.

Absence of Common Sense in Claims Reviews

The absence of human involvement in reviewing claims means the absence of applied common sense. In the paper-based processes, claims that were patently absurd, visibly peculiar, or strikingly similar to other claims the reviewer had recently seen, would be set aside for review. By contrast, claims submitted electronically would be filtered out for review only if the particular absurdity had been predicted in advance and built into the automated checks.

With paper-claim forms, straightforward visual clues often reveal fraud schemes. Many of the more common visual indicators of fraud will be lost altogether under electronic claims submission, including the following:[10]

- Documents showing signs of alteration of dates, descriptions, amounts, and so on
- Similar handwriting of patient and provider
- Misspelled medical terminology or improper use of medical forms

- Photocopies provided but originals cannot be produced
- Mixture of type styles on same form, or combination of different handwriting
- Use of a post office box for payment destination
- Frequent name changes, aliases, different spellings of names
- Illogical age/occupation combination
- Undue pressure to pay claims quickly
- Hand delivery of claims or use of private mail systems [to avoid the provisions of the mail-fraud statute]
- Repeated accidents of a similar nature
- Provider is not in insured's geographic area.
- Physician's signature is a name stamp
- Insured provides more information than is necessary
- Illogical prescription number sequence, or consecutive numbers on different dates
- Large amount of prescription drugs with little or no other bills submitted
- Various pharmacies visited by insured on same date or within short range of time
- Prescriptions in even dollar amounts
- Accidents at home by owners of companies

The loss of such visual clues is not the only, or necessarily the most important, loss in terms of detection capability. The human brain, quite apart from its ability to spot these familiar clues, also possesses the most extraordinary pattern recognition capabilities, unlikely to be matched by any automated detection systems within the foreseeable future. The human brain's strength—when it comes to fraud detection—lies in its ability to detect patterns *that it was not looking for*; to spot things that look suspicious, even though they might never have been seen before and do not appear on any list of standard fraud indicators.

For example, one claims examiner detected a fraud scheme when he noticed, within the space of one week, bills from two different Nigerian hospitals. In each case patients living in Oakland were seeking reimbursement for treatment of "severe left-side lobar pneumonia" during May 1990. The two bills were identical except that the hospital letterheads and patients' names were different.[11]

Once again, there was the examiner at Company X who noticed a pregnant woman's weight entered incorrectly on a claim form. The provider who submitted the bill had never seen the patient, and just guessed at her weight. (Such descriptors would not normally be included in electronic claims submission, much less reviewed by automatic edits, because they do not constitute an essential data field for claims processing.)

Another remarkable demonstration of the human capacity to spot unusual patterns is provided by a Medicaid fraud investigator who examined a pile of 800 used prescription forms subpoenaed, among other documents, from a pharmacy office. He noticed that none of the prescription forms had ever been folded, which struck him as odd because most people carry them from doctor's office to pharmacy in their pockets. Medicaid had already paid for every one of the prescriptions, and they all turned out to be fraudulent.

With electronic claims submission, not only is routine human inspection lost; many of the data fields most useful in fraud detection are also lost. The standard formats developed for EDI eliminate textual descriptions and signatures.[12] Numeric codes take the place of diagnoses, procedures, and drugs; so virtually every field except for the patient's name is numeric. An examiner from Company X complained that the use of these new forms provides "no keys to the brain to raise suspicions."

If examiners at Company X are justified in their concerns about loss of these fraud-detection opportunities, then why are the managers of larger claims-processing operations not equally concerned? Managers at major Medicare contractors, for instance, seemed quite unconcerned about the effects of EDI. They did not feel EDI posed any significant new threat.

Why such a different view? Why do organizations running high-volume claims-processing operations not fear the same loss as the examiners at Company X? The most plausible explanation is that, with their production-line approach to claims processing, high-volume organizations have already lost the fraud-detection benefits of routine human scrutiny.

Contrast, for instance, the processing arrangements for paper claims at one major Medicare contractor. The mail room is so busy that it has its own dedicated zip code! Each item of mail is slit open by envelope-opening machines. Human operators remove the contents from the envelopes, staple them together, and assign them sequential numbers (containing the date). Then bundles of claims are carried by conveyor belt to the imaging room. The documents are optically scanned, and a high-speed optical character reader reads all the standardized typewritten claim forms. In another room, human operators stand by to help the OCR machine with any fields it could not quite make out. On their computer screens the operators see an electronic image of the fields in question, one at a time, and out of context. Any nonstandard or handwritten claims forms go to another room for manual data entry. The data entry is performed by clerks who have received no fraud-awareness training of any kind, whose incentives revolve entirely around throughput and data entry accuracy, and who will never see any of the claims again.

The automated claims-processing system does the rest; automatically rejecting, adjusting, or paying the claims. The only claims to receive any further human review would be those flagged by a system audit for suspension. Suspended claims are queued to another section, called "claims development," where examiners follow a predefined sequence of steps to determine the fate of the suspended claim. The system audits (or flags) focus on all the normal issues: eligibility, medical appropriateness, pricing, policy coverage, but not fraud.

None of the groups involved in this process has any responsibility for fraud detection, or any relevant training. The issue of effective fraud control was never considered in the design of these systems. They are designed to pay claims, fast and efficiently. The real sense of achievement for employees involved comes from keeping up with the extraordinary volume of incoming claims. One private insurer had a giant electronic scoreboard in the company cafeteria, connected to the central claims-processing system, which displayed the multibillion-dollar figure of total claims paid, year to date for everyone to enjoy with their lunch. The electronic clock, as employees called it, stood as a symbol of what counts.

Managers presiding over such systems, if asked about fraud detection, make the assumption that the system's edits and audits do the work of fraud detection. They do not. And, in these automated operations, neither do humans. The remaining few humans involved in the process do not have the necessary opportunity, the incentives, the time, the experience, the tools, or the training.

The companies that perceive EDI as a threat to effective fraud control are the ones that have so far managed to preserve effective human scrutiny within their claims processes. Many others have lost this tool already.

Three New Threats

Apart from the general loss of human scrutiny, the advent of electronic claims processing brings some distinctively new threats.

Rapid-Fire "Cash Machine" Schemes

With totally electronic claims-processing systems the fraud perpetrator faces a machine, not a thinking opponent. Fraud artists will be curious to know how the machine behaves, what kind of claims it will pay, and which ones it will not. So they will fire a variety of exploratory shots at the system to see what happens. The checks or direct deposits will help fraud artists understand what worked, and the helpful auto-reject notices will tell them what did not.

After using the shotgun approach to find the holes in the system, fraud artists can train their rifles on whatever holes they found. They can use even very low-value loopholes to generate significant payments, by submitting hundreds or thousands of claims. The loophole might be something as simple as "claims under $20 are paid automatically without query." With human claims examination, 10,000 claims from the same provider at $19.95 each, all for the same item, would undoubtedly raise some alarm even if the patient name was different each time. But with electronic processing, there is no obvious reason why such a scheme should ever be spotted. The same loophole can be exploited many times over before anyone realizes that anything is wrong.

Computer-Generated Schemes

Second, technically competent fraud perpetrators will be able to use computers to generate and dispatch thousands upon thousands of claims, each designed so as not to attract attention or review, and with some degree of random variation built in to prevent easy detection of duplicate profiles.

Lest some readers be tempted to write this off as science fiction, perhaps it is worth pointing out that computer-generated fraud schemes have been with us since the late 1980s. In 1988 a Bronx shoe store owner was sentenced to between one and three years in prison for bilking $1.1 million from the state Medicaid program. His computerized billing system, automatically preprogrammed according to a recipient's sex and age, added such extra items as heels, lifts, arches, and supports to thousands of orders for women's and children's prescription footwear and billed for scores of men's shoes the store did not even stock. The owner of the store also set up a second billing company on Long Island so that state auditors would not detect the jump in his Bronx store's claims from $103,114 to over $1 million in a few months.[13]

In November 1988 another New York court convicted Dr. Sheldon Weinberg and his two sons of stealing $16 million from Medicaid between 1980 and 1987. The Weinbergs falsely billed Medicaid for close to 400,000 phantom patient visits by programming their medical center's computer to generate phony claims and backup medical charts for as many as 12,000 fictitious visits per month.[14]

We know about these cases, because by some good fortune they were detected. But there is every reason to believe electronic claims-processing systems all across the country might be processing thousands upon thousands of computer-generated claims—all of them utterly fraudulent—that avoid all system audits because they have been billed correctly and make medical sense.

High-Dollar Quick-Hit, Or "Bust-Out," Schemes

If fraudulent providers get too greedy, post-payment utilization review will eventually catch up with them. Excessive or extreme utilization patterns will show up through provider profiling. But utilization review fails to provide an adequate defense for a number of reasons. First, not all insurers have any effective capability for provider profiling. Second, provider profiling usually pays attention only to the extreme outliers, typically the top 2 percent or so within any specialty. Providers that never deliver any service at all can remain quite safe from detection if they bill at the rate of, for example, the seventieth percentile for their particular specialty. Third, utilization review is only useful in the context of a continuing business relationship with the provider and comes much too late for the modern quick-hit style fraud scheme. High-dollar-value quick hit schemes, or bust-outs, represent the most serious new risk under EDI. EDI makes it possible for fraud perpetrators to steal millions of dollars in a single day and be gone.

An example helps show how such a scheme might work. Suppose a perpetrator submits a modest $1,500 claim for some trauma or accident-related treatment (the kind of accident that could befall anybody). A week later they get a check in the mail from the insurer. The provider may or may not have seen the patient; it does not matter. The important thing is they have established that this claim went through the system to payment, without tripping any kind of review. In other words, the diagnosis, the treatment, the coverage, and the pricing are all within normal parameters.

Now the perpetrator takes his computerized file of eligible patients, which he purchased on the black market, downloaded from a hospital database, or obtained from a corrupt employee within the insurance company. He programs his computer to generate 10,000 claims, all identical to the original, but using different patient identities each time. He submits all 10,000 claims on the same day, using free software provided by the insurer.

Question: Will the perpetrator receive a check for $15 million (10,000 × $1,500) at the conclusion of the next processing cycle? We all would certainly hope not.

Post-utilization review probably will not pick up on this scheme until at least three months later, by which time the perpetrator will have long since vanished. Is there any prepayment check that would flag such a scheme and prevent the loss?

There are a number of prepayment controls that, if implemented, would eliminate this risk. For example:

1. An automatic suspension of high-dollar-value checks (above some arbitrary threshold), pending human review of the contributing claims
2. Provider-level monitoring, where a provider's payments in each cycle are aggregated and reasonable thresholds are set for each specialty
3. Acceleration rate checks, which compare a provider's aggregate activity in one cycle with their previous billing patterns as a way of watching for sudden accelerations
4. Random review of some modest percentage of claims (so that at least some of the 10,000 would come up for routine verification), involving some external validation methods such as calling the patients
5. Cluster-detection software, which could spot unnatural similarity in the provider's claims even though they each referred to a different patient

Any of these five prepayment controls would easily detect the scheme. Unfortunately none of them are standard in the industry. Random review with external validation is unheard of. Provider-level profiling and acceleration rate monitoring are increasingly common, but do not occur prior to payment; they are done several months later, under post-utilization review. And cluster-detection methods cannot currently be found anywhere within the industry.

That leaves only the first item: review of the big checks. Managers at three of the top five Medicare contractors in the country and also at one of the largest private payers in the country, presented with this scenario, all expressed a vague hope that somebody, somewhere within their organizations, reviewed big checks before they were sent out. But in each organization no one could identify who it would be, which department would be responsible, or what the dollar threshold was that would trigger such a review. They all conceded it probably did not get done at all. So, for the time being, with these processors at least, the fraud perpetrator probably would get his $15 million check at the end of the week.

After discussing this scenario and similar risks, senior management at one of the Medicare contractors stated their determination to implement prepayment provider-level controls without delay. The controls are planned to be implemented before this book is published. For the rest of the industry, however, the vulnerability to computer-generated bust-out schemes remains a chronic weakness. It symbolizes the lack of attention paid to prudence and caution as the industry rushes headlong for administrative cost savings.

Managers at Company X said they thought the industry would never realize "what a monster they had created with EDI" until some company somewhere took a $20 million hit in one weekend. Only then would the industry wake up to the threat. But that assumes, of course, that someone would notice the $20 million hit. If anyone happened to be in the air-conditioned computer room at the time, probably the only thing they would notice would be the hum of the cooling fans. Perhaps post-utilization review would pick up the anomalous pattern a few months later, but by then the money would be untraceable, and the fraud perpetrators would have long since abandoned that particular business front.

It also assumes that the company taking the loss, even if it managed to detect the scheme, would make the facts public. Many, conscious of their shareholders and afraid of appearing incompetent, would not. Such multimillion-dollar losses could conceivably occur with some regularity throughout the industry without the ultimate losers—the taxpaying public and premium-paying policyholders—ever hearing of it.

Can Technology Provide Appropriate Safeguards?

Investigators at several different sites, talking about their unit's budget and what it would take to persuade management to provide additional resources, observed that the modern trend is to invest in automated controls rather than additional staff: to put faith in machines, not people. In some instances budget requests for fraud-control resources had been rejected on the explicit basis that the company preferred to invest the money in the next generation of electronic controls.

The prevailing vision of how EDI can be made safe combines two different ideas. The first: that machines can do a lot more monitoring, and more cheaply, than people can. The second: that prevention is better than a cure. When you put these two ideas together, you come up with a vision that sounds something like this: "The long-term vision is to have a system that kicks out claims electronically and prevents payment." That is how one private insurance company put it. But this seems to be the emerging vision for all the major high-volume processors, especially as they wade deeper and deeper into electronic claims submission. It also seems to be HCFA's vision for the Medicare program, because it combines their recent emphasis on "stopping the bleeding" (rather than trying to recover payments after the fact) with their technology investments in the new nationwide Medicare Transaction System.

The idea is that totally electronic claims-processing systems can be protected from fraud by implementing comprehensive batteries of up-front edits and audits that will keep fraudulent claims out of the system altogether. Provided the up-front preventative controls are good enough—so the theory goes—there should be less and less need for review or investigation. The controls would become increasingly automated at the same time as they move forward in the processing cycle toward "up-front prevention." The core of the prevailing vision, therefore, lies in *automated prevention*. And the realization of this vision, so the theory goes, will redeem EDI from its criticism as an attractor and facilitator for fraud.

"Automated Prevention": A Fatally Flawed Vision

This vision, unfortunately, is fatally flawed. It assumes that a particular set of automated controls (edits and audits), once implemented, can provide adequate protection against fraud. That assumption underestimates the opposition and ignores the fundamental nature of the fraud-control game.

Fraud Control Is Dynamic

First of all, this vision assumes fraud control to be a static game; in fact it is highly dynamic (as discussed under The Pathology of Fraud Control in Chapter 1). Given any set of up-front controls, fraud perpetrators will very quickly adjust their billing to fit. Making such adjustments and testing out the systems' latest capabilities will take someone bent on committing fraud a week or two at most. Which means any static set of controls provides very temporary protection. Relying on static controls is as foolish as expecting to find the perfect defensive configuration of chess pieces that, once implemented, will remain safe without the need to move again, or to watch what the opponent is doing.

Transaction-Level Monitoring Is Inadequate

The prevailing vision also imagines that fraudulent claims can be distinguished from legitimate ones through some analysis of their information content. Often they cannot. A criminal investigator at the IRS once held up two tax returns. The figures on the two returns were identical. Only the taxpayer identities were different. He said, "One of these is completely fraudulent, and the other is perfectly genuine. You tell me which is which; or show me a system that can tell them apart." Most fraud schemes cannot be detected at the transaction level (i.e., by reference to the information content of the transaction alone). Only the least sophisticated attempts at fraud can be detected by examination of the claim information in isolation. In most cases the information content has either to be compared with other claims to detect unusual patterns, or it has to be checked against external information to verify its truthfulness.

Lack of Common Sense

However artfully constructed, automated defenses can never substitute for human common sense and will never be able to spot patterns that they were not looking for.

Lack of Useful Intelligence

Automated defenses, especially where they rely mainly on auto-rejects, provide the fraud perpetrator with complete information about what the detection systems can and cannot see. At the same time, they provide little or no opportunity for anyone inside the organization to gather intelligence about what the fraud perpetrators are doing.

Some companies do keep records of auto-rejections for a short time, within their claims databases. Some even perform superficial analysis of them (e.g., flagging providers that have unusually high rejection rates). But the vision for electronic fraud prevention seems to provide no place for humans at all. Without a human fraud-control operation to do the analysis, only one side in this game is gathering any useful intelligence.

Auto-Rejection Is a Poor Fraud-Control Tactic

Automatic rejection of claims up front is a perfectly fine tool for dealing with nonconformist billing practices or for rejecting claims that contain some obvious mistake (e.g., the procedure code does not match the diagnosis). For the most part, the audience for such rejections is honest and happy to be corrected.

But relying on automatic up-front rejection of claims as the principal tool for fraud control is foolish. A fraudulent audience has only one objective: to find a way around the defensive systems. It would be naive to try to protect a country's borders from invasion by constructing impassable barriers along the entire border; or to try to prevent illegal immigration from Mexico by constructing a fence all along the border and then leaving it unstaffed. It is just as naive to assume that even the most sophisticated set of up-front rejection criteria, left unstaffed, can provide effective protection.

In order to defend borders, students of military doctrine would suggest different tactics. They would advocate the use of trip wires— advance warning posts strategically located to provide early intelligence of enemy troop concentrations or movements. Then, behind the trip wires, the defending country would arrange its defenses with a view to funneling invading forces into killing zones.

Effective fraud control needs early warning systems too: systems designed to warn the *defenders*, not the attackers. And that assumes some cognitive (human) being is available to be warned. Once warned, fraud-control tacticians need the opportunity to evaluate the threat and implement the best response.

Usually, auto-rejection is a lame and feeble response to a new fraud threat, because it leaves the perpetrator unscathed and free to try something different tomorrow. The defending system would be much better if it delivered a sting of some kind that would make the perpetrator think twice before attacking the same target again.

Lack of Identified Fraud-Control Responsibility

As far as one can tell, the pervasive vision for fraud control under EDI provides no place for a human fraud-control team as such. In the absence of such a team, who will be responsible for gathering information about emerging fraud threats? And who can coordinate effective responses? If the vision for fully automatic fraud-prevention systems really does have no place for human strategists, the advent of EDI will finally cement in place two of the major failings of fraud-control systems today: no one is in charge and no one is responsible for fraud control.

Predictability as a Weakness

In many ways computerized payment systems and effective fraud control do not sit comfortably together. One uses technology to achieve efficiency; the other uses human powers of observation to achieve prudence and control.

At the heart of the dilemma, however, lies the issue of *predictability*. Fully automated payment systems are completely predictable. And predictability is welcomed in such processing systems as a product of consistency, procedural correctness, and data-processing accuracy. But in the business of fraud control, perfect predictability is a flaw. Perfect predictability makes the target static, transparent, and easy to attack. Effective fraud control requires *unpredictability*, an element of mystery, and has to put the fraud perpetrator at some substantial risk. Just because one claim went through unchallenged today, a perpetrator cannot be allowed to rely on the system handling 10,000 similar claims exactly the same way tomorrow. Predictability in fraud control is a major weakness.

Can EDI Ever Be Safe?

It seems unlikely, approaching the turn of the second millennium, that EDI will be rolled back. Clearly by the year 2000 most claims will be submitted and paid electronically. So the issue is no longer should we encourage EDI, but how can EDI be made safe? The following few minimal elements of a fraud-control strategy would help to make EDI somewhat safer.

Risk of Random Review

There *has* to be an element of unpredictability. Every claim submitted should suffer at least some small risk of random selection for human review and verification. A risk somewhere in the range 1 percent to 5 percent might be reasonable.

External Validation

The human-review process must include external validation and be sufficiently rigorous to establish a claim as fraudulent. The object is to verify the claim. At a minimum the validation process should normally involve contact with the patient or their relatives, if the claim is submitted by a provider. The validation process should include contact with the provider when the claim is submitted by the patient. It should also include contact with the prescribing physician where appropriate.

Capacity to Suspend Large Groups of Claims

Whenever a potentially fraudulent claim is detected, all other claims that might be associated with it should be suspended immediately. They should remain suspended until inquiries establish where the source of the deception lies: with the provider, the patient, the prescribing physician, the billing agency, or with some other intermediary. In other words, if a randomly selected claim turns out to appear suspicious and might be part of a larger scheme, what is needed is the opportunity to stop the *scheme,* not just the claims initially selected.

Payment Cycle Not Too Short

Payment cycles should be slow enough, and verification procedures fast enough, so that bust-out schemes can be detected and stopped before the payments go out.

Fraud-Control Team

A *human* fraud-control team should be allowed to operate up front, and prepayment. They should have day-by-day control over claims-selection criteria so that they can arrange for the suspension and review of any categories of claims they want to see. Fraud-control teams should have their own dedicated review staff to conduct the external validation of claims. The fraud-control claims-selection criteria, their resources, and their reviews should never be confused with those relating to the medical review function, because medical review is a quite different function.

Appropriate Query Tools

The fraud-control team should have all the technical tools they need to be able to launch ad hoc queries within the claims databases. They need to be able to interrogate paid claims, rejected claims, and claims pending payment.

Prepayment Aggregate Monitoring Systems

The fraud-control team needs to have access to a variety of prepayment monitoring systems. They should include at a minimum:

1. Provider-level aggregation of claims with thresholds, so that any unusually active provider in any one period is flagged for review
2. Provider-level acceleration rate monitoring
3. *Duplicate address listings* to detect multiple payments being sent out to the same address and the equivalent for payment destinations under direct deposits

Many post-utilization review units use these forms of monitoring, but for the time being virtually no one operates them on a prepayment basis.

Review of All Large Checks or Payments

All checks or payments above some reasonable limit should be reviewed before being dispatched. The limit should fluctuate day by day, so as to be unpredictable.

Absence of Basic Controls

Hopefully the reasons for each of these basic controls seems clear enough in light of the foregoing discussion. Perhaps some readers assumed that controls like these were already in place. Sadly, the industry's consideration of EDI, to date, has paid a great deal more attention to processing efficiencies than to sensible controls.

In the absence of these basic controls, EDI produces the most attractive fraud targets imaginable—payment systems that are fast, efficient, and totally predictable. If an electronically perpetrated fraud scheme is reasonably well planned, no human will intervene, and no human need ever know. In the case of government programs, the U.S. Treasury sits on the end of the line.

Unfortunately, even such basic controls cost money. In particular, reinserting human claims examiners back into the system will sorely dent the administrative cost savings promised by EDI. For that reason alone, many government officials will deny the vulnerability and reject such controls as too slow, too cumbersome, and too expensive.

And if they reject them, and proceed nonetheless to make EDI the basis for claims payment nationwide, then what? According to the senior investigator at MFCU-1, who had been trying to sound the alarm about EDI for so many years, "Then the only hope for taxpayers is to buy shares in the companies that will rip into the Treasury." The right way to play the fraud-control game is to rely on people and to equip them with the very best technical tools available. If our major health insurers make the mistake of trusting *systems* to play the fraud-control game for them, we all lose. Fraud perpetrators run rings around such defenses.

7
Managed Care

Many within the industry believe that managed care eliminates the fraud problem. Many times, during interviews with senior managers at both private and public payers, they would acknowledge some of the more serious weaknesses in their fee-for-service controls and then close the discussion by pronouncing it irrelevant anyway: the inevitable expansion of managed care would eventually consign fee-for-service, with all its associated problems, to the history books.

Managed-care systems certainly alter the financial incentives for providers. Under "capitation" arrangements—where a fixed fee is paid per month per patient, regardless of usage—the traditional financial incentives for overutilization are indeed eliminated. Capitation, therefore, should eliminate the incentives for provision of medically unnecessary services. Capitation fees, moreover, are paid regardless of the level of service provided and thus eliminate the possibility of false claims.

By eliminating the incentive for overutilization and the possibility of false claims, managed care—so the argument goes—should eliminate fraud. This chapter seeks to test that hypothesis and to clarify the impacts that managed care will have on opportunities for fraud and on methods for fraud control.

Expansion of Managed Care

No one can deny the rapid growth of managed care. As of January 1, 1995 over 50 million people in the United States were enrolled in health maintenance organizations.[1] The Medicare program had 3.1 million beneficiaries under managed-care plans of one kind or another, representing 9 percent of the Medicare population and accounting for roughly $11 billion of the Medicare budget.[2] Approximately 65 percent of the workers at medium and large companies were covered by managed-care plans in 1994.[3] The Federal Employees Health Benefits Program, which pays over $16 billion in annual premiums, now has more than one-third of its recipients under managed care.[4]

With industry-wide penetration of managed care at roughly 25 percent,[5] growth remains rapid, even without any formal national health care reform. Under Medicare, the number of managed-care organizations contracting with HCFA rose by 21 percent from 1993 to 1994; and increased a further 41 percent in 1995.[6]

The fastest-growing type of contract under Medicare is the "Risk" program (fully capitated), where Medicare pays a per capita premium for an agreed-upon package of benefits. The package generally includes some services not traditionally covered by Medicare, such as routine physical examinations, immunizations, plus eye and ear examinations. Additional services available within a smaller number of plans include outpatient drugs, dental care, foot care, and health education.[7] The attractiveness of managed-care plans for beneficiaries stems from inclusion of these extra (preventive) services, a minimal paperwork burden, and small or no out-of-pocket expenses.[8]

Managed care is also advancing rapidly through the Medicaid program. Thirteen states have already obtained their "1115 waivers" (which means they are exempt from the normal Medicaid requirements mandating freedom for beneficiaries to choose any doctor).[9] As of March 1996, nine more states had submitted waiver requests, and another three states were preparing them.

Major Types of Managed-Care Plans

Managed care comes in many shapes and forms, with a seemingly endless variety of financial arrangements. The major categories are discussed here.[10]

Preferred Provider Organizations (PPO)

PPOs are basically fee-for-service organizations, with incentives for the beneficiary to stay within a defined pool of providers. Providers discount their rates in exchange for a guaranteed, steady stream of business.

Exclusive Provider Organizations (EPO)

An EPO is the same as a PPO, but with tougher restrictions on out-of-network services. There may be no coverage at all for out-of-network services and stricter utilization review.

Health Maintenance Organizations (HMO)

The HMO receives capitated payments—a set premium per patient per month. Enrollees designate a primary-care physician and subsequently pay a small, fixed fee per office visit. Some HMOs (Open-ended HMOs) provide some benefits with respect to use of out-of-network providers. Others (Network Model HMOs) do not. HMOs sometimes bear all the financial risk, compensating their network physicians on a claims-submitted basis (usually at discounted rates). Alternatively the HMO might share the risk with its providers, or distribute it to providers entirely, paying them at least in part on a capitated basis.

Individual Physician Associations Model HMO (IPA)

An HMO receives capitation payments and bears the financial risks. The HMO then contracts with a network of physicians (as does a PPO or an EPO) to provide services on a discounted fee-for-service basis. There may be year-end bonuses (in the form of cash disbursements) or penalties (usually in the form of reduced fee schedules) depending on whether aggregate cost-control goals were met across the network.

Staff Model HMOs

Staff model HMOs are hospital-or clinic-based HMOs, whose providers are salaried employees working almost exclusively with HMO enrollees.

Structural Solution to the Fraud Problem?

Those who believe managed care solves the fraud problem assume that the solution would be structural. In other words, they believe that the contractual and financial arrangements peculiar to managed-care plans remove the opportunity for fraud; and that detection, investigation, or any other dedicated fraud-control functions or systems would consequently become unnecessary.

The National Health Care Anti-Fraud Association commissioned a task force to examine managed health care and to address the hypothesis that the structure of managed-care plans eliminates the opportunity for fraud. Their report, published in November 1994, works through each of the major managed-care plan categories in turn and then roundly rejects the idea: "Experience of managed care organizations contradicts the myth that managed care, by its nature, eliminates incentives to commit fraud. It merely eliminates some of the more familiar methods of committing fraud, and replaces them with others."[11] The NHCAA report explained logically the different forms of fraud that might appear under each type of plan, pointing out that, under capitated fees, the predominant nature of fraud will involve diversion of capitation fees, resulting in underutilization.[12]

In practical terms, however, the hypothesis that managed care provides a structural solution lives on. Few cases of fraud under managed care have been prosecuted, so there is little accumulated experience within the industry as to the practical forms fraud will take. The absence of cases, by itself, fails to answer the question either way. As always with fraud control, you see only what you detect. So the dearth of cases under managed care, to date, could mean that fraud has become less prevalent; or it could mean that existing detection methods fail to detect the new forms of fraud, leaving them invisible.

With the continuing rapid expansion of managed care, the industry urgently needs to know which of these two explanations to accept. If managed care structurally eliminates most fraud, then the industry can finally breathe a sigh of relief and worry about fraud a little less. But if fraud has merely changed its form, then the industry needs to understand why existing detection systems fail to find it and move quickly to design alternatives that work better.

Practical Experience

Two of the Medicaid fraud control units examined had substantial experience with fraud under managed care. In particular, the state Medicaid program with which MFCU-3 was concerned had 80 percent of its recipients under managed care plans. The majority of payments made by the state Medicaid agency were capitated fees.

So, what forms of fraud had these MFCUs seen? One early case, investigated by MFCU-3 involved a plan run by two doctors, who were eventually indicted in 1989. The case demonstrates a wide variety of mechanisms for diverting capitation fees. The two doctors formed a corporation that won a contract for managed-care provision under the state Medicaid program. They operated under the contract for two years.

After the corporation had been operating a short while, the fraud unit started getting complaints from frontline providers (physicians) that they were having trouble obtaining reimbursement from the plan for their services. The fraud unit also received a tip from the FBI that the plan had purchased a bogus reinsurance policy from a con artist who faked Lloyd's of London policies, so they had two reasons to take a look.

Investigators from MFCU-3 set out to "follow the money" and found that 24 percent went, one way or another, to the two doctors who owned the plan. (The state expected contracting plans to make roughly 5 percent profit and to use another 5 percent of the capitation payments for administrative overhead.) The doctors paid themselves huge salaries and management fees. They owned seven other corporations, which acted as subcontractors. The doctors failed to declare the related-party transactions to the state.

One of the subcontracting entities provided eyeglasses on a capitated basis. Dividing the contract cost by the actual number of pairs of eyeglasses issued gives a cost per pair of $952. The doctors also acted as providers of specialist care themselves and were reimbursed on a capitated basis; but, because they were in a position to manage their own referrals, they were able to keep the number down to a minimum.

According to investigators, none of this activity showed up in the plan's financial statements. Depreciation schedules did reveal, however, that fat-suction equipment and other items that would only be used on private patients, were being charged under the Medicaid contract. The owners also gave sweetheart deals to their friends and families. One of the doctors allocated 6,000 capitated patients to his sister (a physician) for primary care and then employed a physician's assistant to help her cope with the load. One owner put his mother (who had retired) on the payroll as office manager, and the other put his eighteen-year-old girlfriend on the payroll as office manager as well.

There was not a single "false claim" as such. Just an intricate web of corporate arrangements designed to siphon resources away from the Medicaid patients. The principal investigator in the case commented, "And these are the things that *unsophisticated* people do. The sophisticated ones can create much more complex schemes, even harder to detect and to prosecute." A critical issue in oversight of managed-care plans is the proportion of funds reaching the frontline providers. But, even if that proportion is controlled and monitored, then managers can use related party contracts to insert themselves into the food chain again at the provider level.

In another major case, an Individual Physician Association Model HMO used dozens of phony consulting contracts to siphon money off to shell companies with hidden ownership. In a more recent case investigated by MFCU-2, a dental contractor working on a capitated basis skimmed off 62 percent of the fees for administration. Investigators struggled to prove fraud, however, because no patients had actually reported suffering.

Investigators at MFCU-3 were concerned about the role some county agencies had assumed under managed care. Some counties had exercised the right to become providers of long-term health care. As public agencies, they were able to operate with deficits, completely defeating the idea of cost control. According to investigators, the county agencies were "rapidly bleeding to death . . . through lack of effective controls."

Public corruption was another major concern, and it took many forms. For example, MFCU-2 saw instances of state and county personnel selling lists of eligible beneficiaries to contractors. The contractors would then cream off the good risks by offering inducements to healthy patients. Investigators also expressed concern when they saw officials from the state contracting office leave their public positions for jobs with contractors, who would then quickly win, or be in a position to win, a series of lucrative state contracts. "These people have intimate knowledge of the way the state agency operates and intimate knowledge of the ways in which that operation breaks down. They can obviously use that knowledge to their advantage." Investigators could do little but worry, though, because the states in question had very limited "revolving door" statutes.

The mental health program in MFCU-3's state provides an example of how vulnerable populations, who are unlikely or unable to complain, may not receive medically necessary services. HCFA conducted a review of the program in 1993 having heard various allegations. "We, as well as various other Federal offices have received a variety of complaints including nonpayment of provider claims, non provision of services to children, the existence of multiple case managers for one beneficiary, and the inadequacy of reimbursement levels [to providers]."[13] HCFA's review also revealed the erection of bureaucratic obstacles designed to deter patients from obtaining treatment. Parents had complained that intake procedures had been made so difficult in some areas that families and patients alike felt that treatment was not worth the effort.[14] At the same time, HCFA auditors confirmed allegations that between 35 percent and 48 percent of the capitation rate in the children's mental health program was being spent for administration and case management.[15]

In June 1995, fraud under managed care finally followed where so many fee-for-service frauds had gone before: the front page of the *New York Times*.[16] The story concerned high-pressure, misleading, and illegal marketing practices that some HMOs had begun targeting at Medicaid recipients in New York. Marketers had told recipients "Medicaid is coming to an end. Sign up for this HMO now or lose your medical coverage." The HMO of course protected itself by firing the saleswoman subject of the story, saying she had acted out of line.

In the same month, Maryland's Attorney General J. Joseph Curran Jr. announced charges against fourteen HMO marketing representatives, two HMO supervisors, and eight employees of the Department of Social Services. The state employees had accepted bribes to disclose confidential information to the HMO marketing agents, who then used the information to enroll Medicaid recipients' into HMOs (who thus began collecting capitation fees) without the recipients knowledge.[17] The state employees received roughly $0.50 to $1 for the name, address, names of dependents, and welfare status of each patient. The marketing agents received around $28 commission per patient enrolled.

Another front-page story in the *New York Times* (November 17, 1995) drives home the danger of underutilization.

> Posing as patients, New York State health investigators called the 18 largest managed care programs that serve Medicaid recipients in the state and asked to see doctors for such basic but essential services as prenatal care, immunizations of babies, and annual checkups. At 13 of the 18, the investigators had so much trouble just getting an initial appointment, that the Department of Health cited them for providing substandard care.[18]

The National Association of Medicaid Fraud Control Units prepared a report for the president's task force on health care reform in 1993. They summarized nationwide fraud-control units' early experience with fraud under managed care:

> No health plan is immune from fraud and indeed fraud does occur in managed care plans. Rather, fraud simply takes different forms, in response to the way the program is structured.
>
> While the traditional Medicaid provider fraud investigation focuses on overutilization of services and fraudulent billing . . . in managed care organizations the evil more likely lies in the underutilization of services. Unlike the typical Medicaid provider fraud case, the human cost in terms of reduced access to quality care may be tremendous."[19]

The report listed the various categories of fraud that had already been seen somewhere in the country under managed care plans:[20]

- Embezzlement of capitation funds paid by the state
- Theft of funds, equipment, and services
- Fraudulent subcontracts (for example, where no services are provided, or there are phony management contracts)
- Fraudulent related-party transactions
- Excessive salaries and fees to owners or their close associates
- Bust-outs (money goes in, no money goes out to the vendors, and the entrepreneur claims bankruptcy or simply disappears)
- Bid-rigging by state personnel (involving collusion with the bidders)
- "Self-dealing" by state and county employees (awarding contracts to friends, relatives, or close associates)
- Miscellaneous conflicts of interest by state employees in their dealings with the plans
- Improper enrollment practices (attracting good risks or refusing bad risks)
- Improper disenrollment practices (deliberately eliminating bad risks—persuading or forcing sicker patients to leave)
- Presenting bureaucratic obstacles to prevent dissatisfied (good risk) patients from disenrolling
- Falsification of new enrollee registrations (either fictitious patients or fictitious enrollments)
- Kickbacks for primary care physicians for referrals of sicker patients to fee-for-service specialists (perhaps out-of-network providers, under the Preferred Provider Organization structure)
- Extortion, conspiracy, bribery, and tax evasion

This list provides some interesting clues as to how fraud is different under managed care. Most of these methods center on diversion of capitation fees into the pockets of entrepreneurs. None of these methods involves a false claim as such. And frauds perpetrated by beneficiaries or frontline providers do not feature high on the list. Most of these frauds are corporate frauds, committed somewhere within the complex layers of intervening businesses, which now separate payers from frontline providers. These corporate frauds resemble procurement frauds more than they do traditional fee-for-service frauds.

The National Association of MFCUs also reported another set of behaviors, not so indisputably criminal, yet equally 'destructive of adequate medical care. These behaviors have all appeared under Medicaid managed-care plans and are all committed by contractors:[21]

- Arbitrarily excluding identifiable groups of beneficiaries (e.g., those with mental problems, children, infants, elderly) from service
- Regularly denying treatment requests without regard to legitimate medical evaluation
- Establishing policies that require an appeal before treatment will be given
- Measuring performance only in terms of absence of specific breaches of the contract language
- Failing to notify assigned beneficiaries of their rights, yet retaining the capitation payments
- Failing to procure health practitioners, so no service is ultimately provided
- Retaining exorbitant administrative fees, leaving inadequate provision for services
- Assigning unreasonably high numbers of beneficiaries to providers of service, making adequate service impossible

One managed-care provider went on vacation and left a message on his answering machine telling his patients that, if they had a medical problem, they should seek assistance at a nearby hospital emergency room.[22]

Shifting Locus for Fraud

Frontline service providers, insofar as they retain a fee-for-service component of business, retain the capacity to commit all the regular forms of fee-for-service fraud; assuming they can bill the payers direct. But physicians that work for managed-care plans and bill the plans on a fee-for-service basis, have more restricted opportunities to commit fraud. Commission of fraud by physicians would make physicians expensive to the plans, and the plans are not of a mind to tolerate physicians that become expensive for *any* reason. Physicians can generally be discharged from a plan, without cause, within ninety days or less. If cause can be established, discharge can be even quicker.

Expensive frontline providers will soon find themselves thrown out of managed-care plans. It makes no difference whether the reason for the high expense was pure greed or professional diligence. A thoroughly conscientious doctor who, under constrained resources, does more thorough testing than normal will meet the same fate as a dishonest colleague who tries to steal from the plan through excessive billing. Fee-for-service frauds committed by frontline physicians against the plans will be effectively controlled. Curiously, though, such frauds will be controlled not because they are frauds, but because they are expensive. Fraud control, in this context, is subsumed under the goal of cost control.

One investigator, noting the ability of the plans to control fraud by frontline providers, remarked that this heralded a new form of fraud control. He defined it as "having the ability to control *who* can commit fraud." Managed-care plans clearly have this power, and those so inclined will keep the opportunities for committing fraud to themselves. Hence the locus for commission of fraud moves upward, from the frontline service provider to the corporate middle layer.

Shifting Locus for Fraud Control

The locus for fraud *control* shifts too. The responsibility for fraud control used to rest with the payer. In cases where plans receive capitated payments and assume the financial risk, the payers may assume that fraud will hurt the plans, not themselves. So payers may pass the responsibility for fraud control down to the level of the plans. The plans, after all, should have a financial incentive to control fraud in order to protect their profit margins. If the plans, receiving fixed capitation payments, allow themselves to be defrauded by their providers, it will be their loss. This argument holds up if false billings remain the predominant form of fraud, as they were under fee-for-service arrangements.

But payers make a major mistake if they leave the responsibility for fraud control in the hands of the contracting plans. The trap payers fall into looks like this: mindful only of the old forms of fraud, the payers recognize the contractors' financial incentives to control it. They relax their scrutiny of the plans, thinking that the plans are the ones who will suffer any consequences of fraud. What payers fail to realize is that *the locus for fraud control has now shifted to precisely the same place as the locus for fraud commission*: to the intervening corporate middle layers. Those with myriad opportunities to commit new types of fraud are also the ones being trusted or expected to police the system. The payers end up leaving the fox watching the henhouse.

MFCU-3's experience illustrates this problem. With much of the state's Medicaid program under managed-care contracts, the state Medicaid agency was winding down its own internal fraud section. In

1992 the fraud unit had ten to twelve staff members: by 1995 it was down to three. The agency had taken "fraud and abuse" out of the unit's title, renaming it "Internal Audit and Program Investigation" so as not to offend the plans.

The plans themselves were required to refer any fraud and abuse they detected to the state agency, but they were not required to have any fraud-detection apparatus. The plans generally did not regard having a fraud and abuse section as a priority, so whenever the pressure to cut costs came along, the fraud unit was the very first thing to go. The relevant state administrative code spelled out the requirement for referrals but had nothing at all to say about detection or control systems. "All contractors, providers, and non providers shall advise the Director [of the paying agency] or his designee immediately in writing of any cases of suspected fraud and abuse."[23] The bottom line: none of the plans ever made a fraud referral. If they detected any fraud by providers they would deal with it the way corporations normally deal with fraud: quietly, secretly, and with the image of the corporation foremost in mind. A senior investigator at MFCU-3 said she was not the least bit surprised at the lack of referrals: "Now why would you want to create a situation where the middlemen, who are in league with the providers and working with them, are responsible for oversight? It's unbelievable." Another senior investigator at MFCU-3 said the residual fraud-monitoring capacity at the state Medicaid agency remembers only false claims and so focuses on the wrong things:

> Whenever they talk about fraud they focus on *claims*. But the kinds of fraud that arise now are more white-collar, corporate fraud: bid-rigging, public corruption, conflicts of interest . . . and so on. Monitoring by [the state agency] is superficial and focused upon claims.
>
> The other mistake everybody makes is to assume that the pressure to control costs will act to control fraud. In fact, fraud merely results in worse underutilization than we would have had without it.

Corporate Middlemen Not Bound by Professional Ethics

The locus for fraud and the locus for fraud control come together, in the middle. And who are these middlemen? They are corporations, not bound by any set of medical ethics; in the health care business, *for profit*. In 1994, for the first time, for-profit HMOs overtook not-for-profit HMOs as the dominant force in the market.[24] Dr. Arnold S. Relman, editor emeritus of the *New England Journal of Medicine*, has said, "There's

never been a time in the history of American medicine when the inde-
pendence and autonomy of medical practitioners was as uncertain as it
is now. I think that in this process *businessmen and their agents* will begin
to exercise unprecedented control over the allocation of medical
resources."[25] Managed care brings allocation of medical resources more
under the control of businessmen than ever before and also shifts
health care fraud firmly into the domain of big business.

Investigative and Prosecutorial Difficulties

Under managed care, fraud will become much harder to detect, investigate, and prosecute. This section discusses five reasons why this is so.

Investigators Will Have No Way In

Corporations will have the opportunity to commit fraud, and the
same corporations, in theory, will have the obligation to uncover and
refer fraud. Investigators will have little or no way in.

Investigators at MFCU-3 already experienced this "lockout." The
state Medicaid agency took the view that the MFCU had little or no
reason to interact with the managed-care contractors and discouraged
contact between them. At the same time, the state agency produced
very few referrals of any substance, having delegated the responsibility for fraud control to the plans. And the plans, for their part, would
never call in law enforcement voluntarily. If the plan did find a physician had been cheating them, they would simply remove him or her
quietly and discretely, conscious of the need to preserve both their
network of providers (their major selling point) and their corporate
reputation.

So the investigators received almost no referrals. Occasionally
physicians would contact the investigators to complain about the
operations of the plans. In these cases the MFCU had to tread very
carefully, because physicians could be expelled immediately if the
plan suspected them of passing information to law enforcement.
MFCU-3 had seen instances where physicians had been blacklisted for
ratting on their plans, which meant other plans subsequently refused
to take them on.

All told, investigators found useful information extremely hard to
find. And they found they had no allies anywhere. No one wanted them
involved; not the plans, or the politicians, or the Medicaid agency. The
director of MFCU-3 concluded, "I see law enforcement being further and
further removed from fraud control in a managed care environment."

Frauds Will Involve Complex Webs of Contractual Arrangements

The NHCAA report on fraud under managed care pointed out the need for investigators to acquire skills in interpreting complex contractual arrangements. "As a first general rule, investigators must develop a much more sophisticated understanding of the variety and complexity of contractual arrangements between managed-care payers and providers."[26] In evaluating the risks, investigators and auditors need to understand exactly the infinite variety of financial arrangements: capitated payments, withholding of a certain percentage of each claim payment as a hedge against excess costs, incorporation of fee-for-service components, bonus schemes, risk distribution schemes, and so on.

Investigators at MFCU-3 pointed out that financial audits of managed-care plans usually do not uncover fraud. They say the CPAs who do the audits are more concerned with the plans' financial stability and are not generally looking for fraud. (HCFA confirms that the purpose of such audits is not to find fraud, but to ensure financial stability.)[27] The auditors have little or no training in fraud detection. As one fraud investigator explained, "you have to get in there and examine expense reports, ownership arrangements, relationships. You have to follow the checks, check the cash register, and so on." Reviewing financial statements is not the same as figuring out who finally gets the money, and how they get it.

As if investigating corporate arrangements were not difficult enough already, investigators will most likely have to confront legal issues of antitrust as well. Physicians and plans alike increasingly seek to protect themselves from the effects of competition by forming larger and larger bargaining entities.[28] Investigating fraud under managed care will demand a range of skills and a degree of sophistication never previously required in the traditional fee-for-service environment.

Fraud Will Be Revealed in Patterns, Not in Single Transactions

Under capitated systems, a fraud case will almost never rest on a single transaction. There will be no false claim, around which indictments can be constructed. Rather, as the NHCAA report observed, "many preliminary indicators of newer managed care frauds will be statistical in nature ... taking the form of quantitative anomalies in provider-performance data related to such things as number of patient encounters, number of referrals, patient-outcome and satisfaction statistics."[29] The need to prove fraudulent patterns, rather than fraudulent transactions, worries investigators a great deal. An investigator at MFCU-1 described how judges often disallowed comprehensive printouts or computer-generated statistical summaries in fee-for-service cases. Some judges even insisted that investigators should obliterate every item on a printout that did not relate directly to the fraudulent transaction detailed in the indictment.

Proving fraud under managed care will depend upon the ability of the courts to assess the significance of broad patterns, not individual transactions. Many investigators reported that they find prosecutors reluctant to accept such complex cases. "They want a false claim." The result, investigators claimed, was that complex and sophisticated fraud schemes (such as those under managed care) never went to court. If they were dealt with at all, it was through administrative remedies.

Data Required to Establish Patterns Will Be of Poor Quality

Determination of patterns will rest heavily on analysis of *encounter data* provided by the plans. Such data might be of poor quality, late, or even falsified. "Bear in mind that unscrupulous providers, minimizing the time and treatments expended on patients in return for a fixed monthly income, thereby maximizing profit . . . might also misrepresent the services he or she has actually provided in order to appear to meet the HMO's quality-of-care standards."[30] Encounter data, unlike claims data under fee-for-service, does not form the basis for payment. Therefore the plans will feel little urgency to provide such data to payers (unless required as a condition of the contract), and they will not have any financial incentive to guarantee its quality. Encounter data, within fully capitated systems, serves the purposes of internal managerial cost-control and utilization analysis.

Investigators at MFCU-3 described the encounter data available to them as "an absolute mess." Encounter data could be submitted up to 240 days (9 months) after the fact without being officially late. Even if encounter data was sent late, or was missing or inaccurate, there seemed to be no meaningful sanctions in place to remedy the situation. As always with data, if it is not routinely used for some important purpose, its quality will invariably suffer.

One investigator at MFCU-3 had asked the state agency to tell her how much Medicaid had paid in total for one particular pregnancy. The state agency replied that they could not answer the query because they did not have the data in any form that could be aggregated. In the end, the investigator had to go to the contractor (the plan), which, "after making a huge fuss, supplied data that was virtually indecipherable."

Proving Fraud Will Hinge on Questions of Medical Quality

In the absence of false claims, fraud prosecutions will require proof of systematic and conscious failure to provide adequate medical care—with the money being improperly diverted. It will become enormously difficult to distinguish criminally fraudulent practice from poor-quality medical practice. Criminal diversion of funds will be difficult to distinguish from inflated administrative overhead. Proving fraud, and distinguishing it from sloppy practice, will become exceedingly difficult.

Nevertheless, some unscrupulous contractors who care nothing for patients or their health and whose sole intention is to pocket as much as possible just as fast as possible from capitation fees, will remain in this business. One would like to imagine that they would remain vulnerable to prosecution. In practice, prosecutions based on systematic underutilization will probably be exceedingly rare.

Unambiguous measures of medical quality do not yet exist. The medical profession itself has just begun the task of designing systematic measures of medical quality, but even within the medical community itself this is recognized as a difficult and inexact science. Even if unambiguous measures of medical quality did exist, investigators would have to acquire substantial medical knowledge themselves in order to be able to make cases. In the absence of such measures, however, the criminal justice system seems largely powerless to deal with many forms of fraud under managed care. Investigators will find themselves lacking for information, for opportunities to get involved, and for the necessary skills. Prosecutors will fight shy of cases that have no central fraudulent transaction and that rely upon expert medical testimony. Over time the criminal justice system will become less and less relevant to fraud control.

Reevaluating the Health-Care Consequences of Fraud

Many of the prevalent forms of traditional fee-for-service fraud do not affect patient care at all. Billing for services not rendered, entering fictitious diagnoses, and "upcoding" often pass without the involvement or even the knowledge of the patient. Fraud, under fee-for-service, is predominantly a *financial* crime.

Under managed care, patients in the United States should worry about the increased cost of fraud in terms of human health, especially if law enforcement is really being squeezed out of the fraud-control business. Fraud under managed care will produce underutilization, which most experts agree is generally more dangerous to human health than overutilization; and certainly more dangerous than false billing.

Under managed care, fraud will claim *lives*. Testing will not be conducted when it should. Operations will not be performed when they should. Procedures will be carried out by inadequately qualified staff. Bureaucratic obstacles will be erected to deter patients from seeking treatment; and some patients will be deterred. Sick patients will be driven away.

It may take a little while before the health care consequences of fraud under capitated systems can be clearly seen. At the outset, capitation rates are typically set just slightly below historical fee-for-service costs. Medicare capitation rates, for example, are set at 95 percent of the Adjusted Average Per Capita Cost (AAPCC)—an actuarial estimate of expected cost under fee-for-service, taking into account beneficiary's county of residence.[31] At such payment levels, HMOs can earn huge profits. There is also plenty of room to fraudulently divert funds without stripping medical service provision too badly.

But when payers see the wide profit margins, they will inevitably ask themselves whether the rates are too high. "Previous studies have shown that HMOs can earn large profits from their Medicare/Medicaid contracts. The question arises, therefore, whether Medicare/Medicaid capitation payments are, therefore, too high. We plan to do an extended review of the overall process used in establishing reimbursement rates."[32] Moreover, during the honeymoon period for managed care, HMOs have enjoyed the extra profitability that results from favorable selection, enrolling younger, healthier patients.[33] As the penetration of managed care increases, so risk-bearing contractors will be forced to accept a broader mix, including sicker, costlier categories of patients.

Over time, intense competition within this lucrative industry will drive capitation rates down. Once the fees paid more accurately reflect the cost of providing reasonable service, and once the opportunities for favorable selection diminish, then there will be far less room for fraud. Whatever fraud takes place will begin to claim its human victims.

Under fee-for-service, the most damaging forms of fraud are perpetrated by providers, at the financial expense of payers. Under managed care, most fraud will be perpetrated by the middle layer of intervening corporations, and the victims will be the patients. Not only will the new forms of fraud be more damaging to human health; they will be extraordinarily difficult to detect, investigate, and prosecute.

Part Three

Prescription for Progress

8

A Model
Fraud-Control Strategy

The preceding chapters have focused on diagnosis of the problems, rather than on prescription. If the book were to end here, the parting picture would be gloomy indeed: criminals feeding off the health care system, largely with impunity; criminal fraud in the system essentially uncontrolled; the public and insurers placing their faith in control systems that turn out to offer little or no protection; the advent of electronic claims processing creating the opportunity for theft on a massive scale, and at the speed of light; and managed care producing forms of fraud potentially much more dangerous to human health.

The goal of those earlier chapters was to produce a clear understanding of the challenge and complexity of fraud control and to provide an honest and realistic evaluation of existing approaches. Nevertheless, many prescriptive observations were made along the way, and it is time now to pull these together and present them as a coherent whole. But the task for this chapter is more ambitious than merely compiling and presenting miscellaneous prescriptive recommendations. The task here is to define a model fraud-control strategy. To be of any use, the strategy must be one that clearly offers the promise of effective fraud control and is suitable for implementation within the health care industry.

Almost all of the elements of this model strategy can be found somewhere, in certain private insurance companies or in some particular government programs. But the strategy as a whole can be found nowhere. It does not yet exist. This control strategy is new, and implementing it will require enormous managerial courage, commitment, and persistence. For most insurers, adopting this kind of fraud-control strategy would involve radical change in the way they approach the whole business of fraud control.

The strategy described here is most relevant under fee-for-service systems, where payment systems are driven by incoming claims, and where fraud schemes involve the submission of bogus or inflated claims. Why the focus on claims-based payment systems, when managed care continues to grow so fast? Would it not be better to focus on managed care as the wave of the future?

First, despite the growth of managed care, for the time being the majority of payments to providers are still made under fee-for-service systems, and that will probably remain true at least until the turn of the twenty-first century.

Second, most managed-care plans are only partly capitated, with major components of the total care package remaining under fee-for-service arrangements. (Of course, where managed-care plans retain fee-for-service, they tend to do it within the context of more restricted provider networks.) So the continued expansion of managed care is unlikely to eliminate claims-based payment systems.

Third, claims-based payment systems are a familiar and attractive target for fraud perpetrators, and the perpetrators have developed a host of methods for attacking them. Present defenses are woefully inadequate. Claims-based payment systems are the principal mechanism through which criminal fraud currently bleeds the health care system. The job of stanching that flow is urgent and cannot be put off in the vague hope that managed care will one day solve the problem.

In any case, most of the more general aspects of this fraud-control strategy apply equally well within the context of capitated systems. After all the elements of the strategy have been laid out, a later part of the chapter will identify those pieces that apply to capitated systems.

The individual elements of this strategy are not arbitrarily selected. Each one arises as a direct consequence of the nature of the fraud-control business and from an understanding of the way fraud perpetrators think and act. In trying to design defenses, it may be worth taking a moment—as any serious chess player would—to put oneself in the opponent's shoes and to work out what they are trying to achieve, and how. So ponder, for a moment, the intentions and tactics of criminal fraud perpetrators.

Specifically, it might be useful to remember two particular categories of fraud perpetrators, so our control strategy can be tested against each of them. In some ways these two categories represent opposite extremes of the fraud spectrum, and considering them both helps to produce a control strategy of sufficient breadth and versatility.

One of these categories represents a comparatively new phenomenon: the "hit and run" scheme, where high-dollar-value, quick hits are the goal. The rule is "get in quick and get out with the money," then vanish from sight before anyone realizes what happened. These so called "fly by night" operations are not interested in providing any medical service at all. They simply want to get themselves into a position to bill and to be paid. They set themselves up in any way that creates an opportunity to bill insurers, public or private, and usually both. They may act under the guise of being DME suppliers, home health care suppliers, physicians, laboratories, pharmacies, transportation companies, radiological services, or virtually any other type of provider that fits a small-business model.

Hit and run operations will rent an "office" only if they need one to obtain certification. If they can operate with mail drops or prestige boxes, they will. They enroll medical staff only so far as is necessary for program eligibility and may list qualified individuals as affiliated even without their knowledge. The principals of the operation may use fictitious names or may usurp the identities of other reputable individuals.

In order to bill extensively, these operations need lists of patient identities, which are available on the black market or can be downloaded from databases kept by hospitals or clinics. Sometimes the lists are obtained through collusion with insurance company employees.

Once properly registered as a supplier of services or products, fraudulent operators obtain the necessary billing software and go to work, exploring the payment systems with a variety of claims. They test to see which edits and audits are turned off and pile massive volumes of claims through any openings they find. They prefer to submit claims electronically in order to avoid the risk of human scrutiny. And they search for the combinations of procedure code, diagnosis, and price that guarantee auto-adjudication all the way through to payment.

Hit and run operations bill fast and furious, knowing their time is limited. Post-payment utilization review will eventually show them up, even though it may take several months to do so. If they receive system-generated requests for supporting documentation, they do not respond (knowing that those particular claims will then be disallowed). But they watch closely for any sign that an insurer has discovered their fraudulent activity. If they see any sign of a human investigation of their activities, they take that as their signal to leave. By the time investigators eventually come calling, the office has been vacated, the money is untraceable, and the principals are in business somewhere else under a different name.

At the opposite extreme lies a more traditional kind of villain: the white-collar criminal who lives by the maxim that the way to get rich is to "steal a little, all the time." These are typically providers running legitimate businesses and providing genuine services. But they use the bulk of their legitimate business transactions to hide their stealing. When they steal they use familiar methods, such as billing for services not provided, billing for more expensive services or products than those actually provided, and falsifying diagnoses to support more expensive claims. Mindful of post-utilization review, they moderate the volume of fraudulent claims so as to avoid the statistical extremes under provider-profiling. They prefer to cheat, if possible, in the same ways that others in their specialty cheat, because it makes their own behavior less likely to appear abnormal.

If any of their bogus or inflated claims are challenged these white-collar criminals take one of two tacks. If challenged on something as blatant as services not provided they confess their mistake immediately, offering repayment or restitution, and blaming clerical error. Otherwise they would deny any culpability, bemoan the complexity of the regulations, feign ignorance of the particular point in question, and eventually acknowledge the education. In either case, they would then abandon that particular method of stealing and quickly replace it with others. They would carefully figure out the detection mechanism that caught their last scheme and figure a way to circumnavigate it in the future.

The white-collar criminal's strategy is to exploit to the full the respectability of the medical profession, acting at all times and responding to any query as if, utterly trustworthy and well-intentioned, they made administrative mistakes just because they were too busy caring for patients; at the same time they abuse that trust—constantly, deliberately, and systematically. This strategy is used by individual providers and corporations alike.

These represent just two of the opponents' possible strategies. There are many others and many variations on these themes. But these two—the "quick-hit" and the "steal a little all the time" strategies—are major classes of fraud not adequately controlled by existing systems. It is useful, therefore, to hold at least these two in the back of one's mind in reviewing any new fraud-control strategy. If the new strategy does not work for these two major types of fraud, then it cannot be the right answer.

Components of a Model Fraud-Control Strategy

A model fraud-control strategy would comprise the following characteristics.

1. Commitment to routine, systematic measurement
2. Resource allocation for controls based upon an assessment of the seriousness (i.e., measurement) of the problem
3. Clear designation of responsibility for fraud control
4. Adoption of a problem-solving approach to fraud control
5. Deliberate focus on early detection of new types of fraud
6. Prepayment, fraud-specific controls
7. Every claim faces some risk of review

Commitment to Routine, Systematic Measurement

To control fraud, you have to be able to see clearly. Without systematic measurement, a fraud-control operation flies blind. Without measurement, no one can tell whether an increased detection rate represents good or bad news. No one can tell whether the time and expense devoted to investigating and prosecuting cases is producing any real deterrent effect. No one can tell whether one health care insurer or program is any more or less vulnerable than any other; or whether payment safeguards are better or worse than they were last year. And, in the absence of measurement, the debate about fraud rattles loosely and uselessly around the extent of the problem, rather than getting the facts on the table and proceeding to the design of appropriate solutions.

Hence the importance of measurement—a point explored in detail in Chapter 3. Suffice it to say here that a commitment to routine, systematic measurement is the cornerstone of any effective fraud-control operation. Without it, no one can see what they are working on, and they cannot tell how they are doing. Without measurement, no one can demonstrate either the importance of the fraud-control task or the benefits of doing it well.

The mechanism for measurement, using random audits, is well understood and has parallels in many other environments. In the context of health care fraud it would involve:

1. selection of a statistically valid random sample of claims, with
2. rigorous audit of each one, involving
3. external validation of the information within the claim, sufficiently rigorous to identify any fraudulent claims.

Perhaps it is worth pointing out that the sampling should be done immediately after the routine operation of existing control systems and just prior to payment. In other words, all existing edits and audits and other claim-suspension and development systems (including medical review) should each be allowed to complete their own review procedures before the random sample is taken. After all, fraudulent claims that the system already rejects are of relatively little interest. The important measure is the volume of fraudulent claims paid, as a proportion of total claims paid—which represents the proportion of program costs lost to fraud.

Only by allowing existing detection systems to operate first, before taking the sample, can one determine what those systems miss. For precisely this reason, the U.S. Custom's "Compliance Measurement Program" sets up random inspection programs that operate behind all normal inspectional procedures. When the Customs service wants to know, for example, what kinds of contraband their inspectional processes along the Mexican border miss and with what frequency, they establish an inspection program half a mile down the road from the inspection booths at the border. They do it out of sight of the primary inspectors and without notifying them. (If alerted, inspectors' behavior might change, which would invalidate the measurement). At the secondary site, cars and trucks are pulled over at random and searched thoroughly—not because it is an efficient way of finding contraband (it is not), but because it is the only way to measure the level of compliance and to assess the value of existing inspection procedures.

Just as it would be a mistake to take the samples too early, it would also be a mistake to take them too late. Retrospective studies, where a sample of last year's paid claims are picked out for review, suffer greatly from the effects of elapsed time. Fraud perpetrators may have moved on. Patients may have died, moved away, or simply forgotten what happened. The best time to contact claimants is when they are waiting to be paid. They remain uncommonly available during that period. The best way to organize such sampling is to do it in real time, with the claims being extracted for review at the very last stage in the processing cycle, but before payment is made.

Some officials hold the position that such measurement is not technically feasible because of the ambiguity of the distinctions between fraud and abuse. They say it is impossible to classify a claim as fraudulent or merely abusive, because the intentions of the claimant cannot be reliably determined. The IRS successfully dealt with that issue when measuring the refund fraud problem (based on false claims for the earned income tax credit). They picked their random sample, sent a criminal investigator to each taxpayer's home address to investigate, and allowed investigators to use their professional judgment in categorizing the outcome. Investigators were not asked to make cases, or to prove them in court. But they were asked to determine whether or not the children claimed as dependents actually lived with the claimant, whether the employment could be verified with the employer, and whether or not the reported income was correct. Each claim that was not clearly valid also underwent full "examination" by a tax examiner, who subsequently validated or adjusted the investigator's original opinion, using the traditional range of outcome classifications for IRS examinations.

In designing the classifications it is important to be clear about the goal. The goal is not to prove criminal intent beyond a reasonable doubt, as in a court of law. Rather, the goal is to see how bad things are and determine whether they are getting better or worse; and how fast. The professional judgment of experienced auditors or investigators provides a perfectly adequate basis for such measurement. Not only are these officials best placed to classify claims reliably; they are also best placed to design classification systems that make practical sense. They know which distinctions can be drawn, and which cannot.

One other point on technical feasibility should be made: there seems to be some misperception within the industry concerning what constitutes a "statistically valid random sample." Among Medicare contractors in particular, I was told several times (in several different companies) that a sample, in order to be statistically valid, should include at least 10 percent of the claims. Such a notion would make routine random sampling prohibitively expensive. If it were true, this belief would kill any prospects for routine measurement. Fortunately the notion is completely erroneous. To be statistically valid, a random sample has only to be of a specified size, not a specified proportion of the claims. It does not matter how large or small the underlying population of claims.

Calculating necessary sample size is quite straightforward when the purpose of such sampling is to answer simple binary questions with respect to each claim, such as:

- "Was the service or product supplied as claimed?"
- "Did the patient suffer from the condition corresponding to the diagnosis entered on the claim form?"

- "Can the referring physician confirm his or her referral?"
- "Does the claim, in the investigator's best judgment, appear to be fraudulent?"

Such sampling seeks to establish an estimate of the proportion of claims from the whole population for which the answer to any one of such questions is "yes" or "no." The simple rule of thumb is that a sample size of around 1,000 will give you such estimates plus or minus 3 percent and that a sample size of 5,000 will provide estimates plus or minus 1 percent.[1]

The IRS, in their first study of refund fraud in 1994, randomly selected just over 1,000 tax returns, resulting in answers with a 3 percent margin of error. In subsequent years the IRS enlarged the sample to give greater accuracy and to support more detailed (segmented) analysis of the results.

Even with misconceptions about statistical validity aside, no one should imagine that measurement of health care fraud will be straightforward. The technical problems may be more easily overcome than the political. Many managers will remain exceedingly nervous about the prospects of having to reveal the results of such measurement. And many managers would worry that, even if they discovered the true extent of fraud, they would be unable to bring it under control. Some would prefer not to know.

The model fraud-control strategy, however, begins with an emphasis on seeing clearly, which requires a commitment to systematic measurement—painful and difficult as it may be.

Resource Allocation for Controls Based upon the Seriousness of the Problem

In the absence of systematic measurement, the level of resource allocated for fraud controls is normally based on the volume of the reactive workload, sufficient investigative capacity being established to keep pace with the caseload generated by fraud-detection and referral systems. But that caseload is tiny compared with the size of the problem, because the detection and referral systems do not work very well, and they typically uncover only a very small proportion of the fraud schemes. So, if the referral volume remains the basis for investigative resource allocation, massive underinvestment in controls will persist.

Under a model fraud-control strategy, investment in control systems (people and technology) would be related in some direct and obvious way to the size of the problem, as determined by measurement. If the proportion of fraudulent claims within a program was confirmed to be 10 percent, then it would make no sense to maintain investment in controls at a level of 0.1 percent of program costs, or thereabouts; especially when the ratio of return on marginal investments in controls exceeded three to one.

Some recent initiatives at the federal level (and a sequence of legislative proposals) have embraced novel ways of producing additional funding for fraud investigation and prosecution. For example, the U.S. Department of Health and Human Services announced "Operation Restore Trust" in May 1995. This operation targets Medicare fraud and abuse in California, Florida, New York, Texas, and Illinois. One feature of the plan is the reinvestment of court-awarded penalties from health care antifraud activities. Money awarded by the courts in Medicare cases would be placed in a health care fraud-control reinvestment fund, used to support further antifraud enforcement efforts.[2]

Use of these funds would strengthen efforts to fight fraud in much the same way that asset forfeitures are used by law-enforcement agencies against drug dealing. The establishment of such funds certainly represents progress. After all, anything that increases the level of resources available for fraud control from their current, pitifully low levels has to be seen as progress. But such a system is no substitute for rational resource-allocation decisions based fairly and squarely on the size of the problem. In fact, creation of funds of this type will inevitably produce some rather odd dynamics. The rate at which resources for controls grows would be directly proportional to the volume of monetary recoveries. In other words, when control systems are small and feeble (when rapid growth is most urgent) the rate of growth would be slow; whereas control operations that came anywhere near optimal size would be flooded with additional resources because of their larger caseload.

There are other reasons why the use of funds gained from penalties provides a less than ideal basis for resource allocation. For one, having a budget that depends to a significant extent upon reactive successes provides a disincentive for preventive work. Any desire to maximize the budget might produce a temptation to deliberately leave room for fraud to occur, focusing on the production of recoveries and penalties after the fact. Such a system offers no reward for preventive work at all. Another objection might be the danger of creating the impression of an enforcement bureaucracy feeding on its own success, operating "on a bounty-hunter principle," raising the question of whether "enforcers will be motivated by a desire to protect the integrity of the health care system, or will they be encouraged to prey upon the unwary and unconventional as a means of increasing their coffers."[3]

Despite these potential objections, more resources for fraud control is still better than less resources. And the creation of such a fund represents one major step toward the situation where returns on investment can be considered more seriously as a basis for resource allocation. In setting up this fund, legislators have finally broken loose from the strictest segregation of funds. Previously any court recoveries and penalties in Medicare had to be returned to the Medicare Trust Fund; setting any of that money aside to supplement fraud control—which was paid for out of the administrative budget—was inconceivable. This step loosens that rule, permitting recoveries to support enhanced fraud controls. This is a significant move forward, even though focusing on court-awarded penalties allows the step to be made without increasing the administrative budget at all.

But it would be an enormous mistake for lawmakers to assume that establishing these kinds of arrangements (which essentially costs them nothing in budgetary terms) relieves them of their obligation to provide controls commensurate with the seriousness of the problem. The requisite level of control will never be established without substantial increases in the relevant pieces of the administrative budget. Within public programs, both at the federal and state levels, the current budget climate makes any such increases quite impossible for now. And increases will remain completely out of the question until the fraud problem is finally measured—so the true costs of fraud can be laid out plainly for all to see.

Clear Designation of Responsibility for Fraud Control

Somebody has to be responsible for fraud control. A collection of loosely connected functional components cannot constitute a coherent fraud-control strategy. Someone, or some team of people, needs to be in charge. Someone has to be responsible for playing the fraud-control game, for grappling with its complexity, and for coordinating the contributions of the various functional tools.

A common mistake is to equate fraud investigation with fraud control. Investigation, and the whole business of preparing cases, is one valuable tool in the control toolbox. But it is not the whole toolbox. The performance of an investigative unit tends to be measured in terms of the number and seriousness of the cases it makes. But the performance of a fraud-control unit should be measured in terms of its success in lowering or suppressing the level of fraudulent claims being paid by the payment system, which would be measured periodically. Target levels would be set, which could be lowered year after year as the control operation matured, until the level of the fraud in the system was low enough to be regarded as "an acceptable price of doing business." For the credit card industry that level is roughly 0.1 percent of transaction volume, and fraud volume is generally kept down close to that mark.

When the IRS realized how serious their refund fraud problem was, one of their first actions was to create a new position, which they called the "fraud control executive."[4] They already had executives in charge of each of the relevant functional branches—criminal investigation, examination, audit, information systems, and so on. But it was the fraud control executive's job to focus on the fraud rather than on the internal functions. The fraud control executive was given overall responsibility for all aspects of fraud control, with freedom to design new policies and procedures, to target investigations and examinations on particular aspects of the problem, and to propose changes in regulations.

The simple test is to ask "who here is responsible for fraud control?" In most organizations nobody has that responsibility. In which case the fraud perpetrator, in designing scams, has only to chart a course around each isolated function; then there will be nobody left to oppose them.

A Problem-Solving Approach to Fraud Control

Many officials, both within private and public programs, were keen to explain how they were deliberately shifting away from a predominantly reactive stance and putting greater emphasis on prevention. Medicare contractors, for instance, reported that HCFA's new maxim was "stop the bleeding," borne from a powerful realization that "pay and chase" (trying to recover the money after it had been paid out) was a losing strategy.

On occasions the preventive and reactive philosophies come sharply into conflict. Whenever a major fraud scheme is discovered, investigators confront a dilemma: should they stop the bleeding immediately, cutting the perpetrators out of the payment system in order to minimize further losses; or should they allow the scam to run on for a while, under their surveillance, so they can collect evidence and make a compelling case? A traditional law-enforcement approach would favor the second action and would ask managers to continue paying out for the sake of the opportunity to build a high-quality case. But a pure preventative approach would favor the first action, cutting losses immediately even at peril of alerting the fraud perpetrators and ruining the prospects of a successful prosecution.

Clearly there is much to be said on both sides. On the face of it, the reactive strategy serves the goals of justice on a case-by-case basis better than the preventive strategy. But prevention appears to serve the goal of cost control better than the reactive strategy.

The task of defining an effective control strategy is more complex than simply choosing between reactive and preventive philosophies. Switching from a traditional enforcement approach to prevention as the guiding maxim would be quite dangerous—and could be viewed as leaping straight from one ineffective extreme to the other, jumping right over much more promising middle ground. It may help to lay out the two extremes first and to show why neither one can constitute effective control, before trying to define a better position.

The Reactive, or Enforcement, Approach. At one extreme lies the purely reactive approach. This incorporates a classic enforcement mentality, based on the fundamental assumption that a ruthless and efficient investigative and enforcement capability will ultimately produce broad compliance, through the mechanism of deterrence. The way to get people to obey the rules is to pick some offenders, prosecute them vigorously, publicize their convictions, and then rely upon the resulting publicity to bring everyone else into line. The reactive approach waits for the fraud to occur, then steps in to repair the damage. It deals with control failures, case by case, after the fact. It seeks justice, case by case, but places little emphasis on control.

Defenders of the reactive approach, if asked why vigorous case-making has so clearly failed to control fraud, point to inadequate resources, the failure of the courts to keep up their end of the bargain, and the absence of sufficient jail space. What is needed, they would say, is more of the same: more investigations, more cases, more convictions, more jail terms.

In the context of fraud control, the flaws in a purely reactive or enforcement strategy have become quite apparent. There are too many violations; too many violators. Making cases is laborious, difficult, and expensive. Due to the limited capacity of the criminal and civil court systems and the reluctance of many prosecutors to take on any but the most straightforward of health care fraud cases, only a small minority of cases prepared by investigators ever get into court. The resulting deterrent effect, based largely on the probability of being caught and convicted, turns out to be minimal.

The resources of the justice system available for health care cases, in terms of court time and jail space, are unlikely to increase anytime soon. Health care fraud may be the number two priority of the Department of Justice, but the number one priority—violent crime—does not leave much room for number two. In October 1995 the *Washington Times* quoted Newt Gingrich defending GOP efforts to reduce penalties and enforcement efforts against Medicare fraud: "For the time being I'd rather lock up the murderers, the rapists and the drug dealers. Once we start getting some vacant jail space, I'd be glad to look at [increased attention to Medicare fraud]."[5] A strategy that relies on the capacity of the justice system is a necessarily limited one. Some particular types of fraud are clearly better controlled by instituting new eligibility criteria, operating additional edits and audits in processing systems, by running education and information campaigns, by instituting requirements for supporting documentation, or by other procedural or administrative changes. In other words, a wide variety of tools turns out to be useful in a variety of fraud-control contexts; and many fraud problems can be eliminated most efficiently by using methods other than enforcement.

Those who emphasize the goal of cost control also criticize the enforcement approach on the basis of its failure to recover funds. Even in the relatively few cases that make it to the civil or criminal courts, stolen funds remain notoriously hard to recapture. Often the proceeds of fraud have already been squandered on the high life, secreted in off-shore accounts, or invested in foreign assets. And, for smaller insurers, pursuing civil or criminal cases makes poor economic sense. The costs of bringing the cases often outweigh the insurer's losses and nearly always exceed any likely recoveries.

The most critical deficiency of a reactive approach to fraud control—in the context of health care fraud—is its reliance on existing detection systems. A reactive strategy can only deal with those instances of fraud that detection and referral systems uncover. Anything that detection systems miss, a reactive strategy does not address. Investigative units only investigate what they are fed. Given the ineffectiveness of existing detection and referral systems, the investigative caseload therefore represents only the tiniest sliver, and a very biased sample, of the whole fraud universe.

If existing detection systems only scratch the surface, then a reactive strategy can only scratch the surface. Given the painstaking nature of case preparation and the constraints of the justice system, a purely or predominantly reactive strategy not only scratches the surface but does it slowly and in a very limited number of places. It accomplishes too little, too late.

The Pure Prevention Approach.   At the opposite extreme lies a philosophy of pure prevention. The preventative strategy focuses on the construction of systems that prevent losses up front: comprehensive batteries of automated edits and audits designed to keep fraudulent claims out of the system altogether, significantly diminishing the subsequent need for claims review, audits, and investigation.

Chapter 6—Electronic Claims Processing—examined the automated version of the preventative vision. That vision, centered on automated prevention, seems to be gaining popularity within the health insurance industry as a possible antidote to the deficiencies of the reactive approach. But Chapter 6 described the flaws of such a vision, pointing out that no static set of controls will ever constitute an effective defense; that discrimination between legitimate and illegitimate claims cannot be accomplished solely by examining their information content; and that exclusive reliance on systems—rather than humans—to play the fraud-control game is a serious error.

At its most extreme (and most dangerous), a philosophy of prevention can undermine the investigative and enforcement capabilities. By stressing other tools and remedies, it diminishes the importance of the investigative and enforcement apparatus and may explicitly transfer resources away from them. Often investigators perceive the shift to prevention as an assault on their status and the importance of their work. They see their evidence-gathering sabotaged through premature termination of providers, or other administrative actions that warn perpetrators. They see investments being made in systems in preference to, and sometimes at the expense of, their own units. And they hear the language of prevention, which seems to hold no place for investigation or prosecution.

Familiar Dichotomy.   The tension between enforcement and prevention appears in many contexts other than fraud control. In a wide range of regulatory and enforcement professions—including policing, environmental protection, tax administration, customs, and occupational safety and health—the traditional enforcement approach has come under considerable stress. These professions also face the realization that there are too many violators, too many violations, and never enough resources to get their job done. They have also discovered that lining up violators for prosecution was more successful in jamming up the justice system than it was in making streets safe, the environment clean, or in eliminating major patterns of noncompliance with tax or trade regulations. These professions have each recognized that the enforcement strategy waits until the damage has been done and then reacts, case by case, violation by violation, failure by failure. They have begun to recognize the foolishness of organizing their work around failures rather than around opportunities for intervention.[6]

In response to the perceived deficiencies of a purely or predominantly reactive strategy, many of these regulatory professions have begun exploring alternative strategies, many of them emphasizing voluntary compliance and using a broader range of tools including education, outreach, and voluntary programs. They seek to influence compliance more broadly, stressing prevention rather than counting their success solely in terms of specific outputs (such as inspections, audits, prosecutions, convictions, or jail sentences—the traditional measurements of an enforcement operation).

Certain predictable dangers beset any regulatory agency that attempts to make this strategic shift. Experienced investigators and enforcement officers perceive the new emphasis on prevention as an attack on their own role and status. Moreover, mindful of the egregious bad actors with whom they have traditionally dealt, investigators express skepticism about the usefulness of tools such as persuasion, education, and the new machinery of "voluntary compliance." Many members of the regulated public will comply, they say, only if *made* to do so; take away the threat of enforcement, or diminish the capacity of the investigative unit, and law-breaking will run rampant.

Enforcement officers also point out, correctly, that no preventative operation can be sufficiently successful to render a reactive capacity completely unnecessary. However much effort goes into making the highways safe, accidents will still happen. However good pollution prevention technology, many industries will choose to pollute simply because it is still in their own private economic interest to do so. However diligent the IRS's taxpayer education programs, many people will still cheat. Investing everything in prevention is as foolish as investing everything in enforcement.

What follows, unfortunately, can be an extremely bitter and destructive internal battle. People divide into camps—joining the enforcement camp or the prevention camp—depending on their experience and functional loyalties.

Problem-Solving. But many of these regulatory professions are now finding their way out of this uncomfortable predicament, exploring a new strategy which has been broadly labeled "problem-solving".

They discover, eventually, that the internal battle between enforcement and prevention is actually a battle over tools, not goals. Both the enforcement and prevention camps can be persuaded that the ultimate goal is broad compliance; and that the remaining argument is about the comparative effectiveness of different tools. They realize that the argument turned bitter when it turned into a competition between different functions, for resources. Then the issue became: how much to invest in investigative units, how much in outreach programs, how much in the development of preventative systems. What started out as a philosophical or strategic debate over the best way to procure compliance had quickly degenerated into a functional fight over money, status, and jobs.

The problem-solving approach rescues regulatory agencies from these destructive tensions and provides a constructive way forward. It dismisses the inward-looking focus on tools and replaces it with an outward-looking focus on important areas of noncompliance.

The problem-solving approach was first laid out explicitly by Professor Herman Goldstein (of the University of Wisconsin), widely acknowledged as the father of problem-solving policing.[7] In the context of police work, Goldstein argued that policing becomes much more effective when it pays attention to the persistent problems or patterns that underlie individual incidents, rather than by dealing with the incidents one by one, in isolation.

Goldstein suggested some useful definitions of problems—as "a cluster of similar, related, or recurring incidents rather than a single incident," "a substantive community concern," or as "the unit of police business."[8] He also explained that problems came in many shapes and sizes and could be defined in a variety of different dimensions. For example, some policing problems are concentrated in particular locations and at particular times of day or night (known as "hot spots"). Others might concern common patterns of behavior, or involve a particular class of offender, a particular type of victim, a repeat offender, a repeat victim, or a particular type of weapon.[9]

The problem-solving approach turns out to be relevant to many more professions than policing.[10] Just as it allows policing to get to the heart of important, persistent or recurring problems (which therefore generate multiple calls), so it also allows environmental agencies to identify and focus upon important environmental problems. The problem-solving approach allows tax and customs agencies to identify and concentrate on important patterns of noncompliance, and it allows occupational safety and health professionals to identify and focus upon significant workplace hazards.

In each case, the goal of problem solving is to *identify important problems early and fix them.* The strategy permits the complete range of available tools to be considered with respect to each problem and demands the use of creativity and innovation in fashioning tailor-made responses to each identified problem. With respect to each problem nominated for attention, the object is to design an intervention that fixes the problem, preferably for good, thus diminishing the reactive workload and enabling the agency to shift its attention to the next set of problems.

In fashioning a solution for any particular problem, the enforcement tool (making cases) is always available, but is never assumed to be necessarily the most effective or the most resource-efficient approach. For some problems, the most effective intervention may well include a campaign of vigorous and well-publicized enforcement. But for others, the solution might be a procedural or policy change, or the requirement for additional information or a second opinion. Problem-solving, recognizing the scarcity of the resource, uses enforcement surgically, incisively, and in the context of a coherent control strategy.

Problem-solving quiets the functional, tool-centered arguments. The foolishness of those arguments becomes immediately apparent once an organization develops a clear focus on its work. No one would dream of telling a furniture maker "next year I'd like you to use the lathe a little less and the hammer more." How much a craftsman uses a lathe depends entirely on what he is making, and the essence of craftsmanship includes knowing when to use what tool.

A problem-solving strategy picks the most important tasks and then selects appropriate tools in each case; rather than deciding first which are the important tools and then picking the tasks to fit. A problem-solving operation organizes the tools around the work, rather than organizing the work around the tools.

Problem-Solving Approach to Fraud Control.   Adopting a problem-solving approach to fraud control accomplishes a number of things. It places the emphasis firmly on fraud *control*, rather than on any of the more functionally specific goals, such as fraud investigation, fraud detection, or fraud prevention. It also provides a rational framework within which all of the different methods and tools can take their proper place. And it makes much more efficient use of available control resources: partly by providing a formal system for focusing attention and resources on the most critical problems; partly by changing the unit of work from cases to problems, giving staff the opportunity to design lasting solutions rather than plodding through their caseload; and partly by bringing the whole toolkit to every problem, so that the most efficient combination of tools can be used.

Stages of Problem-Solving.   The problem-solving process has been laid out in great detail by Herman Goldstein in his book *Problem-Oriented Policing.* The following stages are slightly condensed from his and adapted for the fraud-control context:[11]

1. Nominating problems for attention by grouping fraud incidents as problems
2. Disaggregating and accurately labeling fraud problems
3. Analysis of other parties' views
4. Capturing and critiquing the current responses
5. An uninhibited search for a tailor-made response
6. Establishing a mechanism for measurement, specific to the problem
7. Implementing the tailor-made response
8. Evaluation, feedback, and adjustment

All of which sounds like common sense. Health care insurers might be tempted to assume that the process to be followed, once a problem has been appropriately identified, is obvious.

But experience within policing and a variety of other regulatory agencies suggests the process, while intellectually logical and straightforward, is entirely foreign to traditional bureaucratic behavior. Implementing a problem-solving approach is far from easy.[12]

Stage 1 involves the nomination of fraud problems for attention. Problems can be defined in a great many ways. Some problems may be defined in terms of repeat offenders: providers, patients, or corporations who are persistent in their attempts to cheat. Sometimes persistent offenders can be detected initially through aberrant utilization patterns. Often they cannot.

Some problems may be defined in terms of particular fraudulent practices within specific industry segments. For example: home health care agencies billing for two-person home visits when only single-person visits were conducted; durable medical equipment suppliers billing for motorized wheelchairs when a cheaper version was supplied; pharmacy chains deliberately billing for prescriptions even when patients fail to pick them up; or cosmetic "nose-jobs" that are not usually covered by insurance being billed as septoplasties (medically necessary repairs), which are covered.

Some problems may be defined in terms of improper use of particular diagnoses, or procedure codes. For example the diagnosis "dysphagia" (difficulty swallowing) appears in connection with one of hottest forms of DME scam, involving provision of equipment and supplies for feeding patients through tubes—either "enteral feeding" (through the gastrointestinal system) or "perenteral feeding" (directly into a blood vessel).

Thus there are many different ways—or dimensions—in which problems can be defined. A mature problem-solving approach can recognize any of them and organize around them.

The health insurance industry is no stranger to the idea of grouping claims together so that attention can be focused upon particular problems. Focused medical review, which is widely practiced, does exactly that: defining the units of work as patterns of abuse. However, focused medical review teams—like medical review more generally—pay attention to issues of medical necessity, treatment orthodoxy, and policy coverage; not fraud. And their audit procedures normally assume the truthfulness of the claim content and lack the rigorous external verification processes required to uncover fraud. Nevertheless, the project approach to identified issues, as practiced by Focused Medical Review teams, is exactly what needs to be produced with respect to the control of criminal fraud.

Stage 2 of the process—disaggregating and accurately labeling problems—seems, at first glance, to run counter to the initial stage of grouping them meaningfully together. The object of including this second stage is to make sure that the level of aggregation is not only high enough but is in fact the right one.

Whenever agencies begin learning the art of problem-solving, they often give way to the temptation of defining problems in exceedingly broad terms.[13] In the context of health care fraud, examples of such excessively broad categorizations might be "chiropractic fraud," "DME fraud, ""medical transportation fraud," or "pharmacy fraud." Such problem definitions are really too broad to permit the construction of any sensible plan of attack and too vague to permit any rigorous assessment of whether or not the problem has been adequately controlled.

Stage 3—analyzing the views of other parties with respect to the problem—makes sure that all other parties who have a legitimate interest in the area or practice under scrutiny have their perspectives properly considered before an action plan is finally agreed-upon. Failure to consider such legitimate interests early in the process can lead to frustration and failure later on.

Stage 4—capturing and critiquing the current response—is also straightforward, but demands a dose of honesty. Which control systems or procedures currently deal with this problem? Do they work? How do we know? Why is the current response structured in this way? Which pieces of the current response appear to have some effect? Exactly what effect?

Some components of the current response might be extremely useful and should not be lightly discarded. Others might simply be based upon tradition, on erroneous assumptions about the nature of fraud control, or on nothing more solid than "this is what we do." In any case an honest appraisal both of the nature of the responses and their impact lays a firm foundation for the design of better solutions.

Stage 5, an uninhibited search for a tailor-made solution, tends to run afoul of the enforcement mentality. Many investigators feel they know the solution: continue to make cases; just "lock the bastards up!" They resent further discussion. They feel their traditional tactics would work perfectly well if only the courts and the prisons had the necessary capacity. Truly uninhibited searches demand that officials let go of many firmly entrenched views about what works and what does not.

Stage 6, establishing a mechanism for measurement, runs contrary to traditional practice in the industry. The norm—in the absence of any systematic measurement—has been to implement new controls from time to time and then leave them in place for ever. Everyone would assume they were having their intended effect, and that they should continue operation exactly as they did on day one. The problem-solving process demands that problem-solvers decide before implementing any solutions how their impact is going to be measured. In some cases the impact may produce a decrease in the number of claims of a particular type, or a decrease in the frequency of beneficiary complaints in a particular category. In other cases intelligence reports or undercover operations might report, from the perpetrators' point of view, that a particular modus operandi has become too difficult and has therefore been abandoned. In some cases, randomized programs of audits (targeted on the particular problem area) may be the only method of getting reliable information about practices that cannot be detected without external validation.

With respect to each fraud problem, the fraud control team needs to decide what to measure and how, and they need to get some initial baseline measurements so that changes for better or worse can be detected. Finally, there has to be a commitment to measuring the impact of solutions once they have been implemented. False claims of success ultimately backfire, and there is little merit in replacing ineffective responses with other equally ineffective ones. Measurement needs to be followed by adjustment, and adjustment by measurement, and so on until substantial progress is made. The temptation is always to defend the effectiveness of whatever particular policies, systems, and procedures happen to be in place. Genuine honesty about operational failures is both painful and difficult. But such honesty is the prerequisite for progress in any area.

Problem-Solving Requirements. The previous description of the problem-solving methodology does not do justice to its complexity. The central idea—picking important fraud problems and fixing them—seems simple enough. Yet institutionalizing that simple idea presents significant organizational challenges.

With respect to broad national or regional fraud patterns, it also requires major changes in the manner and depth of cooperation between different agencies. Tackling major fraud problems, which do not fit neatly within the responsibility of a single organization, will require insurers, policy makers, and law-enforcement agencies to work together around the common goal of effective fraud control. On several major cases they have already demonstrated their capacity to work together on specific, high-profile, prosecutions. Working together to produce effective control will be harder still.

It is best to deal with one step at a time, however. Figuring out the more complex implications for interagency relationships is not the first priority. For now, the health care industry could learn a great deal about effective fraud control if one or two major insurers would develop models of a problem-solving approach, within the confines of their own claims-processing system; others could then examine, imitate, and adapt those models to their own organizations.

At a minimum, successful implementation of a problem-solving approach to fraud control will combine the following features:

- A deliberate and continuing commitment to search for new and emerging patterns of fraud
- A person or team of people clearly designated as responsible for fraud control, with access to and influence over the whole range of functional tools—from the design of eligibility criteria at one end of the process, to investigation and prosecution at the other end
- Conscious recognition of the fraud *problem* as the relevant unit of work, producing a project focus rather than a case-by-case focus
- A focus on effectiveness (as opposed to outputs) of controls implemented, with a commitment to monitor the impact for each problem tackled

Deliberate Focus on Early Detection

The real promise of the problem-solving approach stems not just from the capacity to analyze important fraud problems and tackle them creatively but also from the opportunity to intervene early before too much damage has been done. But intervening early requires the ability to spot new fraud trends at the earliest possible moment. Like the child playing the mushroom game, holding a rubber mallet in her hand, successful fraud control depends on the ability to see clearly and to react quickly. All too often, as the continuing supply of health care fraud scandals attest, fraud problems often become endemic before existing control systems respond. So a model fraud-control strategy must stress early detection of emerging fraud problems, rather than remaining in a reactive posture and waiting until the problems, much enlarged, threaten to overwhelm them.

Thus scanning for emerging problems becomes a priority. Resources must be set aside for proactive outreach and intelligence-gathering operations, and these resources must be protected from the demands of the reactive workload—otherwise these proactive activities will never survive.

Proactive outreach requires the use of many tools. Some of the more familiar ones are described here:

- Establishing and maintaining a network of contacts with other insurers and law-enforcement agencies, providing early warning of any fraud trends already spotted by others
- Undercover operations, such as "undercover shopping" of newly established storefront clinics (the object being to find out what kinds of services are really being provided, and to whom)
- Development of informants within criminal networks, who can report on emerging practices
- Interviewing convicted fraud perpetrators, who may be willing to describe a variety of fraud methods and who may be able to point out remaining vulnerabilities in payment systems
- Data mining: using a broad range of analytical tools to search for anomalous patterns. (Chapter 9 examines the analytical tools currently available and describes the need for a broader range of analytical methods.)
- Focus groups, providing the opportunity to pick the brains of patients and providers about system vulnerabilities and observed patterns of suspicious behavior
- Educating claims processing staff (those few who retain the opportunity to examine the contents of claims) about indicators of fraud
- Creation of "tiger teams" within the organization (whose job is to come up with creative new ways to cheat the system), as a way of testing and refining defenses

A collection of such activities constitutes an intelligence operation. These activities may very well generate cases, but they are not case-based. The objective is to discover emerging fraudulent practices, so that the control operation can find antidotes.

All of these intelligence-gathering mechanisms have already been used within the health care industry, but they are used only sporadically, and they are quickly displaced when the caseload builds up. Whenever and wherever these methods have been used, investigators report they uncover far more trouble than they can possibly deal with. In several quite separate organizations, investigators described their experience in exactly the same way, using one particular mixed metaphor that seems to have become conventional wisdom: "Every rock we look under, we find a whole new can of worms."

The critical need to spot emerging patterns earlier shifts greater emphasis onto these proactive methods and intelligence-gathering tools. Timely and accurate intelligence feeds the problem-solving strategy, ensuring that the resources and creative energies of the defending organization focus on the right things, and at the right time. In the control business, intelligence counts. Even more than cases.

Fraud-Specific Prepayment Controls

The fraud-control team needs to be able to operate prepayment. That means they should be able to insert their own fraud-specific edits and audits into the processing system; and they need the resources to be able to validate suspended claims themselves rather than relying on medical-review teams (which are already overburdened and focused on different issues) to do it for them. They should be able to design and operate their own focused reviews, randomly selecting claims within fraud-prone areas and using external validation procedures—telephone calls, visits, on-site audits, and the like—to check them out.

In particular, the fraud-control team must be in a position to prevent rapid, high-dollar-value fraud schemes, characterized as bust-outs. So they must have the capacity and opportunity to operate the controls that Chapter 6, Electronic Claims Processing, pointed out were invariably missing. These would involve, at a minimum, automatic suspension of high-dollar payments (above some arbitrary threshold) pending human review of the contributing claims; provider-level monitoring (looking for sudden accelerations in aggregate claims levels, or totals in excess of reasonable norms for that specialty); and the routine random selection of a small proportion of claims for validation.

Chapter 9 provides a much more detailed discussion regarding the design of detection tools and their operation at different stages of the claims process. Suffice it to say, for now, that whoever is given responsibility for fraud control needs the freedom to intercept claims prepayment, rather than operating entirely post-payment.

Every Claim Faces Risk of Review

Every claim submitted for payment should suffer some risk of review for fraud, regardless of its dollar amount, regardless of its medical orthodoxy, and regardless of the reputation of the claimant. Part of the responsibility of the fraud-control team, reviewing claims prepayment, would be to extract claims for random review and make sufficient inquiries to establish the legitimacy or illegitimacy of each one. This provision would go a long way toward eliminating the vulnerability of payment systems to bust-out schemes, the major new threat under electronic claims processing. Under such schemes, fraud perpetrators test claims to establish which ones the system will pay automatically (auto-adjudicate). Then they generate thousands or tens of thousands of similar claims and submit them electronically, safe in the knowledge that the system will treat each of them exactly the same way. The utter predictability of the payment system works to the fraud perpetrator's advantage.

Some risk of random review eliminates this vulnerability. If prepayment inquiries showed a claim to be even a little suspicious, and did it reasonably quickly, then the fraud-control team could immediately suspend all other claims pending from the same source, pending more detailed scrutiny.

The industry will raise two principal objections to such a practice. First, they will say that random selection, with external validation, constitutes an arbitrary and unwarranted intrusion into the affairs of perfectly respectable providers. But that intrusion may be part of the price society has to pay for reasonable protection of the health care system. Insurers cannot possibly control costs if they give up the right to verify the truthfulness of claims.

Secondly, industry officials will point out that scarce audit and investigative resources would be far better used on focused claims review than on random review. But focused reviews cannot offer this particular protection, because fraud perpetrators watch very carefully to see where insurers are focusing and deliberately play elsewhere.

Both of these objections can be mitigated somewhat by pointing out that the risk of random review does not need to be particularly high. A base probability of 1 percent might be reasonable. Insurers that commit to systematic measurement will see double benefit to such sampling. Not only does it protect against multi-claim scams but it could also act as the foundation for systematic measurement.

Outside the context of measurement (which requires a uniform risk across every claim), it makes sense to devote additional resources to higher risk providers. Brand new providers might start off at a higher risk of review, say 10 percent, and work their way down to the 1 percent floor only by establishing a record of accurate and trustworthy billing. In other words, providers would need to establish their trust-worthiness. Similarly, the risk could be increased for any providers whose randomly selected claims did not seem to be legitimate. Providers would no doubt explain such phenomena as isolated billing errors. But the price for such billing errors would be an increased risk of review—until, over a period of time, they can once more demonstrate that they deserve to be trusted.

The fraud-control team would maintain and operate this selection system as an integral part of their prepayment operation. They would maintain a file of selection probabilities, one for each claim submitter, which would automatically control the random selection of claims for review. They would be able to control the overall volume by adjusting selection probabilities, up or down, for different categories of claimant. But the probability of review should never be zero. Not for any provider, no matter how reputable; nor for any claim, no matter how small.

Applicability to Managed Care

Admittedly this description of a model fraud-control strategy applies most directly to claims-payment systems. Nevertheless, some features of the general control philosophy apply equally well to capitated plans.

The idea that the extent and nature of fraud should be systemati-cally measured applies equally well. Measurement is just that much harder to do under managed care, because of the extra difficulties in distinguishing fraudulent diversion of capitation fees from other areas of underutilization.

The idea that fraud-control resources should be based on the size and seriousness of the problem holds true as well. The erroneous belief that managed care provides a structural solution to the fraud problem threatens to strip away existing control resources, even though the new forms of fraud pose significant threats to human health.

Clear designation of responsibility for fraud control and adoption of a problem-solving approach are both equally valid. For payers to assume that managed-care plans themselves will take care of fraud control is utter folly. After all, it is the plans themselves that have the greatest opportunities to commit fraud.

Proactive outreach and intelligence-gathering, under managed care, becomes more critical than ever. The reactive workload will be minimal, as almost nobody has any incentive to report fraud; and there will be no claims-payment process within which detection and referral systems can be embedded. So, in the absence of such proactive outreach and intelligence-gathering, fraud will remain completely invisible.

Under managed care, intelligence will come from different sources. The locus for fraud will shift to the corporate middle layers that separate the payers from the frontline service providers. The best informants will be physicians and other providers who find themselves in a position to report on the policies and practices of the plans. Many of them will obviously prefer to do this anonymously. Some of them would *have* to do it anonymously, because some HMOs actually gag their doctors, forbidding them to complain, to tell any of their patients what is wrong with their HMO, or to go to any public body and say anything negative about the HMO.[14] If doctors do speak out they can be expelled from the HMO without recourse or appeal.

Even the sixth component of the model fraud-control strategy—the significance of a prepayment interception—is not irrelevant to managed care. A generalized version of that idea would be "make sure you check things out before you pay the money"; which certainly applies to managed care. Capitated programs face the risk of paying capitated fees to plans, in advance, only to see the corporations evaporate or artfully slide into bankruptcy, leaving someone else to take care of the patients. An effective fraud-control operation would take responsibility for minimizing the risks associated with advance payments by conducting background inquiries before contracts are awarded. Such inquiries should be sufficient to establish candidate plans as bona fide operations, and to flush out any criminal affiliation.

The Prospects for Implementation

The seven features of a successful fraud-control strategy described here—systematic measurement, resource allocation based upon measurement, clear designation of responsibility for fraud control, adoption of a problem-solving approach, dedicated resources for proactive outreach and intelligence gathering, prepayment operation of fraud controls including random verification, and ensuring that every claim faces some risk of review—will strike some officials within the industry as a useless and unrealistic wish list. In the real world of constrained resources, existing systems already creak under unmanageable operational loads. Some may accept the prescription in theory, but still write it off as a practical impossibility—of only academic interest.

The model fraud-control strategy described here is indeed, for the vast majority of insurers, a long way from reality. But that is exactly the point. The whole purpose of describing this model strategy is to show just how much it differs from current practice in the industry. Most insurers, public and private, do no systematic measurement of the fraud problem. They therefore fly blind, remaining largely oblivious of the true magnitude of the problem. None, as far as I have seen, make resource-allocation decisions based in any way upon valid estimates of the size of the problem; and thus continue to underinvest in controls by a factor of twenty or more. Most insurers fail to designate responsibility for control, and many equate control with investigation. They have no one responsible for playing the fraud-control game and little prospect of effective coordination between different functional tools. In terms of explicit strategy, many fraud units are bogged down in a reactive, case-making mode, unable to see the forest for the trees. At the other extreme, some proponents of electronic claims processing are in danger of proposing an extreme version of prevention, which threatens to eliminate human beings from the fraud-control operation almost entirely, and which may decimate investigative and enforcement capacities. Insurers need problem-solving as a rational, integrating, control-oriented framework. Most insurers, even if they believe in the value of proactive outreach and intelligence-gathering, cannot find or protect resources for it. So they operate with a distorted and fragmentary picture of fraud, as revealed by largely ineffective detection and referral systems. And most payment systems remain vulnerable to multimillion-dollar quick-hit scams because they lack the necessary prepayment controls. So this model remains far from reality, at least for now.

Two things must happen before anything close to the model can ever become a reality. First, the complexity of the fraud-control challenge needs to be grasped and understood. Second, the health care industry and the public need to learn the true extent of fraud in the U.S. health care system. (Without that knowledge, nobody can possibly justify the cost or inconvenience associated with operating such controls.) Hopefully this book will help reveal the complexity of the fraud-control challange. Only a commitment to systematic measurement can produce an understanding of the extent of fraud that exists in the health care system today. Until these two things happen, effective fraud control will remain elusive, and health care fraud will continue to plague the United States.

Evaluation Checklist

Many readers of this book, and of this chapter in particular, will be practitioners within the health care system seeking to understand the strengths and weaknesses of their own fraud-control operations. Some of those operations are much better than others. Very few come anywhere near the ideal.

For the sake of those practitioners, this chapter closes with ten summary questions that can be asked of any fraud-control operation and used as a crude evaluation device.

1. Are fraud losses within the payment process systematically measured?
2. Is the allocation of resources for fraud controls based in some direct way upon the outcome of systematic measurement (i.e., on some scientific estimate of the seriousness of the threat)?
3. Is there somebody or some team designated within the organization as responsible for fraud control (as distinct from fraud investigation)?
4. Does the fraud-control operation place deliberate emphasis on discovering new forms of fraud as early in their development as possible?
5. Can fraud-control analysts or investigators implement and operate fraud-specific edits and audits within the payment system, enabling them to suspend claims for external validation?
6. Are resources for proactive outreach and intelligence-gathering adequately protected from the pressures of the reactive caseload?
7. Do members of the fraud-control team routinely communicate with other insurers and law-enforcement agencies in order to update their own knowledge about emerging fraud trends; and do they then test their own claims population to see if such fraudulent practices are present?
8. Does the control operation use a problem-solving approach? (Evidence of such an approach would include: projects as the central unit of work, rather than cases; coordination of responses to particular problems across functional boundaries; and deliberate assessment of the impact of measures implemented in response to specific fraud problems.)
9. Does every claim that comes in run some small risk of being audited in a way that would involve validating the truthfulness of the claim?

10. Suppose a fraud perpetrator tested one claim today, say for $1,500, and discovered that the claim proceeded through auto-adjudication to payment, with no human intervention. Next week they submit 10,000 similar claims, generated by computer, using 10,000 different patient identities and claiming exactly the same procedure with respect to each. Is there anything in the payment system (in terms of prepayment detection systems) that would detect the scheme and prevent an automatic, multimillion-dollar payout?

For each of these ten questions award one point for each "yes" answer and half a point for any questions where the answer is "maybe" or "in some ways." A perfect ten-point total would reflect a mature and effective fraud-control strategy. For lower totals questions prompting anything other than a "yes" answer might indicate where there is still progress to be made.

9
Detection Systems

The last thing in the world I need right now is to detect more fraud.

HCFA official

Given the current state of affairs within the industry, many officials would prefer not to detect more fraud. They have far too many cases and far too few resources. They see too many investigations and prosecutions abandoned for lack of capacity in the court system and see little value in exacerbating the problem. Moreover they suspect any significant increase in the detection rate (which might result from improved detection systems) might be misinterpreted by many as yet more evidence of poor performance. As a matter of course, therefore, few within the industry show much eagerness to upgrade detection capabilities. For many practitioners, existing incentives push the opposite way: their lives would be much easier if the level of detected frauds went down. Hopefully, a better understanding of the nature of the fraud-control business will eventually produce a greater enthusiasm for improved detection systems within the industry. Once insurers start systematically measuring the level of fraud, the inadequacy of existing detection systems will become obvious.

The IRS, in tackling tax-refund fraud, had no idea just how bad their detection systems were until they carried out their first random sampling of EITC-based claims in 1994 (see Chapter 3 for details). During the 1994 filing season they detected 160 million dollars worth of fraudulent refunds. But the statistical measurement of the EITC fraud problem, through random sampling, indicated 3 *billion* dollars worth of fraudulent refunds passing through the system. IRS detection systems were uncovering only a fraction (roughly 5%) of the total. All of a sudden, the need for the IRS to upgrade its detection tools became obvious.

Also, as the emphasis shifts from fraud investigation to fraud control, improving detection tools will become more attractive. Officials will want to see the fraud picture more clearly, and they will feel less obligation to make a court case from every fraudulent claim they find.

This chapter is written for the sake of those within the industry who genuinely want to understand the limitations of existing detection tools and to grasp the opportunities for improvement. It has a slightly more technical flavor than the rest of the book, and some readers may therefore choose to skip over it.

Emphasis on Detection Tools, Not Detection Systems

Earlier chapters have stressed the importance of relying upon humans, rather than systems, to play the fraud-control game. Some will undoubtedly interpret that emphasis as antitechnology. Some readers may interpret the account given of the small private insurer (in Chapter 6) as being an untimely and irrelevant glorification of outdated manual practices.

The issue is not whether to use technology, but how. The model of detection systems currently dominant in the industry—systems select: humans inspect—cannot offer effective protection. The basis upon which systems select seldom has much to do with fraud; and the detection systems are largely static, making them easy for fraud perpetrators to circumnavigate. The vision for automated prevention under electronic claims processing—using technology instead of people—suffers from the same flaws.

A recent article in *American Medical News* described how some insurers were experimenting with modern technologies such as neural networks and parallel processing to improve their fraud-detection capabilities.[1] After pointing out the cumbersome nature of old-fashioned manual claims review, the article noted:

> Today, however, some payers are rapidly moving from the old casual controls to comprehensive computerized ones.
>
> The new intelligent computing systems cast their nets constantly, tirelessly, and more thoroughly than the human examiners and limited computer programs they are replacing. Promoters claim that some of the new systems are so "smart" that they can even train themselves.

In other words, once you buy these new technologies you will not have to *think* about fraud control any more, because these new systems can do the thinking for you! Describing how, with the use of neural networks, "aberrant behavior will bubble to the surface," the article reported "you don't have to define for it what constitutes fraud and abuse. . . the network figures that out for itself".[2]

The vogue new technologies—fuzzy logic, neural networks, artificial intelligence, and advanced technology computing platforms—all have their place in the improvement of detection systems. The advent of such new technologies, as the rest of this chapter will make clear, offers the prospect of a whole new generation of fraud detection tools.

But human beings must decide where these technologies need to be used and in what ways. Human beings must understand what these tools can do and what they cannot. And human beings must operate these tools day by day and deal with their output. These tools can never substitute for human thought. If increased use of technology results in displacement of human analysts and investigators, then it will have done more harm than good. Hence this chapter's emphasis on equipping fraud-control teams with the very best technological tools, as distinct from the dangerous notion that technological systems can actually do the work of fraud control.

The Multilevel Nature of Fraud Control

To analyze the strengths and weaknesses of existing detection tools, one has to understand the many different levels at which fraud can be perpetrated. Frauds perpetrated at one level will not normally be detected by fraud controls operating at any other level.

To illustrate the multilevel nature of fraud, let us turn for a moment to the world of credit card fraud. Credit card fraud falls rather more neatly into distinct levels than many health care frauds, so using credit card fraud as an example makes the underlying framework a little easier to grasp.

Credit Card Fraud: An Illustration

There are basically five distinct levels at which credit card fraud can be perpetrated, which the following table summarizes.

Level 1	Transactions
Level 2	Card (or "plastic")
Level 3	Account
Level 4	The cardholder (holding multiple products or accounts)
Level 5	Multiparty or "RING" level

The first level of fraud control is the simplest. It involves monitoring for fraud at the *transaction* level. A transaction on a card is considered suspect if and only if the transaction itself, considered in isolation, is inherently suspicious. Examples of such suspicious transactions might include ATM (Automated Teller Machine) withdrawals at, or close to, the permitted maximum; or mail-order bulk purchases of portable and valuable resalable merchandise, such as jewelry or electronics; or purchase of expensive domestic or personal items on a corporate card.

Credit card issuers recognize these transaction-level threats, so they design detection apparatus and controls to contain such activity. ATM withdrawals above some threshold will require confirmation of identity via telephone. Or purchases of certain kinds will require additional user-authentication.

In the face of such controls, fraud perpetrators move to the second level. Using stolen or found credit cards, they deliberately keep individual transactions small, but make their money by using the same card many times over. Fraudulent users of credit cards and cash cards have been known to stand at ATM machines for hours, repeatedly withdrawing $50 at a time, believing that monitoring systems will not pay any attention to such small transactions, no matter how many in succession.

To defend against repeated use of stolen cards, the card issuers institute monitoring at the second level, which is the *card* level. These controls watch the overall behavior of the card—aggregating across multiple transactions—comparing the overall pattern with previous history and watching for "out-of-character" spending profiles or sudden accelerations in usage.

So now the game moves to the third level. Fraud perpetrators usurp the identities of account holders, or use fictitious identities to establish accounts. And they deliberately obtain multiple cards on the same account, often by requesting the issuance of supplementary cards. Spreading their activity across several different cards defeats the card-level controls. So the issuing banks then have to institute *account-level* controls to monitor the aggregate behavior across all of the cards. The more sophisticated fraud perpetrators then learn that they can use the same cardholder identity to procure multiple accounts. So they apply for, and obtain, multiple accounts from the same bank (using a fictitious or usurped identity). They also obtain accounts from many different banks in order to frustrate efforts at detection. Any bank that issues multiple products to the same individual now has to implement controls at the *cardholder* level, in order to be able to watch for any alarming trends in the bank's aggregate exposure to that individual.

Even this is not the end. The serious fraud perpetrators—for example, the major counterfeit credit card rings—move to the highest level: the *multiparty* or *ring* level. At this level, fraud perpetrators deliberately spread their fraudulent activities across hundreds or thousands of different accounts, in order to avoid all lower-level detection systems and controls. At this highest level, the credit card industry confronts organized criminal rings, as opposed to the opportunistic petty thieves who deal in one or two stolen cards at a time. These criminal rings may involve collusive merchants, even bank employees, and may involve fifty or more conspiring individuals playing different roles.

The most sophisticated schemes (and the most difficult to control) are global counterfeit card schemes, many of which have their roots in the Far East. These operations obtain credit card account information from members of staff at prestigious restaurants, hotels, or other high-volume service establishments. Those establishments are referred to within the business as "points of compromise." Once a week or so, the "source" at the point of compromise compiles a list of cards that have been used at that establishment, focusing mostly on "gold" or "platinum" or other prestige cards with higher credit limits. The source then transmits the list of account names, numbers, and expiration dates to the criminal counterfeiting organization, in exchange for a payoff of some kind. When the source is a senior staff member, they may also arrange placement of a magnetic stripe reader, hooked up to a personal computer, so that the encoded magnetic stripe information can be read off the cards, stored in a database, and passed on with the rest of the account information.

Another piece of the operation involves "spending teams" that travel from city to city, using the counterfeit cards. Blank counterfeit card stock (much of which is manufactured in Hong Kong) is mailed to them as they travel and comes complete with counterfeit holograms and other security features. The teams carry with them card embossing machines and magnetic stripe encoders, which, given the proliferation of card-based identification and security systems, anyone can buy. They receive lists of card numbers by telephone, passed on from the points of compromise, and spend their evenings in hotel rooms embossing the account details onto blank card stock and encoding the magnetic stripes to match. They then hold a more or less exact physical duplicate of the original card.

They then use these counterfeit cards vigorously, running them up to their credit limits within a day or two, before discarding them. They buy expensive jewelry, designer clothing, consumer electronics, and other items that can be resold for cash. The spending teams seldom stay in the same city for more than two or three days. And the legitimate cardholders have no idea anything happened to their account until they get their statement a month later—by which time fraudulent use of their account has stopped, and the team that counterfeited their card has long since moved on.

The credit card industry has developed reasonably good defenses at fraud levels 1, 2, and 3, but is less well-defended at levels 4 and 5. Some issuing banks have even tried to deny the existence of the counterfeit fraud problem, holding the account holders responsible for all charges, unless they reported their cards stolen. (Account holders are not responsible for such charges, provided they report the unauthorized activity on their accounts reasonably quickly after receiving their statement). In order to improve their detection capabilities, credit card issuers need to focus on two things. First, they should pay special attention to those levels where they are least well protected; and, second, they should look for earlier detection opportunities at every level in order to minimize losses.

The health care industry has precisely the same needs. They have to understand at which levels they remain vulnerable and design tools to plug those holes; and they have to move detection tools forward, to the earliest possible moment, in order to minimize losses.

The Seven Levels of Health Care Fraud Control

The corresponding analysis of health care fraud is a little more complex, and what follows here is oversimplified. There are at least seven distinct levels of aggregation at which fraud-control monitoring is required. The lowest level (transaction level) and the highest level (multiparty criminal conspiracies) of health card fraud are the same as with credit card fraud, but there are more intervening layers. In order, they are:

Level 1   Claim, or Transaction level
Level 2   Patient/Provider relationship
Level 3   (a) Patient level

	(b) Provider level
Level 4	(a) Patient group/Provider
	(b) Patient/Practice (clinic)
Level 5	Policy/Practice relationship
Level 6	(a) Defined groups of patients (e.g., families or residents of one nursing home.)
	(b) Practice (or Clinic)
Level 7	Multiparty, criminal conspiracies

Level 1 concerns claims that are inherently suspicious, even without any broader context or history: men having hysterectomies; infants receiving psychotherapy; doctors treating their own family. These claims can be deemed suspicious purely on the basis of information contained within the claim.

Level 2 concerns the relationship between one provider and one patient and examines the overall volume and nature of services delivered to that patient, by that provider. Detection systems operating at level 2 would compare service frequency with reasonable norms for the provider's specialty and for the patient's diagnosis.

Level 3 requires a broader perspective, either looking at the whole history of the patient (aggregating across all providers), or looking at the overall practice patterns of the provider (across all patients).

Level 4(a) takes account of the fact that several patients may be covered by the same insurance policy and any one practitioner may abuse the *policy*, distributing fraudulent or abusive activity across several patients. Providers may abuse the insurance policies of some other group of patients, such as the residents of a particular nursing home.

Level 4(b) also deals with abuse of one patient's account by a practice (which may involve several practitioners), acknowledging that frauds may be perpetrated by clinic or hospital administrators, who may deliberately distribute fraudulent activity across several practitioners.

Level 5 considers the overall use of a policy (which may cover several patients) by a practice (which may include several providers).

Level 6(a) considers misuse of a particular group of patients more broadly, perhaps by many different medical providers. The group of patients might be a family, all covered by one policy. Or they might be residents of a particular apartment complex, or residents of the same nursing home—any connection that opens the possibility of their insurances being abused as a group.

Level 6(b) concerns patterns of claims activity by groups of practitioners affiliated with one another through practices, clinics, or other cooperative business arrangements. Monitoring at this level would be suitable for detecting the activities of "Medicaid mills," where several providers set up under the same roof and continually refer patients to and fro among themselves for needless tests and services.

Finally, level 7 deals with the operations of criminal networks—such as prescription drug recycling schemes—where the pattern of fraudulent activity is much broader than any restricted set of beneficiaries or providers. The art of detection at this (highest) level involves watching for broad patterns of coincidence or connection between hundreds or thousands of otherwise innocuous transactions.

It is important to note that the higher levels of fraud monitoring are not necessarily *better* than the lower levels; they are just different. A fraud operated at level 5, where a clinic routinely makes claims on a policy, but spreads the fraudulent activity between many different doctors and across several patients, will most likely not be detectable by monitoring at any lower level. Certainly each individual transaction (claim) will look perfectly normal.

But, conversely, if an insurer monitors at level 5 only, then they would fail to catch opportunistic one-time frauds characterized by absurd claims at the transaction level (level 1). The individual fraudulent claims, manifestly unreasonable by themselves, would likely have insufficient impact on the overall use of a policy by a practice to trip any level 5 alarms. The transaction-level frauds would get lost within a much larger set comprising mostly legitimate claims.

So the issue is not one of choice. No one should abandon level 1 controls and move to some other level. And the issue is not simply one of monitoring at a high enough, or low enough, level. The issue is monitoring at the right level for the kind of scheme one intends to uncover, because most schemes will only be revealed at the same level at which the fraud perpetrators design and operate them. Assuming that frauds will continue to be perpetrated at any and all of these levels, then fraud-monitoring capabilities will be required at any and all levels.

Of course the characteristics of fraud schemes perpetrated at these various levels differ substantially. The lower-level frauds are more numerous, often opportunistic, and net relatively low dollar amounts. By contrast, the higher-level frauds can run undetected for long periods, require significantly more technical and organizational sophistication to operate, and are therefore probably less common; but each scheme may net many millions of dollars.

The sensible next question to ask is at what levels are insurers most vulnerable, and what might be done to remedy those vulnerabilities? Which levels are currently well-defended? And which levels are undefended? Sometimes fraud schemes that run undetected for months or years show only too clearly which particular levels of control were missing.

NBC's *Dateline* ran a feature on Medicare fraud in November 1995.[3] Part of the program featured a patient in whose name a supplier of medical equipment had billed Medicare over $10,000 *per month*, for several months, just for surgical dressings. In this case, the principal detection opportunity lies at level 2 (patient/provider relationship). But such flagrant billing could also be picked up at the *patient* level or even at the *provider* level if the provider was abusing a sufficient number of patients' accounts to distort their overall provider profile.

Congressional testimony provided by GAO in 1995, on fraud in the Medicare and Medicaid programs, cited several examples of schemes that, according to GAO, ought all to have been detected and stopped. But they came to light only through tip-offs, rather than through the operation of routine monitoring. In one case, a Medicare contractor processed and paid, without question, $1.2 million in claims from one supplier, all for body jackets supplied to various nursing home residents. The supplier's previous year total for the same item was just $8,500.[4]

Clearly, fairly rudimentary *provider-level* profiling ought to have spotted the anomaly—in particular, provider-level acceleration rate monitoring, had it been present.

In another example, a pharmacist from California had been billing Medicaid for improbably high volumes of prescription drugs and was being reimbursed without question, despite the fact that several recipients had been receiving more than twenty prescriptions per day, each.[5] Had the overall volume of drugs been unusually high for a pharmacy, then provider-level monitoring (level 3[b]) should have revealed the pharmacist as an outlier within the specialty, by total volume. But if the real anomaly concerns a small number of individual patients receiving far too many prescriptions, then the detection opportunity lies at level 2, where the unit of analysis is the aggregate transaction volume between a particular provider and a particular patient.

Two more cases, where rudimentary monitoring at level 2 would have detected the scheme, came to light only through whistle-blowers or some other good fortune. Over a sixteen-month period, a van service billed Medicare $62,000 for ambulance trips to transport the same patient 240 times.[6] And Medicaid paid for more than 142 lab tests and 85 prescriptions for one patient within an eighteen-day period. The lab involved billed Medicaid for more than $80 million over two years.[7]

Another case described in the same testimony shows how some scams are organized around groups of patients: in this case, all residents of the same nursing home. More than $1 million in claims was paid over twelve months for therapy services within a small nursing home, which had previously only had nominal claims for therapy.[8] Conceivably, many therapy providers may have been involved. In which case, provider-level monitoring might not be expected to detect the pattern. And clearly the "therapy" was spread across multiple patients, so *beneficiary-level* monitoring might not have caught it either. In this case, detection would depend on the capacity to monitor groups of patients (i.e., at level 6[a]), the patients being connected in this instance by residence in the same nursing home.

Medicare investigators monitoring DME suppliers report a fairly new phenomenon, which makes monitoring at level 6(a) particularly important. Fraud perpetrators describing themselves as "salesmen" walk into nursing homes and offer "to take care of everything"—the supplies, the billing, the works. . . at no cost to the patients, or to the home. Once allowed in, they begin using the residents' insurance policies as vehicles for passing business to a whole range of providers. The nursing home gets showered with unnecessary services and products, and the insurers—principally Medicare—pay the bill. The salesmen themselves are not licensed in any way. They make their money on a commission basis. Such schemes are organized by the salesmen, around the nursing home. So standard forms of provider-profiling (level 3[b]) may not catch it. The detection opportunity lies in monitoring aggregate claims across the nursing home residents. At that particular level of scrutiny, the activities of such salesmen would stand out quite clearly.

Examples such as these demonstrate the critical need for detection tools at all levels. Fraud schemes designed and perpetrated at one level will normally be detected only by controls designed and operated at precisely the same level.

The Current Emphasis

For the time being, most fraud detection tools used within the industry fall within certain narrow categories.

Prepayment Monitoring

At the prepayment stage, edits and audits within claims-processing systems perform monitoring at the transaction level (level 1) and at the patient level (level 3[a]).

Transaction-level monitoring (edits and audits) pick out those claims where the diagnosis does not match the procedure code; where the age or gender of the patient does not match the diagnosis; or where detectable forms of unbundling or price manipulation have occurred.

Patient-level monitoring examines each claim in the context of the patient's recent claims history. The most obvious question at this level is "has this claim—or one similar enough to be considered a duplicate—already been paid?" Beyond the *duplicate claim* checks, patient-level monitoring examines the *frequency* of certain procedures: childbirths less than nine months apart; more than one hysterectomy or appendectomy in a lifetime; too many visits to the chiropodist in a month. Patient-level monitoring also checks for incompatible treatments: for instance, the billing of outpatient or emergency services during a period that the patient (according to hospital claims) spent as an inpatient.

Post-Payment Monitoring

The vast majority of post-payment monitoring within the industry falls at level 3(b), taking the form of provider-profiling. Profiling systems, used within the context of post-payment utilization review, calculate a set of variables or ratios for each provider descriptive of their overall treatment patterns. These indicators are then used, either one at a time or in various mathematical combinations, to select providers whose treatment patterns appear anomalous against the background of their peer group. Typically, provider-profiling picks off 1 percent or 2 percent of the providers in each group examined.

Once a provider's billing patterns have been identified as suspicious, future claims from that provider can be suspended for review through the insertion of prepayment provider flags into the processing system. Some feedback occurs, therefore, between post-payment review and prepayment claims suspension.

The insertion of provider-flags as a result of post-payment review should never be confused, though, with prepayment provider-level monitoring. The first offers no protection against rapid bust-out schemes, because the prepayment flag only appears after post-payment analysis has been completed—several months after the fact. Provider flags may operate prepayment, but they *result* from post-payment claims analysis. By contrast, true provider-level monitoring on a pre-payment basis would identify suspicious claims patterns on the basis of prepayment claims data and would trip alarms in real time to prevent the claims being paid.

Post-payment utilization review teams vary in how they choose different medical specialties for attention. Some teams routinely work through each specialty in turn, looking for outliers worthy of more detailed scrutiny. Others pick and choose the specialties, first, by monitoring the aggregate behavior of the specialty as a whole. A specialty will receive attention if the aggregate dollar value consumed by that group accelerates rapidly from year to year; or if the aggregate billing patterns for that specialty on a regional basis diverge from national norms.

HCFA's emphasis on focused medical review seems to be exactly this: a way of selecting specialties, or procedures, as a preliminary step to provider-profiling. A 1994 review of Medicare's Post-Payment Utilization Review procedures by GAO summarized the practice thus:

> In 1993, HCFA developed a new emphasis on data analysis. Calling its approach *focused medical review*, HCFA required carriers to better *focus their profiling efforts* (*) and to begin identifying general spending patterns and trends that would allow them to determine the causes for unusually high spending. Carriers are now required to examine spending for specific services or procedures largely by comparing their own spending amounts for certain procedures with these procedures' spending averages across carriers.[9] (*)—author's emphasis.

This approach provides an extremely useful way to drill down into the data, from the top level, to ascertain where program dollars are being spent and where further review or policy re-evaluation might offer key opportunities for cost control. But its limitations as a fraud-control measure need to be understood. First, it is much better suited for identifying broad *utilization* problems (which is its purpose, hence its name) than for detection of fraud. Second, if used as a preliminary filter for subsequent provider-profiling, it substantially reduces the probability of fraudulent providers being detected, unless they happen to be in sufficient bad company or to be so prolific themselves that their fraudulent activities distort aggregate regional trends for their specialty.

Current Developments

For the time being, the bulk of the industry's detection toolkit is therefore focused at levels 1 and 3, with prepayment operation of transaction-level and patient-level monitoring, and post-payment provider-level monitoring some months after the checks have gone out. The following table summarizes this situation, and clearly illustrates the opportunities for development of additional detection tools.

Detection Tools Broadly Available Within the Industry

		Prepayment	*Post Payment*
Level 1	Transaction	X	
Level 2	Patient/Provider		
Level 3(a)	Patient	X	
Level 3(b)	Provider		X
Level 4(a)	Patient group/Provider		
Level 4(b)	Patient/Practice (clinic)		
Level 5	Patient group/Practice		
Level 6(a)	Defined patient group		
Level 6(b)	Practice (or clinic)		
Level 7	Multiparty conspiracies.		

Clearly the industry has plenty of scope for the development of new detection tools. Ideally, payment systems should be protected at all levels and at the earliest possible moment—that is, prepayment. And there are some interesting technologies available that can help to plug some of these holes. Unfortunately, however, the industry falls into the trap of using technology to enhance existing detection capabilities, rather than to build new capabilities. Most recent new applications of technology support either prepayment transaction-level monitoring, or post-payment provider-profiling—two of the three areas best defended already.

This is a very natural temptation, which afflicts many other fraud-control environments. It is much easier to throw fashionable new technologies (such as neural networks, artificial intelligence, or advanced statistical methods) at traditional forms of analysis, than to understand the need for new forms of analysis. Organizations do the former because they generally do not see the need for the latter. Making high-tech investments in existing forms of analysis has an easy appeal. It makes the organization look good (by acquiring the very latest technology). It also requires no fundamental change in the way the organization conceives of or conducts its fraud-control oper-ations. These are the *natural* fraud-control enhancements.

But the most promising prospects for enhanced fraud-detection tools are not necessarily the most natural. Providing state-of-the-art defenses at certain levels is not as important, or as urgent, as providing even the crudest of defenses at other levels, where there is nothing. The vulnerability of most health insurers' payment systems to bust-outs results directly from the complete absence of provider-level mon-itoring at the prepayment stage. Even the crudest of provider-level aggregate monitoring tools and acceleration rate checks would sub-stantially eliminate this threat. Nothing terribly sophisticated is required. Just a broader understanding of the complete detection toolkit and the will to shore up the weakest points first.

Artificial intelligence, neural networks, and other sophisticated technologies do have an important role to play in fraud control. But they offer no panacea. Their acquisition will increase, not diminish, the need for dedicated fraud analysts and investigators. And there are definite limits to the benefits they can bring.

First, and most obvious: applying highly sophisticated models at one level does nothing to help at any other level. For example, hav-ing the very best provider-profiling system in the world only helps with provider-profiling.

Second, and a little less obvious: in "training" the new models, the model-developers often use historical data sets that may contain many undetected frauds (partly because there was no previous capac-ity to detect them, and partly because many fraud types do not reveal themselves even retrospectively). Hence the new models, may be "trained" to faithfully replicate past fraud-detection performance, rather than to take any meaningful step forward.

Third, with the use of sophisticated modeling techniques, the users of the system (investigators, fraud analysts, claims reviewers) lose touch with the grounds upon which claims are being picked out. In such situations tensions can arise between those who support the model and those who do not really understand how the model works and prefer to rely upon their own judgment and experience. The end result, too often, is that a rift appears between the people and the sys-tems involved in fraud control. Use of more sophisticated tools ends up displacing human judgment and expertise rather than equipping it.

Fourth, the more expensive and intensive the model development effort, the more likely the resulting model to remain unchanged for ages. Investment in highly sophisticated filters can, on occasions, result in the production of static fraud controls, which will quickly be outpaced by developments and mutations in fraud methods.

In order to provide broader protection, the industry needs to shift its technological emphasis somewhat. Instead of focusing upon state-of-the-art analytical methods, the industry should focus on providing its fraud-control teams a broad range of flexible, user-friendly, claims-analysis tools. These teams should be able to construct their own searches quickly and easily, slicing and dicing the claims data in many different ways, inserting and deleting different types of search as different fraud threats wax and wane. And the people operating the systems should not need to be technical wizards to get what they want. The most important tools in the fraud-detection toolkit are timely and easy access to claims data (including prepayment data); friendly, easy to use, nontechnical interfaces; and a broad range of analytical tools that can be easily sequenced to answer complex ad-hoc inquiries.

Recently, the problem of fraud detection has attracted several major vendors of analytical systems to the health care industry. They see health insurers, concerned about fraud and abuse, as a ripe market for a new generation of analytical systems. But these vendors, whose interest in fraud detection is most welcome, should be pressed to think seriously about the undefended levels of fraud to figure out what they can offer there, rather than offering highly sophisticated tools that turn out to be of only narrow and marginal utility. First things first!

Defense at the Higher Levels

One major opportunity to apply modern technology to great effect for fraud control lies in the development of detection tools aimed at the highest levels (levels 6 and 7). The health care insurance industry currently has almost no capacity to monitor at such levels, and it certainly has no warning systems that can detect the most sophisticated schemes early enough to prevent major losses. These schemes, involving extensive collusion, operate across multiple patients, multiple providers, and often across multiple insurers too. These schemes are designed and operated so as to be undetectable by lower-level detection tools.

For many institutions facing fraud committed by organized criminal rings—both within and outside the health care context—transaction-level and other lower level defenses are no longer sufficient. As the perpetrators shift their attention to multi-account schemes, so the defending institutions have to develop multi-account or ring level detection systems—preferably systems that can spot major schemes early enough to cut them off and make them unprofitable.

The advent of electronic claims processing actually provides substantial new opportunities for fraud control at the higher levels, and these opportunities have received less attention from the health care community to date than the corresponding fraud threats.

First, the electronic format for data makes it easier to separate the service functions (claims processing) from fraud monitoring. The two processes used to be coincident, because both had to track the physical movement of paper. With the data in electronic format, background monitoring and review by fraud-control staff can be conducted without any kind of interference from, or reliance upon, the service side of the organization.

Second, with so much data in electronic format, it will be possible to run much more complex pattern detection searches than could ever have been attempted manually. When it comes to higher level monitoring, modern processing capabilities will make it possible to aggregate and manipulate massive volumes of claims data in ways inconceivable in a paper-based environment.

One important key to early detection of sophisticated, multi-account schemes involves spotting *patterns of unnatural coordination between different accounts*, which might indicate that they have all come under common control, even when the behavior of each account (or patient) shows nothing suspicious when viewed in isolation. The health care insurance industry has substantial motivation for investing in development of multi-account fraud-detection systems that could exploit this possibility. That motivation arises from two different kinds of promise:

First, that the ability to spot unnatural coordination in the transactional behavior of different policies may make it possible to detect some fraud schemes that were otherwise undetectable. Second, that the ability to spot unnatural coordination in the transactional behavior of different accounts may make it possible to detect some fraud schemes (which would in any case have been detected eventually) much sooner than otherwise possible.

Which of these two kinds of benefit accrues depends on the fraud-control environment and the nature of the fraud threats. With fraud schemes of the non-self-revealing type, the ability to spot the criminal coordination or orchestration of activity across several accounts might be the only clue, even in retrospect, that can reveal the fraudulent scheme.

With other types of fraud, the scheme might come to light eventually, but too late to prevent significant losses. For example, counterfeit credit card schemes reveal themselves ultimately as unauthorized activity spread across multiple cardholders' accounts. But, depending on the billing cycle and speed of subsequent dispute resolution processes, two or three months may elapse before the transactions are confirmed as fraudulent. The ability to spot the fact that a *group of accounts* appears to have come under common control (control by one person or group) may provide an opportunity to detect the scheme very much earlier, maximizing the potential for loss prevention or recovery.

Multi-Account Detection Opportunities

The following three situations illustrate the potential for multi-account detection systems in a variety of different fraud-control contexts, including health care fraud control.

Credit Card Fraud

Suppose that twenty separate credit card accounts belonging to twenty different people all used the same car rental agency in Boston during August, all had supplementary cards with ATM privileges issued during September, and all began using the same ATM machine for cash withdrawals in Seattle during October; suppose also that none of the basic account holders had ever used that particular ATM machine before.

It sounds like an obvious case of "dumpster-diving" (the practice of retrieving carbon copies of credit card slips from trash bins in order to obtain account information), with subsequent fraudulent use of the appropriated account details. This kind of pattern, or network, lends itself readily to detection through network analysis techniques. It is not a behavioral profile as such, because credit card companies would not be much concerned with use of car rentals in general, or use of new ATMs in general, or a sequential combination of the two. The profile is too common, and generally legitimate.

Rather, it is the linkage through a *specific* car rental, followed by linkage through a *specific* ATM location, coupled with common set-up operations (requesting issuance of supplementary cards), that make this pattern interesting. It is the specific *linkages* that make the pattern detectable too, despite the fact that each account's behavioral profile might not be particularly unusual.

Under most credit card companies' current arrangements such a scheme would not show up until the cardholder saw some evidence of unauthorized activity on their account and disputed it. Even then, the different accounts might never be linked together as part of the same scheme, and many issuing banks would not be able to identify the merchant (the connecting link) where the account information had been compromised. If fraud analysts were able to piece the scheme together, it would be far too late to prevent the losses.

In fact this fraud scheme creates a pattern that is detectable fairly early during the set-up stage, even before any losses accrue. The relevant pattern to search for, in this case, would be a set of accounts that have as a common feature the use of one particular merchant in August and that, as a group, show an unusually high rate of supplementary applications during September. With that kind of monitoring, this scheme could be detected in September, and steps could be taken to protect all the accounts at risk. In this case the key to the earliest possible detection of the scheme is to use the point of compromise itself as the key to revealing the scheme. The advantage of this approach is that it informs the credit card company of all accounts that might be similarly compromised, even if the perpetrators have not yet had time to begin manipulating many of them. It permits all of the customers at risk to be warned and protected, even those whose accounts have not yet been touched—offering enormous benefits in terms of customer relations as well as loss avoidance.

Health Insurance Fraud

Criminal rings have developed many methods for obtaining insurance policy details, together with sufficient personal data to support the submission of fraudulent claims for medical treatment. The simplest method involves stealing or buying lists of patients' details from clinics or other providers.

Suppose that medical claims are received by an insurer for a group of seventy residents of Washington, D.C., all of whom purportedly received emergency treatment during October while traveling in Philadelphia. Suppose also that the patients received their Philadelphia treatments from a variety of different physicians, all of whom happen to use the same billing service. Moreover, none of these patients has ever received treatment in Philadelphia before. Apart from these odd coincidences, the only fact that connects all seventy patients is that each one of them used a particular pharmacy in Washington, D.C., at least once during the preceding April.

This pattern—if only one could spot it—is inherently suspicious. It suggests that the Washington, D.C., pharmacy is the point of compromise from which insurance policy information was leaked, and it suggests the Philadelphia billing agency to be the fraudulent user of that information.

But each transaction viewed in isolation is not suspicious. The insurer would not normally reject, or even question, a claim for emergency treatment just because it came from a provider in a city other than the city of residence. Hence transaction or patient-level monitoring could never reveal this scheme. In order to detect this type of pattern one would have to be monitoring for specific patterns that suggest improper distribution and use of lists, which would mean being able to link claims or policies together in ways that could reveal the extraordinary coincidences suggestive of organized multi-account fraud schemes.

Automated Inquiry Systems

The provision of high-tech services to customers, whether in government or private sector financial services, often involves provision of twenty-four-hour automated telephone information systems. Using 800 numbers and Touch-Tone phones, customers navigate menu-driven information services to check their bank balance, their frequent-flier mileage balances, the status of their tax refund, their available credit limit, or details of a variety of other personal service products. Access is often controlled through a password system, but passwords often consist of readily available information such as social security numbers or mothers' maiden names. Fraud perpetrators make extensive use of such systems to gain information about target accounts without having to speak to a human being. They use these systems to avoid arousing anyone's suspicions.

In many instances such automated telephone assistance systems have an ANI (automatic number identification) capability built in, either for billing or record-keeping purposes. Hence a record, which includes the source telephone number, is created for each call.

An account-level fraud-monitoring system might utilize such data to check whether the source number matched the telephone number on the account records. But, assuming genuine customers are allowed to call from anywhere, the fact that they were not at home when they called is not particularly useful information. If the company keeps any kind of "trouble list" (a database of names, addresses, or telephone numbers known to have been associated with fraud in the past), then call-source numbers could also be checked against that list.

But higher-level multi-account fraud-detection systems would ask quite different questions. They would look for any telephone number from which inquiries about numerous different accounts originated, maybe within the same day, or within the same week. The fact that someone had systematically called ten times in succession from the same phone number, asking questions about ten apparently unrelated accounts, would be highly suspicious. Such an observation might be a very early indication that this group of accounts had been compromised in some way and that fraudulent redemption or other conversion to gain was being planned.

As with all multi-account fraud-detection systems, it is the unnatural coordination itself, rather than anything about the behavior of the individual accounts, that acts as the first sign of trouble. Subsequent follow-up inquiries, triggered by such an alert, should continue to focus on the group of accounts as a whole rather than on each in isolation.

So follow-up inquiries would include questions such as, for instance, "what merchants are common to the recent transaction history of these accounts?" (if this is really a multi-account fraud scheme in the early set-up stages, can we identify the point of compromise?) or "what is there in the original applications for these accounts that might support the notion that they are all under common control?" (for example, employer references supplied by same individual, or same address given for next of kin). This example illustrates another feature of multi-account level controls: the cost-efficiency and effectiveness of verification procedures. Callback procedures—inquiring of just one or two of the affected account holders whether it was really them that used the automated inquiry system—would give a very strong indication as to whether or not the whole group of accounts is, in fact, at risk; or whether there is some other legitimate explanation for the series of calls from the same phone. Just one or two callbacks provide valuable information about the exposure of a large group of accounts. Depending on company policies and priorities, the exposure can then either be protected or set up for arrest. If the pattern turns out to have a legitimate explanation, very little human effort has been wasted.

These examples should help clarify the distinction between the potential class of coordination-detection tools envisaged here and the more traditional and familiar kinds of fraud-monitoring systems. Anyone who grasps the fundamental conceptual differences will have no trouble generating their own ideas for application of these ideas. There is nothing inherently complicated about them; they are just different from traditional forms of fraud control and constitute a different way of looking at fraud-control situations.

Health care insurers—whether they be private companies, nonprofits, or government—know they are victimized by many different types of extensive and sophisticated fraud schemes. They acquire that knowledge through a variety of mechanisms. Sometimes they receive unsolicited tip-offs from disillusioned or marginalized conspirators. Sometimes an astute claims-processing clerk happens to notice some unusual and coincidental pattern of linkages between different claims (which may be something as simple as common handwriting). Sometimes a tip-off reveals some fraudulent activity but—through rigorous follow-up investigation—what appeared at the outset to have been a small case of abuse or fraud grows into something very much larger and more sinister. (Such cases are referred to by investigators as "tip of the iceberg" cases and are counted as major investigative successes).

So insurers know from experience that they have, on occasion, been victimized by large, sophisticated, multi-account schemes. But very few insurers, if any, have developed the capability for routine monitoring at the higher levels, and so it remains impossible to estimate the extent of such activity.

There are several pressing reasons for developing multi-account fraud-detection systems in a wide variety of fraud-control environments. First, they address the most sophisticated and expensive forms of fraud threat (where individual schemes, if successful, typically net hundreds of thousands or millions of dollars). Second, fraud-control defenses have traditionally been weakest at the multi-account level (due to the predominance of transaction-level and other lower-level approaches).[10] And, third, a wide variety of U.S. institutions have witnessed rapid growth in the activities of organized fraud rings, particularly the targeting of major payment systems like Medicare and Medicaid, often by immigrant or foreign groups.

Applicability of Network Analytic Tools and Concepts

In developing fraud-detection tools many ideas and concepts from the social science discipline of Network Analysis may turn out to be relevant, especially when monitoring at the higher levels, and at level 7 (organized and collusive multi-account frauds) in particular. Simply put, multi-account fraud schemes are networks of a kind, consisting of a great number of entities (accounts, or transactions, or practitioners) linked together in curious and specific ways.

Network analysis is a small but fast-growing academic discipline, emerging from social science.[11] It has only been recognized as a discipline in its own right for about eighteen years. Since 1978 it has had its own international journal[12] and there is now an international association for network analysts.[13]

Network analysis studies the effects of network structure (which is described in terms of connections of various types between objects, or "nodes") on various processes. The networks might variously show family associations, friendships, professional contacts, membership of different entities, participation in different activities, or communication channels connecting different people or institutions. Network processes studied by social scientists include group behavior, coalition formation, innovation adoption, influence transmission, product awareness and preference transmission, and the emergence of leadership within groups.

Network analysis is now recognized as being of substantial interest not only to social scientists but also to organizational theorists, epidemiologists, anthropologists, psychologists, business strategists, and political scientists—to name but a few. But anyone dealing with organized crime or complex frauds has good reason to pay attention to this field. The key to detection of criminal conspiracies lies in developing the capacity to spot the subtle patterns of linkages that connect the transactions comprising organized frauds. Under present arrangements the necessary data sits within claims databases, but virtually no analytical techniques exist to facilitate extraction of the patterns. Often the linkages may be quite subtle: the appearance of common or similar addresses, permutations of names, same telephone numbers being given for different patients, same or similar bank destination codes or account numbers for payments, or coincidental histories (such as common use of one Washington, D.C., pharmacy followed by unexpected emergency treatments in Philadelphia a few months later). Tools for extraction of such patterns of linkage from massive databases do not currently exist. They will need to be developed.

Here are just a few brief examples of some patterns, potentially indicative of major fraud schemes, which network analytic techniques could extract using available technology platforms. There are a great many other potential applications too.

1. Transfer of pool of patients: identify when one provider or supplier takes over a whole pool of patients from another. Such patterns may reveal the same people doing business under a new business name, when their old business has come under scrutiny or has been excluded from program participation.
2. Detect mill-like activity: identify clusters of providers/patients with unnaturally dense sets of interconnections (using clique-detection methodology), which may reveal so called "ping-pong referral" schemes.
3. Detect fraudulent use of patient/beneficiary lists: identify when a particular group of clients/beneficiaries show up on the billings of multiple providers. Such patterns may either reflect inappropriate referral practices, or the use of lists circulated for billing services not rendered.

Some vendors of "link-analysis" tools and many potential purchasers of such systems misunderstand the real promise of network analysis applied to fraud detection. They focus on the visualization of networks[14] as traditionally practiced by law-enforcement agencies in the context of criminal intelligence analysis.[15] Link-analysis software products currently available offer graphical display capabilities that can present two-dimensional pictures (or "maps") representing networks of connections. Such a map might show, for instance, the network of connections between specified physicians and their respective patients; or might show the patterns and frequencies of referrals between different providers.

In support of the investigation of higher-level frauds, such tools are undoubtedly useful. But the real promise of network analytic tools lies not in data-visualization, but in the prospects for detecting major schemes that would otherwise remain completely invisible. Fraud analysts should be able to define network-type patterns, which detection systems would then search for within massive databases of claims data.

The health care field is perhaps the most pressing and promising application for such tools. Insurers have masses of existing claims data and will be collecting much more data in standardized electronic formats in future years. Insofar as complex fraud schemes are known to exist in the industry, these databases contain the telltale structures—patterns of interconnection and coincidence—that would permit early detection if only the analytic methods for extracting those patterns could be developed.

For all such applications, however, the hard work yet to be done is to build effective bridges between investigators, analysts, and technologists and to design organizational policies, industry incentives, and legislative frameworks that support the design and operation of fraud-detection tools more appropriate to the electronic environment and to the sophistication of organized criminal frauds.

Conclusion

The question this book set out to answer was why health care fraud has not been brought under control, despite the unprecedented degree of attention the subject has received over the last five years.

The answer is clear enough. Health care fraud has not been brought under control because the health care industry has underestimated the complexity of the fraud-control business and has never developed any reasonable defenses against fraud. The defenses currently in place may protect against incorrect billing and certain forms of overutilization, but they offer little in terms of protection against criminal fraud.

Insurers have no way of knowing how much they lose to fraud and have little incentive to find out. Unable to see the magnitude of the problem, public and private programs alike massively underinvest in control resources. Insurers rely upon fraud-detection and referral mechanisms that barely work, and they lack any coordinated fraud-control strategy.

Fraud in the health care system has been, and remains, *out of control*. Electronic claims processing will make the situation much worse unless serious and urgent attention is paid to provision of prudent controls. And managed care will not eliminate fraud as many believe; rather it will make fraud more dangerous and much more difficult to control.

My modest hope for this book is that it will help provide a better understanding of the complexity and seriousness of the fraud-control challenge and help those within the industry see why and how existing control systems fail.

But it would be naive to believe that understanding the situation will automatically lead to progress. Many significant obstacles still stand in the way. The country is not in the mood to increase administrative budgets: neither the government's nor those of insurance companies. The medical associations—already fighting the increased administrative oversight that comes with managed care—are loathe to accept further impositions for the sake of fraud control.

Bureaucrats and managers are unlikely to stick their heads above the parapet in order to tell how serious the fraud problem is and how inadequate existing defenses are. And the public are in no mood to tolerate the inconvenience and imposition of random audits (as evidenced by the 1995 cancellation, under public and budgetary pressures, of the IRS's plans to conduct its TCMP audits).

Reflecting on these obstacles from time to time has led me to question, on several occasions, whether there really is any way out of the current predicament. Maybe, with respect to fraud and fraud control, this is just the way things have to be. Maybe this is just the pathology of fraud control; and maybe this pathology is inescapable.

But before abandoning hopes for radical improvement, we should seriously weigh the consequences. The pressure is on for health care cost control, especially in major public programs. Costs will be controlled one way or another. If the industry learns the art of fraud control, then the industry will have learned a discriminating way to save money—by investing in the capacity to distinguish between legitimate and illegitimate claims. The alternative is to use less discriminating methods, such as across-the-board reductions in benefits, further restrictions on eligibility, or lower reimbursement rates for providers. All these, in theory, hit the honest and the dishonest alike.

In practice, these less discriminating methods hit the honest and the genuinely needy much harder than the dishonest. Restricting eligibility or reducing benefits has a negligible effect on fraud, because fraud perpetrators can easily adjust their billing patterns and patient lists to fit the new rules. And when reimbursement rates drop, it is the honest providers who take the pay cut, not the crooks. In the major public programs such as Medicare and Medicaid, cuts in reimbursement rates drive away honest providers, who can no longer afford to participate. But dishonest providers compensate by increasing their billing volume.

Across-the-board cuts therefore will have a perverse effect. Genuinely needy patients will be denied services, and honest providers will be driven out of the system. What will remain will become more and more rotten, more crooked, more wasteful. Ultimately, in a vicious cycle of decay, only the crooks will remain, and important public programs will be destroyed.

If the health care industry were to learn the art of fraud control, they could cut costs quite substantially without denying the needy, restricting eligibility, or squeezing honest doctors out of business. But effective controls have their costs: both in terms of resources and in terms of inconveniences and intrusions. For the time being, there is little prospect of society paying the necessary price.

The vital first step is measurement. Adequate investments in controls will *never* be made while the facts about the true nature and scope of health care fraud remain unknown. The health care fraud debate desperately needs the transforming effects of systematic measurement. Without that, not much else will change.

In closing, let me briefly anticipate some predictable reactions to this book.

First, some may point out (quite correctly) its narrow focus. It has dwelled heavily on fraud committed by providers, and not so much on fraud committed by patients. That is because the providers steal millions of dollars, whereas patients generally only have the opportunity to steal thousands. Also fraud committed by hospitals has received relatively little attention here. That is because the investigative units I have dealt with so far pay hospital fraud relatively little attention. It deserves a great deal more.

Second, some may regard it as irresponsible for me to have laid out the vulnerabilities of payment systems for all to see, especially having been welcomed in by insurers and shown around. My response would be that meaningful discussion of this whole issue is impossible unless the industry is willing to discuss honestly and openly the weaknesses of current strategies. Such discussion is a prerequisite for progress.

Also a number of specific precautions have been taken to avoid unnecessary exposure. The identity of different companies has been concealed throughout, and all the participating companies received advance copies of reports several months before this book was published—enabling them either to fix specific problems or point out matters they would prefer not to be divulged.

Third, some may claim—almost as soon as the book is published—that it is out of date and therefore no longer relevant. For sure, some officials will say "recent changes are believed to have eliminated the vulnerabilities."

Well, "recent changes," in the fraud-control business, are usually rather minor and of limited impact. Chapter 1, The Pathology of Fraud Control, notes the tendency of officials to place far too much faith in the latest changes. Any who genuinely believe that their fraud-control systems are finally "fixed" may find the evaluative guide at the end of Chapter 8 helpful in determining what progress has really been made and what still remains to be done.

One day, I trust, the health care industry will implement coherent control strategies, obtain adequate levels of resources for fraud control, and design effective detection and referral systems. But that is liable to take many years. For now, fraud control remains a much-neglected science.

Even when the science of fraud control is better understood, no one should expect progress to come fast or to come easily. Fraud control will always remain a miserable business.

Appendix: Site Selection and Interview Subjects

Eight sites were selected for the field research, representing a mix of private and public insurers. Two or three days was spent at each site studying the systems, tasks, processes, and policies that comprised the claims-processing system.

The sites were selected in consultation with an advisory committee including representatives from the National Institute of Justice, The Department of Justice, The Office of Inspector General at HHS, the FBI, the National Association of Medicaid Fraud Control Units (NAMFCU), the Health Care Financing Administration, and the National Health Care Anti-Fraud Association (NHCAA).

All eight sites were selected in part on the basis that they were reputed to be among the very best in the industry in terms of fraud control. The reason for selecting from among the best, rather than picking a broader or more representative sample, was to be able to work from current best practice, so that any guidance ultimately offered to the industry would help advance the state of the art.

The sites were also selected so as to offer, as far as possible with only eight sites, a broad cross section of the industry. The sites examined included three Medicaid fraud control units. These three differed significantly in the extent to which the Medicaid program within their states used managed care arrangements, with MFCU-3 having had the most experience of fraud control in that environment, and MFCU-1 the least.

Two private insurers were included: one comparatively large, with business spread nationwide and health care premium income totaling roughly $2 billion per year; and the other much smaller, with only 17,000 policyholders (mostly rural workers) and with operations confined to just one state.

The remaining three sites were all private corporations acting as major Medicare contractors. All three were among the top five Medicare contractors when measured in terms of total claims volume. One of these contractors serves as a durable medical equipment regional contractors (DMERC) as well as holding broader contracts under both Parts A and B of the Medicare program. As one of four designated DMERC sites, this company processes durable medical equipment claims under the Medicare program for roughly one quarter of the United States.

All eight sites selected agreed to participate in the study and to make managers and staff available for interview. A list of fifteen interview subject areas (reproduced in the following section) was provided in advance to each site, with a request that interview lists be constructed to include personnel knowledgeable in each area. The interviews themselves were not formally structured.

Broad Subject Areas for Interviews

1. Mechanisms for measuring or estimating the scope and nature of existing fraud problems. Statistically valid sampling/audit procedures, or other scientific estimation techniques in use?
2. What is acceptable level of fraud, in a business sense (i.e., level at which institution would not be willing to invest additional resources in fraud controls)?
3. How is budget for fraud-control operations established?
   a. Process
   b. Assumptions and Basis
   c. Policy
4. Fraud-control philosophy/strategy.
   a. Proactive versus reactive.
   b. Justice on case-by-case basis versus economic cost containment.
   c. Tension between processing efficiency and prudent controls. How it gets resolved within the organization.
   d. What is the "unit of work" in the fraud-control operation? (Cases, problems, practices, products, etc.). Evidence of a problem-solving approach?
5. Sources of investigations (cases). Which mechanisms produce what proportion of cases investigated?
6. Staffing/Backgrounds/Resources for fraud-control operations. What kinds of people, skills, experiences, backgrounds?
7. Fraud-detection systems: [Levels]
   a. Present
   b. Experimental
   c. Future (i.e., planned, or anticipated)

   8. How is performance of fraud-control operation measured? How is
      quality defined within fraud-control environment?
      a. Cost benefit analysis
      b. Productivity measures/efficiency
      c. Effectiveness/impact
   9. Nature of fraud threats
      a. Past
      b. Present
      c. Future
  10. Advent of Electronic Claims Processing
      a. New opportunities for fraud
      b. New opportunities for fraud control/detection
  11. Criteria used for case/investigation selection and for decisions regard-
      ing criminal/civil prosecution or settlement.
  12. Relationship with the criminal justice system. Referral mechanisms,
      practices, formal and informal. Tensions, conflicting objectives, and so
      on.
  13. Experiences with managed care. How fraud is different in managed-care
      environment.
  14. What are perceived constraints on effective control? (Resources, prohi-
      bition on information sharing, etc.)
  15. Anticipated effects of various reform proposals. Industry trends and
      their consequences.

Notes

Introduction

1. In 1992, hearings relating to health care fraud were held by the following Senate Committees: Judiciary; Budget. House Committees: Select Committee on Children, Youth, and Families; Select Committee on Narcotics Abuse and Control; Energy and Commerce.

In 1993, hearings related to health care fraud were held by the following committees in the Senate: Judiciary; Special Committee on Aging; Finance. House Committees: Judiciary (Subcommittee on Crime and Criminal Justice); Ways and Means (Subcommittee on Health); Energy and Commerce (Subcommittee on Health and the Environment); Temporary Committee (on "Psychiatric Hospital Fraud and Abuse"); Government Operations.

2. Testimony of Edward J. Kuriansky, special prosecutor, Office of the New York State Special Prosecutor, before the U.S. House of Representatives Select Committee on Narcotics Abuse and Control, July 29, 1992, p. 2.

3. "Health Insurance: Vulnerable Payers Lose Billions to Fraud and Abuse." Report to the chairman, Subcommittee on Human Resources and Intergovernmental Relations, Committee on Government Operations, House of Representatives. General Accounting Office, Washington, D.C., May 1992, GAO/HR—92–69, p. 1.

4. By, among others:

Representatives: Democrats Fortney "Pete" Stark, Charles Schumer, Edolphus Towns, Rosa Delauro, Jim McDermott, Roy Rowland, and Sherrod Brown and Republicans James Sensenbrenner and Robert Michel.

Senators: Democrats Joe Biden, Tom Harkin, George Mitchell, Herb Kohl and Republican William Cohen.

For a summary of specific proposals see "Congressional Advocates of Health Care Fraud Legislation." Paper presented to the Annual Conference of the National Health Care Anti-Fraud Association, New Orleans, La., November 15, 1994.

5. 1995 hearings were held by the following Senate Committees: Special Committee on Aging; Appropriations (Subcommittee on Labor, Health and Human Services, and Related Agencies); Ways and Means; Finance; Appropriations. House Committees: Budget; Commerce Oversight and Investigations; Governmental Reform, Human Resources, and Intergovernmental Relations; Judiciary.

6. GAO report numbers: Series HRD–90, nos. 29, 49; Series HRD–91, nos. 32, 59, 81; Series HRD–92, nos. 1, 26, 52, 69; Series T-HRD–92, nos. 2, 29, 49, 56; HRD–93–92; Series T-HRD–93, nos. 3, 8, 14; HEHS–94–42; Series T-HEHS–94, nos. 106, 124.

7."Statement on Action Against Health Care Frauds." Weekly Compendium of Presidential Documents. June 30, 1992, pp. 1052–1053.

8. "$111 Million Payment Set for Fraud in Health Claims; Large Testing Company Admits to False Billing" (National Health Laboratories, Inc.), Calvin Sims. *New York Times*, December 19, 1992, v. 142, p. 1.

9. "Hospital Chain Sets Guilty Plea: Kickbacks, Bribes Paid for Referrals," Allen R. Myerson. *New York Times*, June 29, 1994, v. 143, pp. C1(N) and D1(L).

10. "National Medical Resolves Last of Insurance Disputes," Milt Freudenheim. *New York Times*, December 14, 1993, v. 143, pp. C5(N) and D5(L).

11. Statement of Louis J. Freeh, director, Federal Bureau of Investigation, before the Special Committee on Aging, U.S. Senate, Washington, D.C., March 21, 1995, p. 1.

12. "From the Health Care Financing Administration: Medicare, Medicaid Fraud and Abuse," Bruce C. Vladeck, Administrator, HCFA. *JAMA*, March 8, 1995, v. 273, n. 10, p. 766.

13. Information provided by the National Association of Medicaid Fraud Control Units (NAMFCU) directly to the author.

14. "Health Care Fraud," Gordon Witkin. *U.S. News & World Report*, February 24, 1992, v. 112, n. 7, p. 34(8).

15. Social Security Amendments of 1994. Section 132, Public Law 103–432, October 31, 1994. Now forms Section 1834a(a)(17)(c) of Social Security Act.

16. "Is Fraud Poisoning Home Health Care?" Linda Himelstein, Gail DeGeorge, and Eric Schine. *Business Week*, March 14, 1994, n. 3362, pp. 70–73.

17. Press release, August 23, 1995, National Association of Medicaid Fraud Control Units, Washington, D.C., pp. 1–3.

18. Statement of a supervisory special agent, FBI, to Special Committee on Aging, U.S. Senate, Washington, D.C., March 21, 1995.

19. Statement of Louis J. Freeh, director, Federal Bureau of Investigation, before the Special Committee on Aging, U.S. Senate, Washington, D.C. March 21, 1995, p. 2.

20. "Phantom Firms Bleed Medicare: Cost of Fraud in Florida is Estimated at $1 Billion." Tom Dubocq. *Miami Herald*, August 14, 1994, p. A1(3).

21. Ibid.

22. Ibid.

23. *Unloving Care: The Nursing Home Tragedy*, Bruce C. Vladeck. Basic Books, New York, 1980, p. 101.

24. "Analytical Perspectives: The Budget of the United States Government, Fiscal Year 1996," Executive Office of the President of the United States, Office of Management and Budget, Washington, D.C., 1995, p. 229.

25. Ibid., p. 236.

26. "From the Health Care Financing Administration: Medicare, Medicaid Fraud and Abuse," Bruce C. Vladeck, Administrator, HCFA. *JAMA*, March 8, 1995, v. 273, n. 10, p. 766.

27. *Dateline*, Tuesday November 7, 1995, NBC, 10:00 P.M. EST, feature on medicare fraud, segment 1.

28. Medicare Carriers' Manual, Section 11,012, HCFA.

Chapter 1

1. *Management Accountant's Guide to Fraud Discovery and Control,* Howard R. Davia et al. Wiley, New York, 1992, pp. 60–61.

2. See for example, the treatment given by *Fraud, Prevention and Detection.* I. K. Huntington. Butterworths, London, 1992.

3. "Fraud by Fright: White Collar Crime by Health Care Providers." Pamela H. Bucy. *North Carolina Law Review*, v. 67, n. 4, April 1989, p. 857. See foot-note 11 for list of symposia on legal issues in health care where the subject was completely omitted.

4. Testimony of Paul M. Allen, "Medicare and Medicaid Frauds: Joint hear-ing before the Subcommittee on Long-Term Care and the Subcommittee on Health of the Elderly of the Senate Special Committee on Aging." Part I. 94th Congress, 1975. Cited in "Fraud by Fright: White Collar Crime by Health Care Providers," Pamela H. Bucy. *North Carolina Law Review*, April 1989, v. 67, n. 4, p. 857.

5. "Data Sources on White-Collar Law-Breaking," Albert J. Reiss, Jr. and Albert D. Biderman. September 1980, National Institute of Justice, U.S. Department of Justice, Washington, D.C., p. 91.

6. Hearing before the Subcommittee on Health of the Committee on Ways and Means, House of Representatives, 103rd Congress, 1st Session, March 8, 1993, Serial 103–3. Statement of Larry Morey, deputy inspector general for investigations, Office of Inspector General, Department of Health and Human Services, p. 35.

7. "Health Care Fraud: Actuarial Report," The Travelers, Hartford, Connecticut. February 1992.

8. The subset of the claims history consisted of all claims for Chicago area providers who had been paid more than $3,000 during the year.

9. For a discussion of techniques for studying the biases inherent in detec-tion systems, so that inferences can then be drawn about the underlying pat-terns of noncompliance, see "Detection Controlled Estimation," Jonathan Feinstein. *Journal of Law and Economics*, v. 33, April 1990.

10. "Welfare Fingerprinting Finds Most People Are Telling the Truth," Kimberley McLarin. *New York Times*, September 29, 1995, v. 145, pp. B1 and B4.

11. Ibid., v. 145, p. B4.

12. Testimony of Edward J. Kuriansky, special prosecutor, Office of the New York Special Prosecutor for Medicaid Fraud Control, before the U.S. House of Representatives, Committee on Energy and Commerce; Subcommittee on Health and the Environment, April 1, 1993, p. 6.

13. See also testimony of Senator Donald M. Halperin, before the New York State Senate, on the same point. "A Partnership Approach: A Prescription for Enhanced Coordination of Medicaid Fraud Detection and Prevention in New York State," Senator Donald M. Halperin. New York State Senate, Albany, New York, June 1993.

14. For example, see "Data Sources on White-Collar Law-Breaking," by Albert J. Reiss Jr. and Albert D. Biderman. September 1980, National Institute of Justice, U.S. Department of Justice, Washington, D.C., p. 91.

15. Quoted in testimony of Edward J. Kuriansky, special prosecutor, Office of the New York Special Prosecutor for Medicaid Fraud Control, before the U.S. House of Representatives, Committee on Energy and Commerce, Subcommittee on Health and the Environment, April 1, 1993, p. 12.

16. "Viewpoints," James P. Pinkerton. *Newsday*, March 18, 1993, p. 118.

17. Edward Kuriansky, quoted in "Health Care Fraud," Gordon Witkin. *U.S. News & World Report*, February 24, 1992, v. 112, n. 7, p. 34(8).

18. For example, see last sentence of *New York Times*, July 15, 1991, v. 140, p. B7(L), "Medicaid Fraud: It Can Be Costly."

19. Modern day enhancements to these filters include the use of logistic regression analyses and, more recently, the application of neural network algorithms in devising the best set of weights to be atttached to different variables.

20. Physicians and physician assistants are assigned unique physician identification numbers (UPINs). All providers have a provider identification number (PIN), assigned by the Medicare contractor for billing purposes.

21. "One Scheme Illustrates Vulnerabilities to Fraud." Report presented by GAO to hearing on Medicare Fraud, Waste, and Abuse, Subcommittee on Health, Committee on Ways and Means, House of Representatives. 102nd Congress, 2nd session, September 10, 1992. Report no: GAO/HRD–92–76. Government Accounting Office, Washington, D.C., August 1992, p. 16.

22. Testimony of Edward J. Kuriansky, special prosecutor, Office of the New York Special Prosecutor for Medicaid Fraud Control, before the U.S. House of Representatives, Committee on Energy and Commerce; Subcommittee on Health and the Environment, April 1, 1993, p. 6

23. Ibid.

24. "A Partnership Approach: A Prescription for Enhanced Coordination of Medicaid Fraud Detection and Prevention in New York State." Unpublished report. Senator Donald M. Halperin. New York State Senate, Albany, New York, June 1993.

25. "Health Care Fraud: Prosecuting Lack of Medical Necessity," Andrew Grosso. *FBI Law Enforcement Bulletin*. October 1992, v. 61, n. 10, pp. 8–12.

26. "$110 Million Payment Set for Fraud in Health Claims; Large Testing Company Admits to False Billing. (National Health Laboratories Inc.), Calvin Sims. *New York Times*, December 19, 1992, v. 142, p. 1.

27. Statement of Louis J. Freeh, director, Federal Bureau of Investigation, before the Special Committee on Aging, U.S. Senate, Washington, D.C., March 21, 1995, p. 15.

28. False Claims Act (31 *U.S.Code* § 3730).

29. "Dracula, Inc.: Bloodsucker of the Decade," Rick Hornung. *Voice*, December 26, 1989, p. 45. Also in press release, State of New York, Deputy Attorney General for Medicaid Fraud Control, June 29, 1989, pp. 1–2.

30. News release, "NYC Blood Trafficking Doctor Gets 5–10 Years in Jail for U.S.' Largest $3.6 Million Medical Lab Fraud," Office of the Special Prosecutor, New York State Medicaid fraud control unit, June 29, 1989.

31. "Lab-Fraud Anemia," D. R. Stone, A. Duran, and K. C. Fine. *New England Journal of Medicine*, September 15, 1988, v. 319, n. 11, pp. 727–728.

Chapter 2

1. "The Control of Insurance Fraud: A Comparative View," Michael Clarke. *The British Journal of Criminology*, v. 30, n. 1, Winter 1990, p. 2.

2. "Healthy, Wealthy and Fraudulent: Doctors and Patients Are in on Scams that Could Bust Clinton's Health Budget," Jill Smolowe. *Time*, August 30, 1993, v. 142, n. 9, p. 24.

3. "Ghost Riders Are Target of an Insurance Sting," Peter Kerr. *New York Times*, August 18, 1993, v. 142, p. 1.

4. Ibid.

5. "Public Attitude Monitor, 1993," Insurance Research Council, Oak Brook, Illinois, 1993, p. 3.

6. Ibid., p. 20

7. Ibid., p. 20

8. See, for example, "A Growing U.S. Affliction: Worthless Health Policies," Barry Meier. *New York Times*, January 4, 1992, v. 141, p. 1. The story describes how innocent victims suffer when insurers refuse to pay, disappear, or go bankrupt.

9. Testimony of Dr. "A," before the Senate Special Committee on Aging, Washington, D.C., March 21, 1995.

10. Hearing before the Subcommittee on Health, of the Committee on Ways and Means, House of Representatives. 103rd Congress, 1st Session, March 8, 1993, Serial 103–3. Testimony of William J. Mahon, executive director, NHCAA, p. 49.

11. Statement of Louis J. Freeh, director, Federal Bureau of Investigation, before the Special Committee on Aging, U.S. Senate, Washington, D.C., March 21, 1995, p. 4.

12. "Health Insurance: Vulnerable Payers Lose Billions to Fraud and Abuse," report to the chairman, Subcommittee on Human Resources and Intergovernmental Relations, Committee on Government Operations, House of Representatives, U.S. General Accounting Office, Washington, D.C., May 1992, GAO/HRD–92–69, p. 23.

13. Opening statement of Senator Tom Harkin, Senate Appropriations Subcommittee on Labor, Health and Human Services. "Stopping Abusive and Inappropriate Medicare Billings," May 5, 1995, p. 3.

14. Medicare Part B is funded from general tax revenues (roughly 75 percent) and from premiums paid by the elderly (roughly 25 percent). See "Medicare at 30: Preparing for the Future," Nancy De Lew. *JAMA*, July 19, 1995, v. 274, n. 3, pp. 259–267.

15. "In the War of Politics, Medicare Spending Has Become the Latest Battlefield," David Rosenbaum. *New York Times*, May 2, 1995, v. 144, p. A14. Republican Newt Gingrich is quoted as saying, "We have decided that we're taking Medicare into a separate box. Every penny saved in Medicare should go to Medicare. It should not be entangled in the budget debate."

16. "Medicare and Medicaid: Opportunities to Save Program Dollars by Reducing Fraud and Abuse." Statement of Sarah F. Jagger, director, Health Financing and Policy Issues, Health, Education and Human Services Division, General Accounting Office. Testimony before the Subcommittee on Human Resources and Intergovernmental Relations, Committee on Government Reform and Oversight, House of Representatives, Washington, D.C., March 22, 1995, p. 12

17. Ibid.

18. One such proposal was included under the umbrella of "Operation Restore Trust," announced by the U.S. Department of Health and Human Services on May 3, 1995. Chapter 7 contains a discussion of this particular proposal and its likely impact.

19. *Prescription for Profit: How Doctors Defraud Medicaid*, Paul Jesilow, Henry N. Pontell, and Gilbert Geis. University of California Press, Berkeley, 1993, p. x.

20. "Doctor Involved in Blindings Is Given a 4-Year Term for Fraud," Robert Welkos. *Los Angeles Times*, April 27, 1984. Quoted in *Prescription for Profit*, p. 20.

21. *Prescription for Profit*, p. 11.

22. "Medicare Case Underlines Importance of Physician Compliance with All Rules When Claims Are Filed," Charles Marwick. *JAMA*, February 3, 1993, v. 269, n. 5, p. 563.

23. Ibid.

Chapter 3

1. Hearing before the Subcommittee on Health of the Committee on Ways and Means, House of Representatives. 103rd Congress, 1st Session, March 8,

1993, Serial 103–3. Statement of Janet L. Shikles, director, Health Financing and Policy Issues, Human Resources Division, U.S. General Accounting Office, p. 17.

2. Medicare-Medicaid Anti-Fraud and Abuse Amendments, Public Law 95–142, 1977.

3. *Prescription for Profit: How Doctors Defraud Medicaid*, Paul Jesilow, Henry N. Pontell, and Gilbert Geis. University of California Press, Berkeley, 1993, p. 12.

4. *The Fraud Control Game: State Responses to Fraud and Abuse in AFDC and Medicaid Programs*, John A. Gardiner and Theodore R. Lyman. Indiana University Press, Bloomington, Indiana, 1984, p. 10

5. "A Partnership Approach: A Prescription for Enhanced Coordination of Medicaid Fraud Detection and Prevention in New York State," testimony of Senator Donald M. Halperin before the New York State Senate, Albany, New York, June 1993, p. 7

6. Ibid., p. 9

7. "The Control of Insurance Fraud: A Comparative View," Michael Clarke, *British Journal of Criminology*, v. 30, n. 1, Winter 1990, p. 2.

8. Ibid., p. 9

9. The last TCMP audit was conducted in 1988. In 1991 the scheduled TCMP audits were canceled as a result of internal and external opposition. The IRS planned to conduct a more extensive TCMP audit (152,000 returns) of 1994 returns, beginning in the fall of 1995 but canceled these plans as a result of congressional pressure and budgetary constraints.

10. For a discussion of the merits and difficulties of performing random audits, see testimony of the author, Malcolm K. Sparrow, and others before the House Ways and Means Committee, Subcommittee on Oversight, U.S. Congress, Washington, D.C., July 18, 1995.

For a broader discussion of the increasing importance of measurement as regulatory agencies focus more and more on impact, or effectiveness, see *Imposing Duties: Government's Changing Approach to Compliance*, Malcolm K. Sparrow. Praeger Books. Westport, Conn. and London, 1994. chapter 4.

11. The IRS uses a stratified random sampling technique to make sure that the sample sizes in each area and industry segment are large enough to support proper statistical inferences.

12. *The Fraud Control Game*, p. 7.

13. "The Control of Insurance Fraud," p. 1.

14. See "Health Insurers' Anti-Fraud Programs: Results of a Survey of the Health Insurance Association of America," Kathleen Fyffe, Thomas D. Musco, and Kristin Witecki. Health Insurance Association of America, Washington, D.C., 1994.

15. "Safe Targets: Fraud and Paperwork. (Clinton's Focus on Fraud in Medical Billing.)" Washington Perspective, Daniel Greenberg. *The Lancet*, September 11, 1993, v. 342, n. 8872, p. 670.

16. The maximum credit was $2,211 for the 1992 tax year. It would be paid, therefore, during the 1993 filing season. For the 1993 tax year the maximum credit was raised to $2,364; and to $2,528 for 1994.

17. Of the $136.7 million fraudulent returns detected during the 1993 filing season, $102 million were found soon enough to prevent payment. The remainder was paid.

18. EITC Compliance Study: Tax Year 1993, p. 5. The study was released publicly as an appendix to the statement of Margaret Milner Richardson, commissioner of Internal Revenue, before the Subcommittee on Oversight, House Ways and Means Committee, U.S. House of Representatives, Washington, D.C., June 15, 1995.

19. A final sample size of 1,059 gave a 95 percent confidence interval around these proportions of plus or minus 3 percent.

20. Internal IRS documents on Earned Income Credit.

21. The results of the study have not been published in their entirety. The facts and figures presented here were released to the author, who acted as a consultant on fraud-control issues to the IRS from 1993 onward. The summary figures have already been made public.

22. Of the $160 million fraudulent claims detected, $117.3 million in refunds was "stopped." The remainder was paid.

23. Statement of Margaret Milner Richardson, commissioner of Internal Revenue, before the Subcommittee on Oversight, Subcommittee on Human Resources, House Committee on Ways and Means, "Federal Income Tax Credit," June 15, 1995, Washington, D.C., p. 8.

24. Ibid., p. 7.

25. USA Today, March 10, 1995, "IRS Puts on the Brakes: Anti-Fraud Slowdown Angers Filers," p. 1

26. Ibid., p. 2.

27. During the 1995 filing season EITC payments totaled $20.3 billion.

28. Statement of Margaret Milner Richardson, commissioner of Internal Revenue, before the Subcommittee on Oversight, Subcommittee on Human Resources, House Committee on Ways and Means, "Federal Income Tax Credit," June 15, 1995, Washington, D.C., p. 6.

29. "Budget Bulletin," July 17, 1995, Senate Budget Committee, p. 1.

30. Meeting of the IRS executive committee, augmented by the regional commissioners, at IRS Headquarters, Wednesday, November 10, 1993. Author was present as a consultant.

31. The Fraud Control Game, p. 28.

32. "Analytical Perspectives: The Budget of the United States Government. Fiscal Year 1996," Executive Office of the President of the United States, Office of Management and Budget, Washington, D.C., 1995, p. 229.

33. "Health Insurers' Anti-Fraud Programs: Results of a Survey of the Health Insurance Association of America," Kathleen Fyffe, Thomas D. Musco, and Kristin Witecki. Health Insurance Association of America, Washington, D.C., 1994, p. 9.

34. Ibid., p. 10

35. "Disability Income Insurer's Anti-Fraud Programs: Results of a Survey of the HIAA," Kathleen Fyffe, Thomas D. Musco, and Kristin Witecki. Health Insurance Association of America, Washington, D.C., September 1994, p. 6.

36. "Analytical Perspectives: The Budget of the United States Government. Fiscal Year 1996," Executive Office of the President of the United States, Office of Management and Budget, Washington, D.C., 1995, p. 236.

37. Congress enacted the Medicare-Medicaid Anti-Fraud and Abuse Amendments, which established the MFCU Program in 1977 (Public Law 95–142). As of February 1996, forty-seven states had established MFCUs. The Omnibus Reconciliation Act, effective January 1995, requires every state to have an MFCU unless the state can prove a minimum level of fraud and abuse or demonstrate adequate protection without an MFCU. Three states— North Dakota, Nebraska, and Idaho—have received such waivers from the Department of Health and Human Services.

38. Testimony of William W. Whatley Jr., president, National Association of Medicaid Fraud Control Units, before the U.S. House of Representatives Committee on the Judiciary, Subcommittee on Crime and Justice, 2237 Rayburn House Office Building, Washington, D.C., July 19, 1994, p. 4.

39. Medicaid fraud control units have responsibility for investigating cases of patient abuse, particularly within nursing homes, hospices, and other institutions.

Chapter 4

1. Testimony of Gregory Kaladjian, executive deputy commissioner, New York State Department of Social Services, before the Senate Standing Committee on Social Services, Albany, New York, March 7, 1991, pp. 2–4.

2. HCFA has stated their intention to move away from strict numeric limitations in 1996, granting contractors greater flexibility in allocating resources between different controls and emphasizing outcomes.

3. "Empire Says It Paid Claims Without Checking," Jane Fritsch. *New York Times*, June 22, 1993, v. 142, pp. A14(N) and A1(L).

4. "Medicare Claims: Technology Could Save Millions," GAO Report GAO/AIMD–95–135, May 5, 1995.

5. The software packages handled four specific categories of code-manipulation abuse:

(1) Unbundling: billing for two or more codes to describe a procedure when a single, more comprehensive, code exists that accurately describes the procedure. (2) Global service period violations: billing separately for services that are incidental to a major service (billed) and that fall within a predetermined time period. (3) Duplicate procedures: billing twice for services provided only once. (4) Unnecessary assistant surgeon: billing for an assistant surgeon when assistant was not warranted.

6. HCFA contested the findings, of course, (Statement of Steven A. Pelovitz, associate administrator for Operations and Resource Management, Health Care Financing Administration, before the Appropriations Subcommittee on Labor, Health and Human Services, and Education, United States Senate, May 5, 1995.) saying it's not so simple, pointing out inadequacies in the available off-the-shelf software, and claiming that the Medicare Transaction System, to be phased in between 1997 and 1999, will allow HCFA to move beyond the state of the art. Pelovitz said, "Thus, as we implement the Medicare Transaction System, we will incorporate capabilities similar to those discussed here today. The question is not whether to proceed, but how and when." Quoted from page 10 of his statement.

7. "Fighting the Unbundlers," Gretchen Morgenson. *Forbes*, August 5, 1991. p. 109. Aetna installed GMIS's system, called "Claim Check," which is now widely used in the industry.

8. "Health Fraud: Computers at war," Mitch Betts. *Computerworld*, September 13, 1993, v. 27, n. 37, pp. 1 and 14.

9. Ibid.

10. HIMR: the Health Insurance Master Records. Beneficiary-based history file showing the status and eligibility of each Medicare beneficiary.

11. *The Fraud Control Game, State Responses to Fraud and Abuse in AFDC and Medicaid Programs*, John A. Gardiner and Theodore R. Lyman. Indiana University Press, Bloomington, Indiana, 1985, p. 85.

12. "Medicare: Inadequate Review of Claims Payments Limits Ability to Control Spending," report to the Chairman, Subcommittee on Oversight and Investigations, Committee on Energy and Commerce, House of Representatives, General Accounting Office, Washington, D.C., GAO/HEHS–94–42, April 1994, p. 18.

13. "Medicare: Antifraud Technology Offers Significant Opportunity to Reduce Health Care Fraud," report to the ranking minority member, Subcommittee on Labor, Health and Human Services, Education, and Related Agencies; Committee on Appropriations, U.S. Senate, General Accounting Office, GAO/AIMD–95–77, August 1995, p. 9.

14. Personal communication with the author, as part of a response by senior HCFA managers to earlier drafts of some of the material contained in this book, September 18, 1995.

15. "Health Care Fraud: The Silent Bandit," Joseph L. Ford. *FBI Law Enforcement Bulletin*. October 1992, v. 61, n. 10, pp. 2–7. Joe Ford was special agent in charge of the FBI's Health Care Fraud Unit at the time.

16. "Health Insurance: Vulnerable Payers Lose Billions to Fraud and Abuse." Report to the chairman, Subcommittee on Human Resources and Intergovernmental Relations, Committee on Government Operations, House of Representatives, General Accounting Office, Washington, D.C., May 1992. GAO/HRD–92–69.

17. Ibid., p. 23.

18. "A Partnership Approach: A Prescription for Enhanced Coordination of Medicaid Fraud Detection and Prevention in New York State," Senator Donald M. Halperin. New York State Senate, Albany, New York, June 1993.

19. 42 CFR, ch. V (10–1–92 edition), Office of Inspector General—Health Care, HHS, § 1007.9.

20. Ibid.

21. *Handbook on Corporate Fraud: Prevention, Detection, and Investigation.* Jack Bologna. Butterworth-Heinemann. Boston, 1993. p. 23.

22. The regulations governing the structure and operations of Medicaid Fraud Control units are contained in Part 1007, 42 CFR ch. V, Office of Inspector General, Health Care, HHS. Authority: 42 U.S.C. 1396b(a)(b), 1396b(b)(3), and 1396b(q).

23. "Federal Funding for State Medicaid Fraud Control Units Still Needed," General Accounting Office, October 6, 1980, p. 32.

24. "Medicare: Antifraud Technology Offers Significant Opportunity to Reduce Health Care Fraud." Report to the ranking minority member, Subcommittee on Labor, Health and Human Services, Education, and Related Agencies; Committee on Appropriations, U.S. Senate, General Accounting Office, GAO/AIMD-95-77, August 1995, p. 19.

Chapter 5

1. The National Health Care Anti-Fraud Association (NHCAA), based in Washington, D.C., maintains an on-line "provider database" for its member organizations.

2. Although, as of November 1995, Company X has two prosecutions pending.

Chapter 6

1. Task Force on Electronic Data Interchange Issues, Status Report, July 20, 1994. National Health Care Anti-fraud Association, Washington, D.C., p. 1.

2. "Medicare: Antifraud Technology Offers Significant Opportunity to Reduce Health Care Fraud." Report to the ranking minority member, Subcommittee on Labor, Health and Human Services, Education, and Related Agencies; Committee on Appropriations, U.S. Senate, General Accounting Office, Washington, D.C., GAO/AIMD-95-77, August 1995, p. 2.

3. Ibid.

4. "EDI and Health Care Fraud." Report of the National Health Care Anti-Fraud Association, Washington, D.C., October 12, 1994, p. 3.

5. The Workgroup for Electronic Data Interchange (WEDI) was established in November 1991 in response to the challenge to reduce administrative costs in the nation's health care system. WEDI, a voluntary public private task force, published a report in July 1992 that outlines the steps required to make EDI routine for the health care industry by 1996. WEDI's 1993 financial

analysis concludes that combining the estimated implementation costs and the gross administrative savings potential, the cumulative net savings over the next six years (to the year 2000) averages $7 billion a year.

6. "Managed Care: Electronic Data Interchange," Barbara Coulter Edwards. *Journal of Insurance Medicine*, v. 24, n. 3, Fall 1992, p. 162.

7. Technical Advisory Group White Paper, presented to the Workgroup on Electronic Data Interchange (WEDI) and included in 1993 WEDI report, Executive Summary, p. 1.

8. "Electronic Data Interchange Issues." Presentation to Board of Governors, NHCAA, Jim Garcia, Aetna, September 12, 1994, Washington, D.C., p. 2.

9. *Fraud, Prevention and Detection*, I. K. Huntington. Butterworths, London, 1992. See chapter 10, The Computer and Fraud: Key Issues for the Investigator, pp. 175ff.

10. "Electronic Data Interchange Issues," Exhibit A, "Health Care Fraud Busters Indicators," National Health Care Anti-Fraud Association, Washington, D.C., pp. 1–7.

11. "Business and Health: Detecting Fraud in Medical Claims," Glenn Kramon. *New York Times*, June 11, 1991, v. 140, p. C2.

12. The two forms in broadest use are the HCFA 1500 for doctors and the UB–92 for hospitals. Providers are required by Medicare to use these forms, and private insurers are required to accept them too.

13. Press release, December 6, 1988, State of New York, Deputy Attorney General for Medicaid Fraud Control, p. 1.

14. "Historical Background of New York State Medicaid Fraud Control Unit," November 1994. Office of the New York State Special Prosecutor, p. 4.

Chapter 7

1. "Physician Incentive Arrangements: Where's the Risk?" Christine C. Boesz, director, Office of Operations and Oversight, Office of Managed Care, HCFA, Washington, D.C., March 1995, p. 1.

2. "Medicare Managed Care Program Update," Office of Managed Care, Health Care Financing Administration, HHS, Washington, D.C., May 1995, p.4.

3. "While Congress Remains Silent, Health Care Transforms Itself," Erik Eckholm. *New York Times*, December 18, 1994, v. 144, p. A1.

4. "Managed Care and Fraud," Joshua R. Hochberg and Scott S. Dahl. Department of Justice, Health Care Fraud Training Conference, Baltimore, Maryland, April 12, 1995, p. 4.

5. Ibid.

6. "Medicare Managed Care Program Update," Office of Managed Care, Health Care Financing Administration, HHS, Washington, D.C., May 1995, p.3.

7. Ibid., p. 9.

8. The Medicare Risk program, allowing HMOs to enroll Medicare patients in exchange for capitation payments, became operational under the Tax Equity and Fiscal Responsibility Act (TEFRA), April 1985.

9. The first seven states to obtain these waivers were: Arizona, Rhode Island, Kentucky, Oregon, Tennessee, Florida, and Hawaii. Source: Medicaid Bureau. Health Care Financing Administration, DHHS, Washington, D.C.

10. For a more detailed, but still summary, listing of plan types see "Fraud in Managed Health Care Delivery and Payment." Report of the NHCAA Task Force on Fraud in Managed Care, NHCAA, Washington, D.C., November 1994. pp. 5–20.

11. "Fraud in Managed Health Care Delivery and Payment." Report of the NHCAA Task Force on Fraud in Managed Care, NHCAA, Washington, D.C., November 1994, p. 1.

12. The emergence of underutilization as the predominant form of fraud under prospective payment systems was forecast very clearly in 1989 by Professor Pamela H. Bucy, in "Fraud by Fright: White Collar Crime by Health Care Providers." *North Carolina Law Review*, v. 67, n. 4, April 1989, pp. 855–937. In particular, see p. 934.

13. Medicaid Review Report, HCFA, 1993, "Review of [Site MFCU-3] Title XIX Mental Health Program," p. 11.

14. Ibid., p. 12.

15. Ibid., p. 14.

16. "New York Acts to Curb Fraud in Managed Care for the Poor," Ian Fisher. *New York Times*, June 23, 1995, v. 144, p. 1.

17. "News release, Office of the Attorney General, Baltimore, Maryland, June 13, 1995, p. 1.

18. "New York Faults Medicaid H.M.O.'s for Poor Service," Elisabeth Rosenthal. *New York Times*, November 17, 1995, v. 145, pp. A1 and B4.

19. "Health Care Provider Fraud: the State Medicaid Fraud Control Unit Experience." Report prepared for the President's Task Force on National Health Care Reform, May 1993, National Association of Medicaid Fraud Control Units, Washington, D.C., pp. 6–7.

20. Ibid., p. 9.

21. Ibid., p. 14.

22. Ibid., p. 15.

23. Site [MFCU 3] State Administrative Code: Title 9, Ch. 22, December 31, 1992, p. 41.

24. "While Congress Remains Silent, Health Care Transforms Itself," Erik Eckholm. *New York Times*, December 18, 1994, v. 144, p. A1.

25. Ibid.

26. "Fraud in Managed Health Care Delivery and Payment," Report of the NHCAA Task Force on Fraud in Managed Care. NHCAA, Washington, D.C., November 1994, Executive Summary, p. 4.

27. Personal communication with the author, as part of a response by senior HCFA managers to earlier drafts of some of the material contained in this book, September 18, 1995.

28. For an excellent and readable discussion of antitrust issues in health care business arrangements see "Legal Issues in Physician Self-Referral and

Other Health Care Business Relationships," Susan Tedrick. *The Journal of Legal Medicine*, December 1992, v. 13, n. 4, pp. 521–561.

See also "Health Care System Reforms Require Coordinated Efforts; Conflicting Policies and Laws Stand in the Way of Change," Steven N. Beck and Gail F. Brandt. *The National Law Journal*, April 26, 1993, v. 15, n. 34, p. 27.

The Department of Justice has issued a statement setting forth antitrust safety zones, describing physician network joint ventures that would not normally be challenged under antitrust laws: they are "exclusive" ventures (which restrict members' freedom to affiliate with other ventures or to contract independently) comprising 20 percent or less of the physicians within one specialty, within one area; or "non-exclusive" ventures comprising 30 percent or less of the physicians within one specialty, within one area. "Statement of Enforcement Policy and Analytical Principles Relating to Health Care and Antitrust." Issued by the U.S. Department of Justice and the Federal Trade Commission, September 27, 1994, Washington, D.C., pp. 66–69.

29. Fraud in Managed Health Care Delivery and Payment." Executive Summary, p. 5.

30. Fraud in Managed Health Care Delivery and Payment," p. 3.

31. Strategic Plan for the Oversight of Managed Health Care," U.S. Department of Health and Human Services, Office of Inspector General, Washington, D.C., June 1994, p. 8.

32. Ibid., p. 7.

33. See for example, "The Medicare Risk Program for HMOs—Final Summary Report on Findings from the Evaluation," Randall S. Brown et al., Mathematica Policy Research, Inc. Princeton, N.J., February 18, 1993, pp. xx–xxiv.

This report examined prior fee-for-service reimbursements for 100,000 Medicare HMO enrollees for the two years prior to enrollment in 1987 and 1988. They found reimbursement rates roughly 20 percent below the average risk-adjusted reimbursements for non-enrollees from the same market areas. Two-thirds of ninety-eight plans experienced highly favorable selection, the remainder experienced slightly favorable or neutral selection. Not one experienced adverse selection.

Consequently, overall costs to HCFA increased when these subgroups enrolled in HMOs. At the same time, HMOs spent roughly 10.5 percent less on services than HCFA would have spent in reimbursements to FFS providers.

Chapter 8

1. These are approximate figures, based on 95 percent confidence intervals and assuming an underlying binomial probability distribution.

2. Press release announcing "Operation Restore Trust," May 3, 1995, U.S. Department of Health and Human Services, Washington, D.C., p. 1.

3. These objections were voiced by Stephen Teichler, in "Reinventing Health Care Fraud and Abuse," *Legal Times*, February 28, 1994, v. 16, n. 41, pp. 36–37.

4. The position was created in April 1993.

5. "Gingrich Places Low Priority on Medicare Crooks: Defends Cutting Anti-Fraud Defenses," Nancy E. Roman. *Washington Times*, October 13, 1995, p. A1.

6. For a description of this broad movement within the professions of policing, environmental protection, and tax administration, see *Imposing Duties: Government's Changing Approach to Compliance*, Malcolm K. Sparrow. Praeger Books, Greenwood Publishing Group, Westport Conn., 1994.

7. Professor Herman Goldstein described the relevance of problem solving to the police profession, and detailed the problem-solving methodology, in *Problem-Oriented Policing*, McGraw-Hill, New York, 1990.

8. Ibid., p. 66.

9. Ibid., pp. 67–68.

10. See chapter 2, entitled Redefining the Unit of Work in *Imposing Duties: Government's Changing Approach to Compliance*, Malcolm K. Sparrow. Praeger Books, Westport, Conn. and London, 1994, for an account of the emergence of the problem-solving strategy within the professions of environmental protection and tax administration.

11. See chapter 4 of Herman Goldstein's *Problem-Oriented Policing* for greater detail. Also see chapter 2 of Malcolm K. Sparrow, *Imposing Duties*, for a slightly more condensed process and for discussion of its suitability outside the world of policing.

12. The description of the problem-solving process that follows in the text is abridged and adapted for the fraud-control environment from *Imposing Duties*, pp. 45–47.

13. Goldstein, *Problem-Oriented Policing*, pp. 38–39.

14. "Beware Your HMO," Ellen E. Spragins. *Newsweek*, October 23, 1995, pp. 54–56. See quotes on page 55 of Whitney Seymour Jr., a New York lawyer with Brown & Seymour, who specializes in insurance and HMO cases.

Chapter 9

1. "Smart-Bombing Fraud: Insurers Turn to Powerful New Computer Tools to Spot 'Aberrant' Claims," Greg Borzo. *American Medical News*, October 10, 1994, pp. 1 and 11.

2. Ibid.

3. *Dateline*, Tuesday November 7, 1995, NBC, 10:00 P.M. EST, Segment 1.

4. "Medicare and Medicaid: Opportunities to Save Program Dollars by Reducing Fraud and Abuse." Statement of Sarah F. Jagger, director, Health Financing and Policy Issues, Health, Education, and Human Services Division, General Accounting Office. Testimony before the Subcommittee on Human Resources and Intergovernmental Relations, Committee on

Government Reform and Oversight, House of Representatives. Washington, D.C., March 22, 1995, p. 8.

5. Ibid., p. 9.

6. Ibid., p. 5.

7. Ibid., p. 5.

8. Ibid., p. 8.

9. "Medicare: Inadequate Review of Claims Payments Limits Ability to Control Spending." Report to the chairman, Subcommittee on Oversight and Investigations, Committee on Energy and Commerce, House of Representatives, General Accounting Office, Washington, D.C., GAO/HEHS–94–42, April 1994, p. 3.

10. In part this results from the legacy of paper-based transaction-processing environments. Where claims processing, or acting upon redemption requests, or payment of tax refunds were essentially paper-based operations, fraud-control systems most naturally consisted of physical diversions (branch points) within physical process flows. Returns or claims would be kicked out for review, based solely on the information content of that particular file. Casting around inside massive electronic databases for patterns of particular types was simply inconceivable.

11. This brief note regarding the relevance of network analytic tools to fraud detection is condensed from a previous paper, "Network Vulnerabilities and Strategic Intelligence in Law Enforcement," Malcolm K. Sparrow. *International Journal of Intelligence and CounterIntelligence*, v. 5, n. 3. Fall 1991, pp. 255–274.

This paper describes potential applications of network analysis within the broader field of criminal intelligence analysis. Another paper covering similar ground, but written for the social science audience is, "The Application of Network Analysis to Criminal Intelligence: An Assessment of the Prospects," Malcolm K. Sparrow. *Social Networks*, v. 13, 1991. pp. 251–274.

12. Called "Social Networks," published by Elsevier.

13. The International Network of Social Network Analysts, supported by a newsletter called "Connections."

14. An analysis of modern fraud-control technologies by GAO, sharing this misunderstanding, refers to Link Analysis as "a powerful visual tool." "Medicare: Antifraud Technology Offers Significant Opportunity to Reduce Health Care Fraud." Report to the ranking minority member, Subcommittee on Labor, Health and Human Services, Education, and Related Agencies, Committee on Appropriations, U.S. Senate, General Accounting Office, GAO/AIMD–95–77, August 1995, p. 11.

15. For a full account of how law enforcement uses link analysis tools, see "Network Vulnerabilities and Strategic Intelligence in Law Enforcement," Malcolm K. Sparrow. *International Journal of Intelligence and CounterIntelligence*, v. 5, n. 3, Fall 1991, pp. 256–274.

About the Book
and Author

Criminal fraud must be factored into the current debates about health care reform, budget deficits, and proposed Medicare/Medicaid cutbacks. As a polity, how can we make good public policy if we don't know how much of the nation's one trillion dollar health care budget is being lost to fraud? The amounts are staggering, measured in hundreds of billions of dollars, but nobody knows for sure exactly how much is being lost.

Malcolm Sparrow, an expert on fraud control, reviews how the health care industry approaches the problem and concludes that fraud is rampant, largely uncontrolled, and mostly invisible to policymakers. The problem will only get worse, he says, unless the industry at all levels changes its priorities, its strategies for uncovering and preventing fraud, and its technological approach.

Many believe that electronic claims processing will save billions of dollars and that managed care will eliminate the major categories of fraud. By contrast, Sparrow shows how electronic claims processing could lead to unprecedented fraud losses, and how managed care makes fraud much more dangerous to human health.

The final section—prescriptions for progress—is a must for policymakers at every level, and for anyone with an interest in the science of fraud control more broadly, in any context.

Malcolm K. Sparrow, author of *Beyond 911* (1992), is lecturer in public policy at the John F. Kennedy School of Government, Harvard University.

Index